PROCESS
50 PRODUCT DESIGNS FROM CONCEPT TO MANUFACTURE

JENNIFER HUDSON

Laurence King Publishing

CONTENTS

PROCESS

Author's acknowledgements

Process is inscribed to my son Willoughby, but is dedicated to the designers in the book, all of whom I admire greatly for making our immediate environment, in turn, so comfortable, interesting, entertaining and practical.

I would like to thank David Bothwell of Hybrid for all the hard work he put into designing a very complicated and detailed book, my editor, Zoe Antoniou, for her patience and perseverance in keeping everything on track and for her unerring eye for detail, Nicola Hodgson the copy-editor and Tessa Clark the proofreader, for helping me appear less of an illiterate, and Felicity Awdry, Director of Laurence King's production department, for her remarkable skill in making the book look beautiful. I owe a dept of gratitude to Dr Russell Marshall for going through my glossary with a fine toothcomb, helping to make it both incisive and independently useful for student and young designer alike, and to Marcus Hirst in Ron Arad's studio who gave me advice on technical details, on more than one occasion, and not only in relation to Arad's design.

Above all, however, I would like to say an enormous thank you to all of the people featured who were so encouraging and spent the time and trouble to, not only be interviewed, but to closely scrutinize the texts for accuracy and detail. Without their support Process would not have been possible.

LAURENCE KING

Published in 2008
by Laurence King Publishing Ltd
361–373 City Road
London EC1V 1LR
Tel +44 20 7841 6900
Fax +44 20 7841 6910
E-mail enquiries@laurenceking.co.uk
www.laurenceking.co.uk

A catalogue record for this book is available from the British Library.

ISBN 978 1 85669 541 1

Designed by David Bothwell at Hybrid 2 Ltd

Printed in China

Picture credits
The publisher and author would like to thank the designers and manufacturers, and the following photographers for the use of their material:

Olivio Barbieri; p110 (illust 1): Alex Barrymore; p61 (illust 14–20): Peter Beard; p98 (illust 1): Antione Bootz; p227, p228 (illust 4–5): Dave Boswell; p229 (illust 12–14): Richard Brine; p64 (illust 2, 4), p65 (illust 9, 10): David Brook; p29, p30 (illust 3): Simon Bruntnell; p47, p48 (illust 2): David Churchill/courtesy Edward Marshall Trust; p30 (illust 1–2): Pedro Cloiudio; p57 (illust 12–13): Frank de Wind; p221 (illust 7–8): EvV; p219, p220 (illust 2–6): Piero Fasanotto for Flos; pp215–217: Frans Feijen/ASP; p149, p150 (illust 1–2, 4): Mitsumasa Fujitsuka; p99 (illust 7): Courtesy The Gagosian Gallery, NY; pp145–146: Getty Images/3D4Medical.com Collection; p22 (illust 1): Getty Images/Nucleus Medical Art.com Collection; p36 (illust 1): Getty Images/Digital Vision Collection/Frank Krahmer; p40 (illust 1), p212 (illust 1): Getty Images/The Bridgeman Art Library; p64 (illust 1): Getty Images/Stockbyte Collection/George Doyle & Ciaran Griffin; p68 (illust 1): Getty Images/Aurora Collection/Ian Shrive; p73 (illust 7): Getty Images/Taxi Collection/Justin Pumfrey; p78 (illust 1): Getty Images/Digital Vision Collection/Mark Gibson; p102 (illust 1): Getty Images/Taxi Collection/Dave Bradley; p142 (illust 1): Getty Images/The Photonica Collection/Silvia Otte; p160 (illust 1): Getty Images/Hulton Archive/Keystone; p170 (illust 1): Getty Images/GAP Photos/Frank Krahmer; p174 (illust 1): Getty Images/Stone+ Collection/Mark Lund; p188 (illust 1): Getty Images/Photodisc Collection/Stock.Trek; p206 (illust 1): Getty Images/Image Source Collection/Image Source Black; p220 (illust 1): Getty Images/Photodisc Collection/Stephanie Dalton Cowan; p224 (illust 1): Getty Images/Dorling Kindersley Collection/Simon Smith; p232 (illust 1): Örjen Henriksson/Fagerhult; p177: Seiji Himeno/Sakai Design Associates; p191, p195: John Hyam; p63: Steve Klein; p221 (illust 9–11): Raoul Kramer; p129 (bottom), p133 (illust 25–26): Yves Krol; p211: Max and Jane Lamb; pp121–123: Laurie Lambrecht; p228 (illust 2–3, 6–8), p229 (illust 16–17): Jonas Marking; p175 (illust 10): Antonio Nascimento; p57 (illust 10): Daniel Nicolas; p115, p117 (illust 5), p118, p119 (illust 13, 15, 16): Marcus Oliveras; p173, p175 (illust 6): Courtesy Opel GmbH; p116 (illust 2–4): Operation: Schoener Ltd/courtesy rAndom International; pp181–185: Lena Palmé/Väveriet; p155: © Panton Design/courtesy Vitra Design Museum; p48 (illust 1): Courtesy Porzellan Manufaktur Nymphenburg; p109 (top): Frank Stolle/courtesy KRAM/WEISSHAAR; p109 (bottom), p112 (illust 8–11): Frank Stolle/courtesy Porzellan Manufaktur Nymphenburg; p113 (illust 14–17): Timecode; pp55–56: Oliver Toscani/Artemide; p170 (illust 2): Tom Vack; p64 (illust 3), p90 (illust 1): Maarten van Houten; p17: Barry Walz; p228 (illust 1): Miro Zagnoli; p141, p143.

INTRODUCTION

The following pages describe the sometimes long, and often arduous, journeys that over 40 designers have undertaken to bring their very varied work to the marketplace. With the proliferation of glossy lifestyle magazines and the publication of bumper compendiums of product design, it is all too easy to believe that the objects of desire with which we seek to surround ourselves are produced virtually overnight: the consumer and aspiring young designer are given little idea of the complexities, trials and tribulations that have gone into their creation. Not only is this misinterpretation and lack of understanding intellectually limiting, it is also dangerous in today's design climate, when courses in some leading schools place an increasing emphasis on the creation of the personal voice to the detriment of a sound grounding in technique and commerciality. Upon completing their studies, graduates of these schools are suddenly faced with having to design something for the real market and real people. Charles Eames famously responded, when asked if he designed for pleasure or function: 'What works good is better than what looks good. Because, what works good lasts.'

For nearly a decade, the design world has been liberated by a pluralistic attitude towards what is permissible, with no single style or trend predominating. Mass-produced and high-tech products sit comfortably with craft-based low tech, along with the individualistic, conceptual approach and the limited-edition design piece sold in galleries and collected by the connoisseur. Modern technology and the increased use of computer-aided design in both the development and manufacture of products have resulted in the research of new and super-pliable materials. These lend themselves to advanced processes such as rapid prototyping, creating complex, organic forms that were unrealizable until recently.

Aaron Betsky, a leading critic and proponent of architectural and design discourse, and current Director of Cincinnati Art Museum,

asserts, 'Design should do the same thing in everyday life that art does when encountered: amaze us, scare us or delight us, but certainly open us up to new worlds within our daily existence.' The downside to the current 'anything goes' attitude, however, is the rise of the specious designer and the overabundance of fashionable and ill-conceived pieces, devised to look good in the media but with little technical integrity.

The designs that follow (from the highly conceptual one-offs, through craft-based pieces to the limited-edition collector's item and the commercially mass-produced) cover the major typologies: furniture, lighting, tableware, textiles and products. They represent the above-mentioned trends but, most importantly, all have been carefully selected to demonstrate their creators' thorough knowledge of design processes, whether they be methodical, research-led, scientific, accidental or even, in some cases, inspirational to the final product. Examining all stages from initial concept, through design and development to production, the work featured proves that design can 'look good and work good'.

Above all, the designs shown here emphasize that the development of a lasting product is 5% inspiration and 95% hard work. To design an object involves problem-solving and creativity, but to produce that object, no matter how innovative, involves a routine or pre-planned process. Having a revolutionary idea is not enough and in many ways is an ego-driven indulgence of the designer. Finding a way to realize a concept through evolutionary solutions is key, as is consideration of the client's brief, consumer needs, market demands, function and practicality. To design in a vacuum with the emphasis on expression would result in ill-thought-out products. For the most part, the stories in this book accentuate the collaborative way in which designers work with manufacturers and, above all, technicians and craftspeople, to develop and produce their initial ideas. In an interview with Fortune Magazine, Steve Jobs, co-founder

and CEO of Apple said: 'Design is the fundamental soul of a human-made creation that ends up expressing itself in successive outer layers of the product...it is a synthesis of the visual and emotional with the functional; it is emotion wrapped within a purpose...an object of desire equipped with a sense of mission.'

Process looks not only at production but seeks to marry the technical with the inspirational; to see into the minds of those we read about in design magazines (plus a few new faces) and examine their design philosophy and modus operandi in order to expose the unknown behind the objects they create. To go deeper into some of the manufacturing techniques mentioned, Chris Lefteri's comprehensive book Making It – Manufacturing Techniques for Product Design (Laurence King, 2007) is a useful companion publication.

The designs featured in this book all stand up to judicious appraisal. They include Stefano Giovannoni's Chair First (which uses an innovative form of gas injection to create an organic form without the structure being visible); Joris Laarman's Bone furniture (a hybrid of creativity and computer software that imitates the precise growth patterns of bones); Reed Kram and Clemens Weisshaar's Breeding Tables (infinite three-dimensional structures generated by algorithmic applications); Satyendra Pakhalé's B.M. Horse Chair (eight years in the making and combining ancient technique with technological innovation); Yves Béhar's Leaf light (whose expressive form is justified by mechanical requirements); and Lionel T. Dean's Entropia light (a milestone in digital manufacturing).

Since the millennium, design society has witnessed its own revolution in what is accepted both inspirationally and technically. As the following pages demonstrate, however, it is only with a sound understanding of the importance of rigorous method that a wannabe designer will be able to translate his or her flights of fancy into objects that will stand evaluation and the test of time.

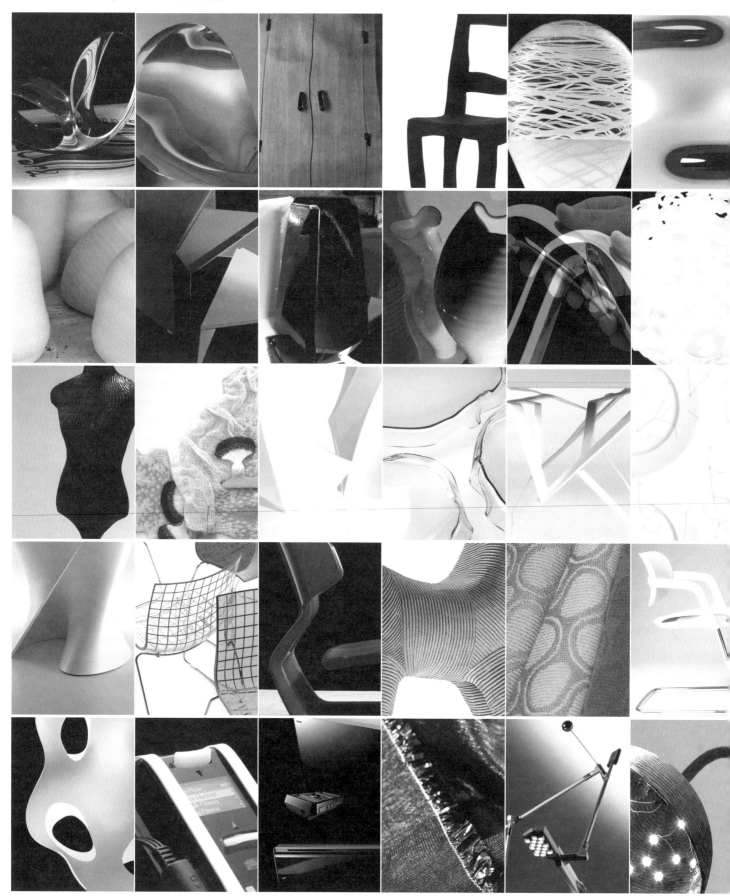

Ron Arad was born in Tel Aviv, Israel, in 1951 and studied fine art at Bezalel Academy in Jerusalem before moving to the UK tempted by the anti-establishment, youth-fuelled punk years of the 1970s. He trained at the Architectural Association and worked for a short time in a small architectural practice before forming his own company, One-Off, producing individual, streetwise and rugged pieces. Teaching himself to weld and beat steel, he produced a series of volumetric chairs that brought him worldwide fame.

Mixing high-tech with low, the Bodyguard series sees a return to those early days. Shaped by the pioneering technique of thermo-forming highly plastic aluminium, the chairs are cut and welded, incorporating the idiosyncrasies of the personal touch, and then hand-finished to achieve brilliant mirror surfaces.

These sculptural objects are not the first time that Arad has experimented with forming aluminium. During 1997 Domus magazine commissioned Arad to produce a temporary landmark for the Milan Furniture Fair (Salone Internazionale del Mobile). Arad responded with the idea of a 10m (32ft) column, the Totem, made from stacking chairs, each cast in one piece. For reasons of time and budget plastic couldn't be used for the installation (although it was later employed when Vitra put the chair into production) and Arad was introduced to Superform Aluminium, a specialist manufacturer of precision-engineered components for the automobile and aeronautical industries. The company had never worked on furniture before but saw no reason why a chair could not be made in formed aluminium. This offered Arad the opportunity of casting the complex shape of the chair in one mould and relatively inexpensively. What was later to be known as the Tom Vac chair was born, along with a collaboration that would see a series of objects produced over the next ten years. These include the B.O.O.P giant vases, the Blo-Void chaise and Bodyguards, which push the innovative process to the limit.

To form convoluted shapes in aluminium, without undue stress being placed on the material, the usual method would be to press it in sequence. This would involve the creation of a number of dies. Vacuum-forming needs just one tool, offering the possibility of producing reasonable-sized runs of rapidly formed objects. The basic technique is to take a sheet of steel into which profiles have been cut. This is lowered on to hot aluminium that has been heated to 400–600°C (752–1112°F) and has the consistency of rubber. Air pressure is then used to force the aluminium through the holes.

Three blowing techniques have been developed to cover the large range of sizes and shapes applicable to the process. All of these were used at times for the various depths of the intricate, organic forms of the Bodyguard pieces. In the cavity method, air pressure and tool movement forces the sheet up into the mould; in bubble-forming, the air pressure forms the material into a bubble, the mould is forced up into it and then air pressure is applied to the top making the aluminium take on the form of the tool; and in back-pressure-forming, pressure is applied by a male and female mould from both top and bottom.

The Bodyguards were developed using freehand sketches that were translated into 3D computer geometry to work out the detailing. Once the definitive shape was created, foam models were produced and then tested for comfort. Adjustments were made and the 3D files, now containing all the information to create the mould, were sent to the tool-makers. A poly-tool model was machined combining Arad Associates' 3D computer geometry and engineering details such as clamp lines. A process of investment-casting was used to make the tools in iron, which were five-axis-machined with a cutting tool to create a good finish. The aluminium was blown, parts ejected from the mould and the flanges trimmed back to achieve the required form. They were then welded. Finally, Arad painted rough forms to determine the positions of the cuts, which were incised by hand. The pieces are finished to create ultrasmooth, shiny surfaces.

BODYGUARDS
RON ARAD ASSOCIATES

Production: Ron Arad Associates
Aluminium
Various dimensions
Design to manufacture: 5 months
Limited edition
www.ronarad.com

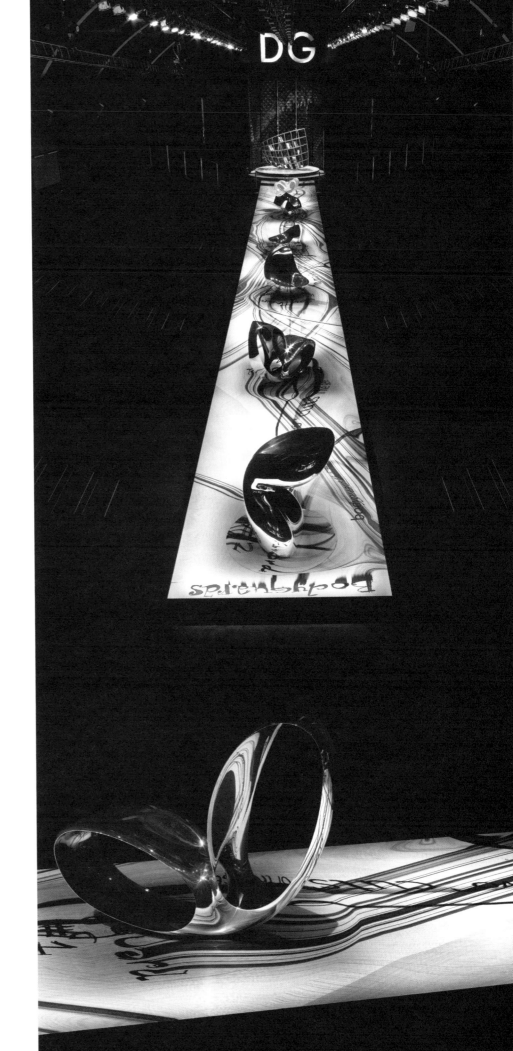

The Bodyguard series is the latest in Arad's experiments in forming aluminium. It was launched at Dolce & Gabbana's showroom during the Milan Furniture Fair, 2007, along with other pieces (including Southern Hemisphere and Afterthought) produced using the same technique.

1–4. Arad's sketches work out the forms of the series.

5–9. 3D computer geometry is used by Arad's studio to refine the shapes. The results are passed back to Arad, who sketches amendments. This ongoing process results in the final form, from which 3D files are created to send to the tool-makers.

10. CAD drawing working out the number of parts needed to cast Bodyguard. Originally it was intended to have only two parts but this put undue stress on the aluminium. In the end, four parts were needed.

11. Renderings of the final form of a Bodyguard.

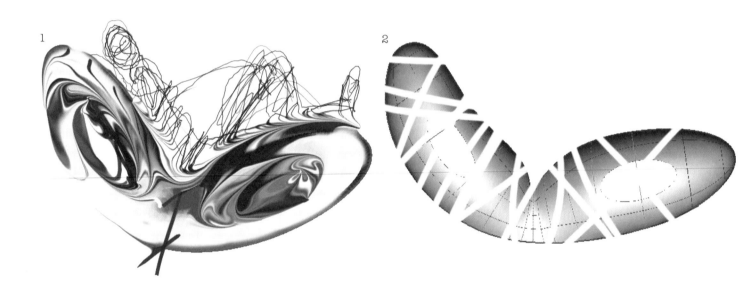

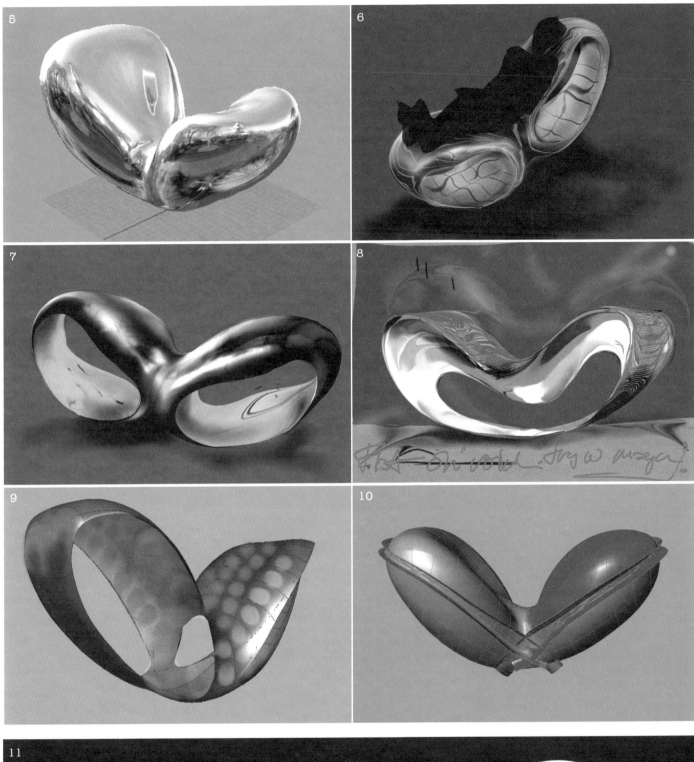

12. Once final forms were created, foam models were made. One of Arad's studio staff tests out the comfort of Bodyguard. Arad's experimentation with initial lines for the trimming can be seen.

13. Foam model of Southern Hemisphere. Physical testing revealed a certain lack of support in the back. Cardboard was added to work out optimum comfort. The information was then calculated and fed back into the computer and further CADs were created.

14–15. The final stage before tooling involves the creation of poly-tool models, here for the seat of Southern Hemisphere (14). Investment-casting is used to make the iron moulds, such as the sphere for Southern Hemisphere's base (15). The moulds are then honed using a five-axis cutting machine to form a perfect surface.

16. The pieces are formed using a range of methods (see text) and in various grades of aluminium from the 5,000 to 7,000 series, depending on the depth and intricacy of the shapes.

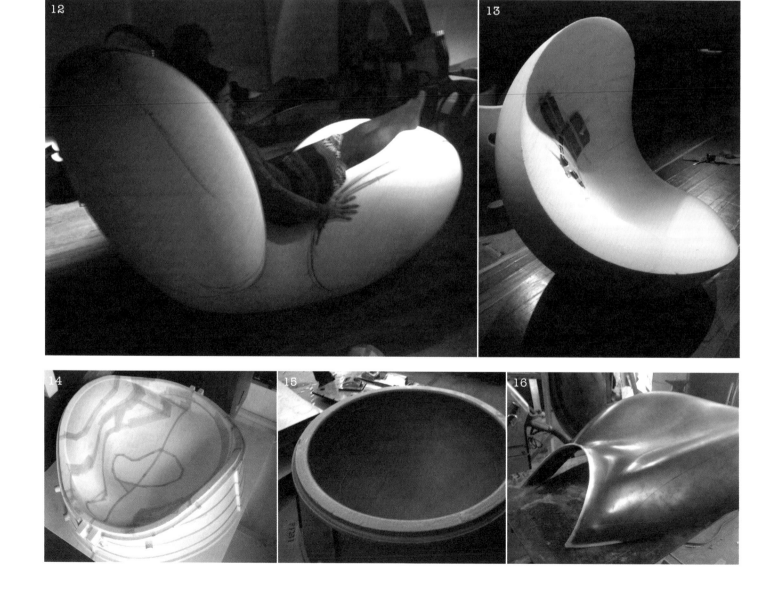

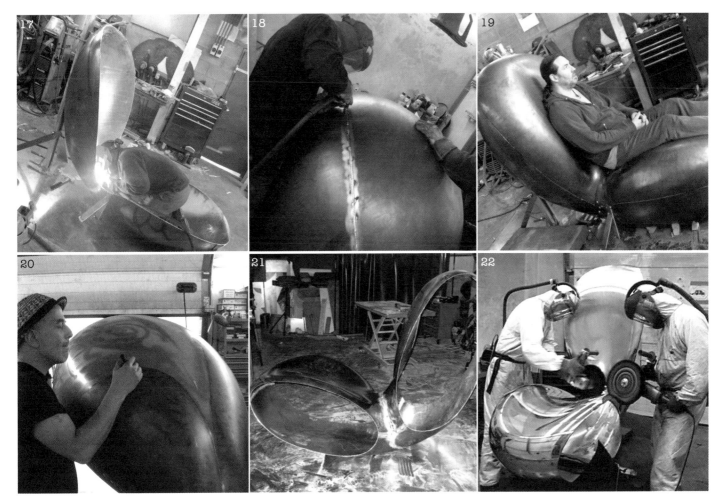

17–19. The parts are ejected from the mould, trimmed to get the desired part and welded together. Here are the four parts of Bodyguard (19).

20–21. Ron Arad paints on the rough object to mark out the lines for the cuts (20), which are then incised by hand (21).

22. The pieces are finished to create a polished mirror effect.

23–25. Additions to the range include Southern Hemisphere, which is cast in three parts: a sphere for the base, the seat and the back. It is finished in a mirror-like surface (23) or with a secret technique to create a weathered bronze aesthetic (24). Afterthought is cast using the negative form of Hemisphere (25).

With the success of his Smoke series, Maarten Baas may for ever be known as the Dutch boy who set fire to contemporary and traditional design classics. However, these beautiful ethereal pieces, which are scorched with a blowtorch and their charred surfaces sealed with epoxy, are only a part of an ever-growing body of work that challenges our preconceptions about design.

Baas refuses to be categorized. He is often asked whether the Smoke series is design or art. His reply that it doesn't matter as long as people like it – or not – is typical of this iconoclastic young designer, whose raw, idiosyncratic approach produces objects that are intentionally imperfect and full of character. Trained at the Design Academy in Eindhoven, Baas has the expected conceptual attitude towards design: Smoke addresses notions of beauty and (im)perfection; Flatpack (a sidetable made of the parts of IKEA's stool Ringo and chair Stefan) compromises the identikit aesthetic of self-assembly mass-produced furniture; Treasure (a series of pieces made from the leftovers of a furniture factory) recreates the spontaneous elegance of a hut he had made as a child using hammer, nail and found boards; and the naïve and colourful Clay furniture, hand-modelled around basic metal structures, carries the idea of functional imperfection to its limits. 'The less the thought, the more the joy' was the leitmotif of the Clay series.

The playful Sculpt range consists of limited-edition hand-crafted and oversized furniture pieces, so far including an armchair, dining chair, table, chest of drawers and cupboard. The basic construction is stainless steel, to which various finishes have been applied such as sand-blasting or powder-coating. The most technically complicated finish was the walnut veneer used in the table and cupboard. The armchair is leather-upholstered.

Each piece begins with a hand-carved 3D sketch/model made from polystyrene foam cut very roughly in five minutes with a Stanley knife. The inspiration for Sculpt comes from the model and embodies the notion that this sketch is often more charming than the eventual, finished object, which loses its spontaneity when it is translated to a 1:1 scale. The sketch retains the notion of creation and is still full of 'life'. To retain this vivacity Baas decided to recreate the model in an oversized scale so that it becomes a real object while retaining the essence of its original character: each item is a model, prototype and end-product in one.

The production was kept as imprecise as the initial inspiration. The pieces do not literally copy the model but rather the atmosphere of the concept; a certain freedom was kept to the manufacturing to allude to the notion of artlessness. Sheet metal was used for the construction as it is strong but retains malleability from which beautiful shapes can be created.

The model was examined to see how it could be made on a bigger scale, and then the parts were cut freehand from the stainless steel and welded together. To create the complicated organic forms, curved edges and uneven surfaces, metal support structures were employed to keep the final shape and avoid the metal denting in and out during the welding. These supports were then removed. The veneering of the cupboard and table proved complicated as it was difficult to measure the undulating dimensions of the metal surfaces in order to accurately cut the veneer, which in turn was hard to bend into the hollow shapes. The unique process was achieved in collaboration with a specialist veneering company who had not previously worked with metal but rose to the challenge.

Asked what others think of his work, Baas replies, 'Opinions differ and I like them all: from very short, impulsive reactions like "Cool!" to more over-thought opinions like "Interesting because...". I even sometimes agree with negative comments. I like it if my works give inspiration to others.'

SCULPT FURNITURE
MAARTEN BAAS

Production: Maarten Baas
Stainless steel, various finishes
Various dimensions
Design to production: work in progress
Limited batch
www.maartenbaas.com

(Previous page). The Sculpt series of furniture includes (clockwise from top left) cupboard, leather-upholstered armchair, powder-coated and sand-blasted dining chairs, chest of drawers and table.

1–3. The inspiration for the range is the initial sketch/ 3D model, which Baas made roughly and quickly in polystyrene.

4. The models are examined to see how the concept can be translated to an oversized scale and the stainless steel sheets are cut freehand.

5–7. The steel is then welded into shape. The cupboard (5–6) will later receive a walnut veneer, while the chair (7) will be left in its raw state and then sand-blasted.

8. The cupboard in the process of welding. Supports are used to keep the organic, hollow form of the final object and to stop the metal denting in and out during the process. The supports are then removed.

9–12. Once the metal of the cupboard is finished (9–10), it is ready to receive the veneer (11–12).

13. The veneered table. The complicated shapes made it hard to accurately measure and cut the veneer to be applied to the metal, while ensuring that the beauty of the grain remained.

Emmanuel Babled's innovative glass vases and lamps are mainly produced by master craftsmen in Murano, Italy. He is fascinated by the nature and demands of the mercurial material. Changes can only be made when the glass is still malleable; the next moment it crystallizes and becomes, as Babled puts it, 'fragile for the rest of eternity'.

The concept behind the Lum lamp was to create a diffuser with an organic, neuronal aesthetic produced by combining a sinuous fibrous element with glass to catch, soften and spread the light from within the shade. Glass is pure and does not mix easily with any other substance. Known for his subversion of the classical ideal of glass design, Babled decided to work on a dialogue between an industrial material and craft technique. During a trip to the Novotomi furnace in the Czech Republic he tried a first combination of two materials, mixing a glass fibre used in boat construction with Czech crystal. The symbiosis was not successful, the 'short' glass reacting badly with the strong fibre, and caused cracks to appear within 24 hours.

Once back in Murano, and with the collaboration of Venini, the world-famous manufacturer of Italian art glass, Babled's experimentations began in earnest. Sheets of glass fibre were combined with 'long' Murano glass. The method seemed to succeed, producing a pattern within the glass, which in turn didn't shatter. However, the result did not have the random fibrous

look that Babled desired. During discussions with an engineer from the Stazione Sperimentale del Vetro, it was suggested that the most commonly used fibre made from glass type E, which has a coefficient of 50, be adopted. As Babled was working with Type A Murano glass with a coefficient of 104, he decided that the two materials would have a better chance of combining if he found a fibre with a similar chemical balance. He finally sourced a fibre, type C, in China with a coefficient of 80, which he thought close enough. A couple of proofs were tried with excellent aesthetic results. However, under the control of a Polariscope, the pieces showed a structural tension that meant mass manufacture was not an option – especially as the lamp would use a halogen light source and the thermal variations would exert even more pressure on the delicate symbiosis. As a last option, Venini's technicians tried shortening the Murano glass to make it harder and as close to 80 as possible. Although the two materials finally coalesced, the fibre dissolved, producing a cloudy effect, which wasn't what Babled had envisioned.

In parallel with the tests to mix the two materials, different methods of optimizing the combination of glass and glass fibre were developed and several techniques were rejected. Rolling the molten glass over the fibres placed longitudinally on the marver before blowing again had the effect of making the aesthetic too regimented. An organic look was achieved by wrapping continuous threads of the fibre

around the circumference of a glob of glass. The only drawback was that, as the fibre does not stick to itself, the cooling glass had to be dipped in glass and heated after every revolution. Once the fibre was added, the glass was placed in a spherical mould and was blown into shape.

The form of the lamp, a sphere sitting within a concave base, was kept as simple as possible. As the process was highly unpredictable, an uncomplicated shape mitigated the chance of anything going wrong in the delicate blowing and cooling stages. The lamp is made entirely of glass, with the sphere supported on a base that progresses from transparent to opaque as it nears the top. The electrics are hidden in a coloured glass tube that adds a strong focal accent to the design.

Unfortunately, after the Polariscope tests, Venini could not take the risk of using the glass fibre. It was decided to keep the form but to add a spiral of white glass, randomly, inside a plain diffuser to recreate the organic patterning of the fibre concept.

LUM LAMP
EMMANUEL BABLED

Manufacturer: Venini SpA
Hand-blown Murano glass
Light source: halogen
H: 20cm (8in) x Dia: 14cm (5½in)
Design to manufacture: 24 months
Mass-manufactured
www.babled.net/www.venini.com

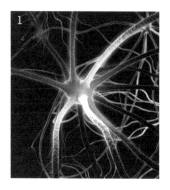

(Previous page). The Lum lamp's base changes from transparent to opaque. The molten glob is rolled to reduce the quantity of white glass on the extremity. A grip is used to further reduce this quantity at the top of the glob. Once in the mould the extremity is closer to the heat and thus softer. As the glass is hand-blown the extremity inflates becoming transparent.

1. The concept behind the Lum lamp was to create a diffuser with an organic, neuronal aesthetic.

2–3. An early experiment mixed glass fibre sheets used in the manufacture of wall coverings with Murano glass. The method (2) did not crack and produced a regimented pattern within the glass. Another experiment

(3) wrapped a fibrous belt around the glass, which was then blown through it. Again, the materials appeared to combine, but the aesthetic did not have the fibrous quality Babled desired.

4. Mixing glass fibre C with hardened Murano glass dissolved the fibre, creating a cloudy effect.

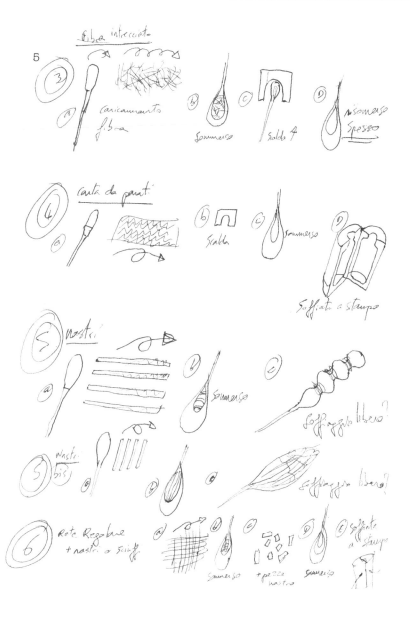

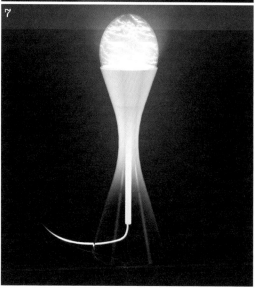

5. Babled used sketches to convey to the craftsmen how he intended the glass to be worked.

6. Polystyrene models were produced to work out the form.

7. Renders were used to present the aesthetic of the design.

8–9. Various methods were tried to combine the glass fibre with the glass. Here (8) they are placed longitudinally on the marver, the glob rolled over them and then blown (9).

10–13. The technique selected was to roll a continuous strand of fibre around the glob (10). As the fibre does not stick to itself, the cooling glass had to be dipped and heated after each revolution (11 and 12). The glass was then blown into a spherical mould (13).

14. The materials combined and the fibrous aesthetic was achieved. However, after random testing in a Polariscope, the glass fibre was found to be too unstable to use as a mass-manufactured technique.

15. The compromise was to keep the form of the original but to add a spiral of glass to the inside of the diffuser. Rather than applying this in a normal way, the craftsman created the spiral in an organic pattern to mimic the fibre.

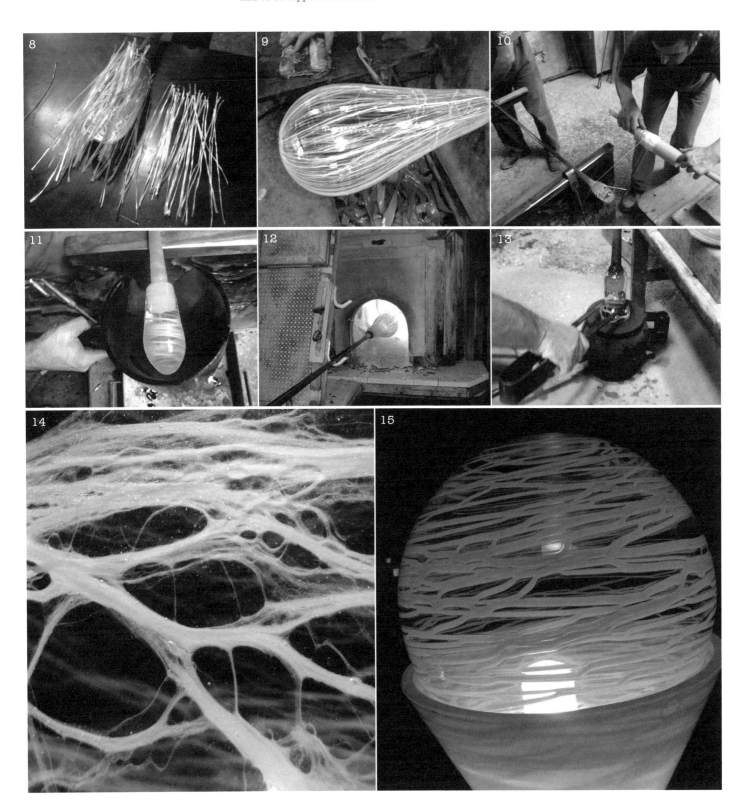

The Units series of sculptural glass pieces was born from Emmanuel Babled's desire to produce works in glass that would provoke questions. Because of the flowing nature of glass in its molten state, it is a material more suitable to organic shapes; a classical aesthetic we have come to associate with the tradition of glass-blowing. Babled wanted to create geometric, mathematical forms that would express modernity and go beyond the merely functional by generating an emotional response. Taking as his starting point the idea of a drop of glass, he began to sketch idealistic, fluid, single-piece forms and came up with the concept of a visionary city. At this stage the drawings were just for fun; he had no idea whether he could make them work in glass. He started to think of different ways the shapes could be conceived physically, finally deciding on a layering technique with the notion of taking away glass to make 'windows'.

With the manufacturer Venini's collaboration, it was decided to launch the series in an exhibition called 'Toys' at the Bevilacqua La Mesa, the most prestigious art foundation in Venice, during the architecture biennale in 2004. The special exhibition of art pieces was to be accompanied with a video celebrating Babled's futuristic vision. The concept was for the series to be seen only side by side with the visionary aesthetic of the animated film, which was realized in cutting-edge 3D Maya computer graphic and After Effect motion graphic programs. By linking the concrete with the conceptual,

the viewer's perception of the objects would change and a bridge be created between the age-old techniques of glass-blowing and innovative computer technology.

Babled's rough sketches were turned into detailed CAD drawings using Rhinoceros® software, which he hand-delivered to the Murano masters. The drawings were refined; adding and subtracting from the curves so the proposed shapes were practical to mould and blow. Polystyrene models were constructed and a series of working sketches produced by Babled to inform the masters just how he wanted the pieces made. Three layers were blown over a mould: first heavy crystal, then coloured glass, and finally white glass. A few examples were made with the coloured glass on top; this is a simpler process but one that Babled thought did not fully express the modernity of the concept.

Each Unit had a complicated form, and a great deal of skill and expertise was needed to make sure the glass reached all the angles and extremities. Failed attempts were broken and examined to test the ratio of the layering and the process refined. Once removed from the mould and cooled, the cold work began. Using a diamond wheel, the master slowly turned the piece by hand, cutting away the white glass and then the colour, feeling the thickness of the material to gauge the depth of etching needed at each stage. Sandpaper was applied to finish and smooth the cut, followed by a cork wheel with abrasive plaster to polish the surface. The

final result appeared as if various layers of glass had been stuck together while, as if by magic, they were created in one piece.

In this project the concept was very much part of the process. Babled wanted the pieces to be appreciated for reasons other than the virtuosity of the glass. His aim was to add a cultural element to make these sculptural objects more contemporary and to give them meaning.

From the Bevilacqua, the exhibition travelled to the Centre Culturel Français in Milan then to the Gallerie Mouvements Modernes in Paris. It was last shown at the Gabrielle Ammann gallery in October 2006.

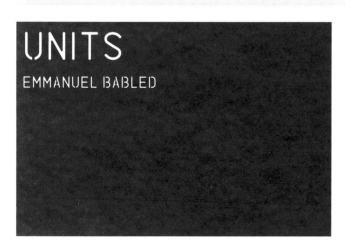

UNITS
EMMANUEL BABLED

Manufacturer: Venini SpA
Hand-blown Murano glass
Various dimensions
Design to manufacture: 12 months
Limited edition, 5 of each colour
www.babled.net/www.venini.com

Units is a modern, geometric series of sculptural pieces that can be used as vases. They are made from three layers of Murano glass hand-blown into a mould.

1

2

3

4

1. Computer rendering of the Unit series of vases, which consists of eight pieces formed in hand-blown Murano glass.

2. First sketches of the architectural forms, some of which would eventually form Babled's futuristic city.

3. Still from the animated film showing an imaginary city, which was made to accompany the presentation of the sculptural pieces.

4. Example of a CAD drawing delivered to the Murano masters to be refined so the pieces could be feasibly blown and moulded.

5–14. The glass layers were prepared (5), the three layers of semi-molten glass were placed in the mould (6–7), and blown (8). After each blowing, the shapes were examined to ensure that the glass filled the extremities of the mould (9). Failures were smashed and the ratio of the layering examined

so it could be refined (10). One of the sculptural pieces before the cold processing (11). The layers of glass were cut away by a diamond wheel (12) and sandpapered to finish the cut (13). Finally, the glass was polished using a combination of cork and abrasive plaster (14).

15. Babled was on hand in the Murano factory throughout the production process.

16. Detail showing the finish and layering: crystal, coloured

glass and then white glass, as for the majority of the pieces.

17. A couple of pieces transposed the coloured and white layers; a far easier permutation to blow and mould.

Edward Barber and Jay Osgerby were awarded the prestigious Jerwood Prize for Applied Arts in 2004; their work was commended by the judges for its 'combination of clarity, coherence and beauty'. They founded their studio in 1996 and received international acclaim following the release of one of their earliest products, the Loop table.

In September 2004, the directors of the De La Warr Pavilion in Bexhill-on-Sea, East Sussex, approached London's Victoria and Albert Museum (V&A) and asked them to recommend a British manufacturer to produce a chair to mark the 70th anniversary restoration of the iconic Modernist building. The initial concept was to produce a plywood chair in keeping with Alvar Aalto's original furniture and Isokon, specialists in plywood manufacture, were put forward. They in turn suggested BarberOsgerby as the designers.

The Pavilion's final brief was for a chair that could be used inside and out, so BarberOsgerby began working on a concept for a metal chair. They took their inspiration from the stunning but austere 1930s architecture of the building itself, in particular the balustrade and detailing within the interior, and the external curved columns on the seafront façade. Unfortunately, Isokon are not experts in metal manufacture and the duo sought the newly founded company Established & Sons, who work only with British-based designers and develop and produce all their products in the UK, to collaborate in the chair's production.

All versions, including the scarlet chair made for the sole use of the Pavilion, are produced in pressure die-cast aluminium for the frame and pressed aluminium for the backrest and seat. Other colour variations are available commercially. In some cases, bespoke upholstery designed by BarberOsgerby and manufactured by the Scottish textile mill Bute Fabrics has been used. Such is the popularity of this elegant and intelligent piece of furniture that it has already become part of the permanent collection of the V&A.

BarberOsgerby used rough sketches, presentation drawings and 3D computer modelling to work up the design. A rough model was made from cardboard and foam, to determine the shape, followed by ergonomic models in polystyrene to test for comfort and solidity. A timber-framed prototype was produced to refine the styling. A full-scale prototype was then CNC-milled from solid aluminium to present during Established & Sons' UK launch during London Design Week in 2005. Various methods of production were discussed, including tube-forming, sand-casting and die-casting, before pressure die-casting the aluminium was selected. Although the initial outlay on tooling was significant, the process makes mass production easier.

The frame is high-pressure die-cast in aluminium. The molten metal is forced under hydraulic pressure into various moulds to form two side pieces, three cross-sections and six cover pieces, which conceal the bolts keeping the frame together.

Fixing details are CNC-milled and all constituents are polished prior to assembly. The chair arms were originally made from aluminium tubing but are now constructed from steel. The steel is bent around a former to determine the required radius and twisted by a high-torque servo motor. The seat and back are laser-cut in a pliable grade of aluminium and then pressed under a two-part steel tool exerting 50 tonnes of pressure to achieve the shape. The pressings are then trimmed and fixing holes formed by a five-axis laser-cutter. Plastic parts used in the assembly are injection-moulded from glass-filled nylon.

Initially, powder-coating and mirror-polishing finishes were used, but the more recent editions adopt an unorthodox industrial process – Vibra Finishing – which involves the parts being shaken for hours with ceramic beads in water to seal the surface and produce a dull galvanized effect. The 25 components are fixed by 44 fasteners; each chair takes 10–12 minutes to put together. 'Assembling the first chair was exciting for us,' says Osgerby, 'that's when we saw the real thing for the first time.'

THE DE LA WARR PAVILION CHAIR
EDWARD BARBER & JAY OSGERBY

Manufacturer: Established & Sons
Cast, tubular and pressed aluminum, steel, nylon, foam, upholstery
H: 78cm (30¾in) x W: 58.5cm (23in) x D: 56.5cm (22¼in)
Design to manufacture: 24 months
Mass-manufactured
www.barberosgerby.com/www.establishedandsons.com

The De La Warr Pavilion chair,
shown here in white next to
an early prototype, is available
commercially in various colours
and finishes.

1–2. The design for the De La Warr Pavilion chair was inspired by the Modernist architecture of Eric Mendelsohn and Serge Chermayeff's Bexhill-on-Sea masterpiece, in particular the tubing of the internal balustrade (1), which was referenced in the choice of cast aluminium for the chair's construction, and the external curved columns on the seafront façade (2), visually referred to in the frame section.

3. Alvar Aalto's original furniture was an early influence, but a plywood chair was rejected for a more contemporary material and aesthetic. The final chair is produced in scarlet exclusively for use in the Pavilion.

4–5. Early hand-drawn sketches of the design.

6–7. Line drawings and 3D computer renderings were used to work up the design.

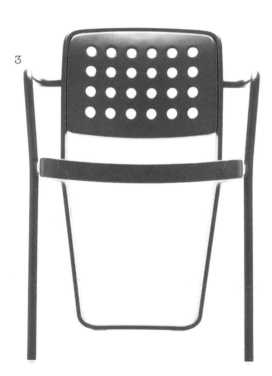

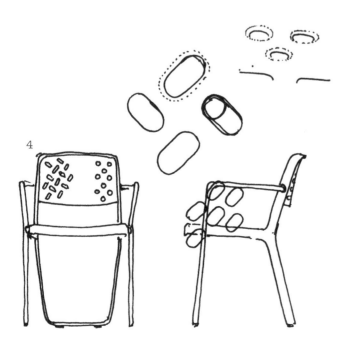

6

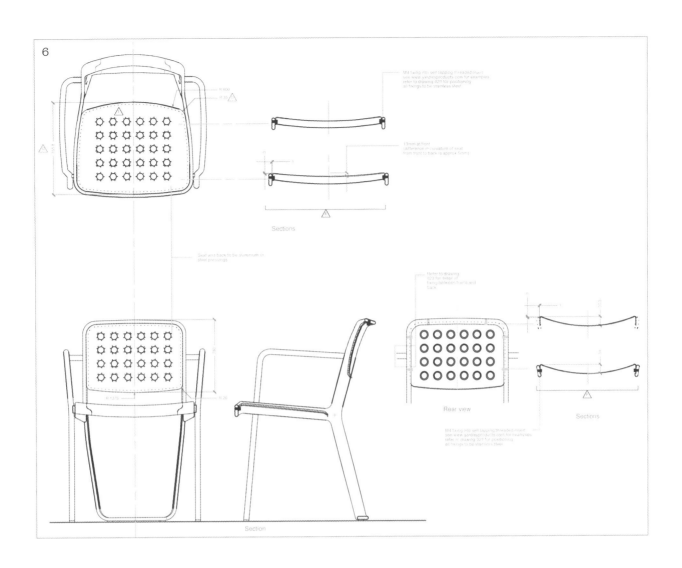

Sections

Rear view

Sections

Section

7

8

9

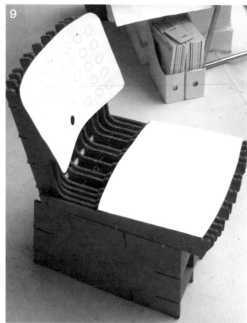

8. The rear profile of the chair is distinguished by the skid leg. This was created in response to the observation that many chairs, particularly dining chairs, are viewed from behind. BarberOsgerby chose to use an enclosed volume; a fluid form rather than a more usual leg type.

9. A cardboard model was made in BarberOsgerby's studio as part of the initial design process.

10. Numerous cardboard models resulted in a polystyrene ergonomic model to determine the comfort and stability of the chair.

11. Blue foam and card mock-up to determine proportions.

12. A second prototype, showing the distinctive skid leg at the rear of the chair, was made in timber by a pattern-maker based in London.

13. The first CNC-milled aluminium prototype was first shown at Established & Sons' London debut in September 2005 during London Design Week.

10

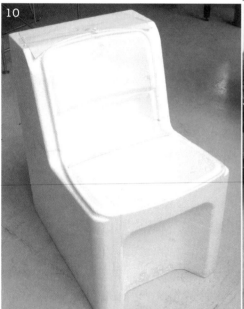

11

12

13

14. The side parts of the chair are high-pressure die-cast. This is the negative mould into which molten aluminium is forced to form a section of the chair's frame.

15. The die-cast machine is made ready for production.

16. The side section is finished to remove the flash lines.

17. Each of the exclusive chairs supplied to the De La Warr Pavilion is engraved with a plaque bearing the designers' names and date of design.

18–20. The unique cherry-red chairs are assembled. The 25 components are fixed by 44 fasteners; each chair takes 10–12 minutes to put together.

21. The fabric for the upholstered version of the chair is the first-ever textile designed by BarberOsgerby and is produced by Bute Fabrics on the Isle of Bute on the west coast of Scotland. The result is a fine-ribbed design combining two contrasting colours. A palette of 34 colourways was eventually selected.

As founder of the award-winning San Francisco-based industrial and branding firm fuseproject, Yves Béhar's mission is to create narratives to develop emotional responses to products. His conviction is that the stronger and more complex the link with a consumer, the longer lasting customer loyalty will be. Béhar's designs are a perfect symbiosis of creativity and technology, which he admits owes much to his bicultural heritage. Born to an East German mother and Turkish father, he says, 'One is functional and modernist; the other expressive and poetic. I always try to marry the two in my projects.'

Aliph is a newly formed developer of mobile audio products. Based in San Francisco, its first offering is the Jawbone Bluetooth headset, built around noise shield technology. The headset only takes notice of speech, which naturally involves moving the mouth and hence the jaw. The headset extends over the muscles that activate the jaw so that when the mouth moves a sensor is activated and any noise that is not generated by the speaker is eliminated, through the use of a military-grade noise-cancelling system.

Béhar started by researching existing Bluetooth headsets. Features such as adjustable earhoops and buds, a choice of colours, and a sleek, contemporary aesthetic became important in his design as they were generally lacking in the market and also sought by the consumer.

Minimalism and simplicity were key to the aesthetic, as was the contrast between high-tech and organic. The outer part of the headset is a pared-down curved surface, with all buttons and sliders hidden within the unit. The inner side, which rests against the jaw muscles, is soft and contoured, emphasizing the functionality of the cheek-touching sensor. The combination of the simplicity and style of the outer surfaces and the soft, ergonomic inner surfaces distinguishes the Jawbone as technological jewellery rather than a mere gadget.

Initial sketches to determine the basic aesthetic of the unit and the earloops were followed by technical drawings, ergonomic studies and material experiments. During these, Béhar worked on the development of a soft moulded band of rubber over a rigid external structure to allow the soft flexible material to fit around the ear while retaining an outer inflexible form. Much iteration of 3D files was made to determine the location of the microphone holes and the smooth shape of the internal parts in the body. Initially the headset was too large; a complete rethink was necessary to shrink the design and the internals by 50%.

The earloop, composed of two different materials, was the most complex element of the headset to manufacture. The process of inserting the zinc metal part into the production machine and injecting the rubber around it needed a lot of refinement: as the intended wall thickness was

only 1mm on either side, the zinc would not always be centred within the tool and would appear on the edge of the rubber, or the rubber would not bond properly to the smooth zinc surface. These challenges were resolved by increasing the rubber section and creating a hole at the bottom end of the metal piece to prevent the rubber slipping. Additionally, due to the varying cross-section of the earloop, stamping was not an option, therefore precluding the use of steel or titanium. The zinc that was eventually employed could not be cast in the traditional way as it became too brittle. Instead it was heated and forged into shape and then taken through a heating and cooling process to limit the chance of fracturing. The shape and softness of the rubber parts took trial and error, during which both earloop and bud were prototyped in three varieties of TPE and tested on a durometer to find the optimum hardness of the rubber for comfort, stability and sensor contact.

To manufacture the hidden buttons on the outer surface of the shield, the tool was progressively machined towards a thinner section. At every 0.55mm, the tool would be injected and the parts fully assembled and tested until an ergonomic and functional balance was achieved.

JAWBONE BLUETOOTH HEADSET
YVES BÉHAR/FUSEPROJECT

Manufacturer: Aliph
Client and program engineer: Alex Asseily
Medical grade ABS plastic, rubber, electro-plated zinc
L: 5cm (2in)
Design to manufacture: 12 months
Mass-manufactured
www.fuseproject.com/www.jawbone.com

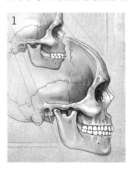

(Previous page). The high-styled outer surface of the Jawbone Bluetooth headset conceals all operating buttons, which are activated by depressing sensors on the silicon board beneath. The sealed controls minimize visual clutter and ensure pure visual and functional simplicity.

1. Jawbone is built around noise shield technology. The headset only takes notice of speech, the movement of the jaw activating a sensor that eliminates peripheral sound.

2. Yves Béhar builds powerful, emotional brand stories to connect with today's consumer. He was made Vice President and Creative Director of Aliph and is involved with all of the creative and consumer experience aspects of the Jawbone while maintaining his fuseproject responsibilities.

3. Early sketches followed thorough research of the Bluetooth headset market, which revealed that customers sought adjustable earhoops and earbuds, and a sleek contemporary aesthetic combined with innovative technology.

4. The headset consists of a high-tech outer surface that conceals the controls, the 'whale' containing the electronics and noise sensor, and the earhoop and bud in zinc and rubber.

5. Exploded computer drawing showing how the unit fits together.

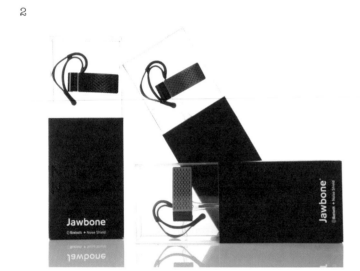

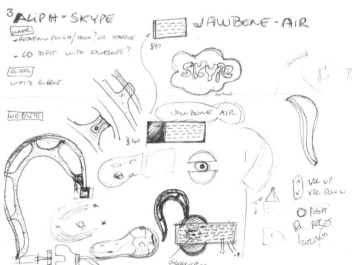

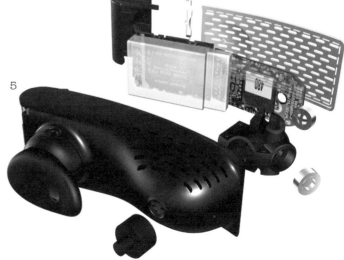

6. Probably the most visually interesting part of the unit is the 'whale', which is a single piece of injection-moulded ABS plastic. The challenge was to make the ventilation holes on the belly perpendicular to its irregular surface. Slides on three different angles were inserted into the mould to achieve this.

7–8. During the development process, Béhar and Alex Asseily of Aliph examined various earloop shapes and sizes (7) and eight different earbud configurations (8).

9. Computer drawing to work out how the earloop and earbud attach to the whale.

10. Workers test the power adaptor to ensure that all units make a connection between the USB port and the charger.

11. Plastic painted face shields are placed in trays before moving to the assembly line.

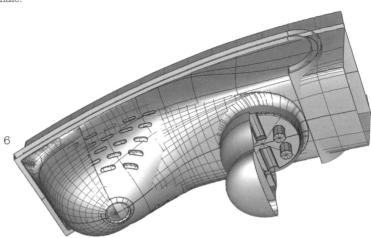

6

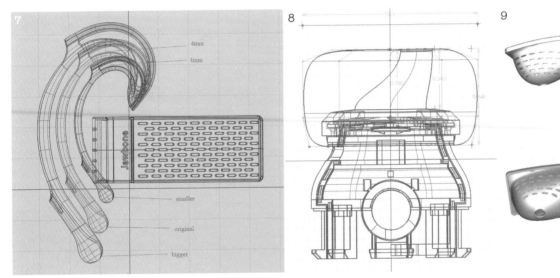

7

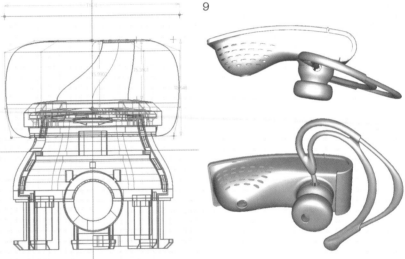

8

9

10

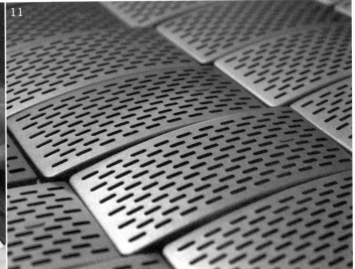

11

Yves Béhar's Leaf light for Herman Miller was introduced during the International Contemporary Furniture Fair in New York in 2006. At that time, Paola Antonelli, the design curator of the city's Museum of Modern Art, wrote, 'LEDs have actually been around a long time but what's most interesting is that the Leaf lamp's very expressive form is justified by mechanical requirements.' Unlike other LED lamps, which burn hot and require complicated cooling systems, Leaf stays cool to the touch through the use of a patented heat-distribution system. This allows the user to grab the head of the light without any worry that they will get burnt.

US-based manufacturer Herman Miller is primarily known for its socially responsible yet innovative seating for the contract market, in particular the ergonomic Aeron Chair designed by Don Chadwick and Bill Stumpf. Although it has been involved in the manufacture of lighting, it was a departure for the company to create a whole new concept in lighting design. They approached Béhar in 2002 and the commission quickly became a personal project for him. 'It is rare to be able to design both the light source and the light. I wanted Leaf to be both futuristic and familiar, like a blade of grass that lights up at night. At the same time, a new technology demands a new expression, and a new function: the ability to change the light from cold to warm, focusing on the experience of the light. In a way the simplicity of the form does enhance the experience. The emotion of light touches you, while one can actually touch the product.'

The lamp uses a biomorphic grid of LEDs to deliver a wide spectrum of light from 2800 to 6000 Kelvin; from the golden glow of a candle to the white light of a task lamp. At the initial stages of the design, the technology did not exist to make this achievable. LEDs were not widely available, and were mainly used in brightly coloured public displays. Herman Miller brought in an engineering firm, Gecko, to help with the technical specifications of the lamp and Béhar, in collaboration with his San Francisco-based design company, fuseproject, experimented with a series of concept lights employing fluorescents, halogen and cold cathodes. These ideas were never put into practice due to the worldwide economic downturn following the dot.com burst and 9/11. The design of the light was put on hold, but the delay proved to be advantageous. By the time work resumed, LED technology had advanced. The development of a compact, white LED meant that Béhar could keep a slim profile for the head of the lamp, which he elongated to showcase these tiny jewels of light. Incorporating a printed circuit board with an integrated microprocessor in Leaf's base gave the user the ability to control both the light's intensity and the warm-to-cool colours within the LED driver circuits by using separate touch controls.

The main problem was eliminating the overheating. During the development engineering phase, the LED lightbulb would fail within 45 seconds. Béhar tried to add a fan, but this meant it quickly lost the sleek profile of its design. The solution came in the form of the LEDs themselves, which Béhar had imitated to create the aesthetic of the stamped, bubbled upper surface of the lamp's head. By punching a hole in each of the bumps, he created miniature flues through which the heat escaped. He also developed a heat-sink linking the LED bulbs to the aluminium body, extending the heat dissipation to the entire light body.

The design was developed using simple sketches and paper models to fashion the slim, flexible arms of the lamp, which could be easily adjusted to create different light effects. The ideas were then translated into CAD drawings from which working prototypes were fashioned to assess functional issues. A simple, easily replaceable, hinge was devised to connect the head to the base to facilitate its removal and replacement at the end of the LED's lifespan, meaning the lamp itself will never be rendered obsolete.

LEAF LIGHT
YVES BÉHAR/FUSEPROJECT

Manufacturer: Herman Miller Inc
Aluminium, plastic
H: 53.3cm (21in) x D: 22cm (8⅔in)
Design to manufacture: 48 months
Mass-manufactured
www.fuseproject.com/www.hermanmiller.com

The aesthetic of the Leaf lamp is biomorphic. Its functions include a flexible arm to give a range of lighting effects and to direct light as needed.

1. The lamp was inspired by a blade of grass.

2. A series of drawings: some address the way the upper arm attaches to the lower to allow maximum flexibility; others develop a hinge to attach the blade to the base.

3–4. The drawings were translated into CAD drawings

(3), from which working prototypes (4) were made to address problem areas.

5. The printed circuit board (PCB), with a microprocessor located in its base, controls the temperature setting of the light.

6. Special software was created to develop an interactive user

interface to control and adjust the brightness and luminosity of Leaf. This is activated by a unique injection-moulded plastic touch sensor located in the base.

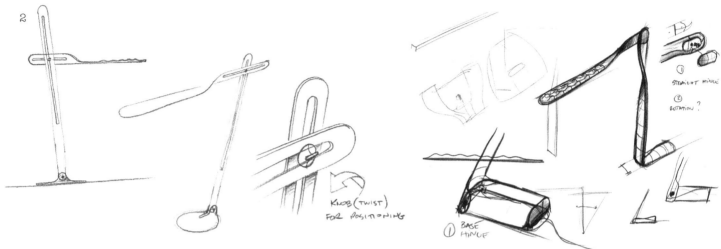

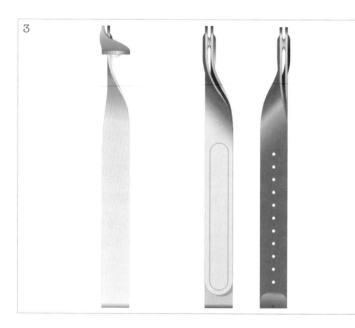

7–8. Sketch and CAD drawing illustrating the patented heat-distribution system achieved through an engineered heat-sink and aluminium blade that allows heat to be dispersed along the length of the lamp.

9. Exploded axonometric diagram showing how the various parts of the lamp fit together.

10–11. Multi-station stamping was used to form the arms of the lamp (10): trim die-cutting for the overall shape and to ensure consistent cost-effective uniformity of form, and stamping die-cut for the internal structural elements where extreme precision was not needed. The aluminium was injection-moulded to ensure consistent wall thickness and good surface quality. Leaf is pressed in several progressive moulds and then slowly bent into its final form (11).

12. Yves Béhar was involved in the marketing and branding of the product.

13. The head was designed to emphasize the grid of LEDs.

14. The arm moves through 90 degrees to direct the light wherever it is needed.

15. The light can be altered from cold to warm.

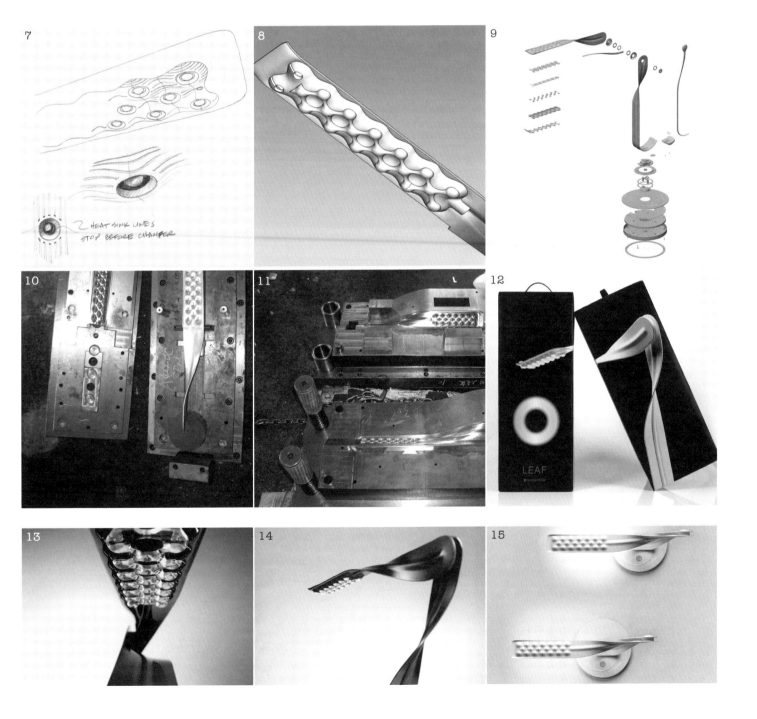

The One Laptop Per Child (OLPC) initiative is a radical scheme aiming to provide low-cost computers to educate children in developing countries and, thanks to antennas that network up to 16km (10 miles) apart, communication between remote communities. Mobile ad hoc networking is used to allow many machines Internet access from one connection, with each computer acting as a router. The brief from Nicholas Negroponte, founder of MIT Media Lab's OLPC initiative, was demanding: to provide a powerful WiFi system with an energy source that permits the computer to run indefinitely without an electrical outlet; to create an accessible cheerful, iconic design that is dust-proof, weather-proof and heat-resistant; and, most importantly, to create a design that would be intuitive to children who had never before been introduced to modern technology. On top of that it had to retail for less than any other computer on the market: it is known as the $100 computer!

Yves Béhar and his company fuseproject became involved in the project after the first design team hired, Design Continuum, had run out of ideas. Béhar started from scratch, with internal layouts and hundreds of configurations to make the assembly work functionally and to also be visually accessible.

Simplicity and efficiency were key. All technological innovations are integrated into a monolithic, clearly defined form that is unmistakably a child's computer, being colourful and possessing whimsical features such as the Rabbit Ears antenna. When closed, it is sealed to protect it from dirt. When opened, it has a soft, tactile quality with a unique rubber-moulded keyboard.

fuseproject is 'idea-centric'. It starts a commission by strategizing first the experience and then the message of a product, before beginning on sketches, rough mock-ups, 3D modelling studies and prototypes that it carries out conjunctionally rather than sequentially to arrive at the final idea. Using a combination of these methods, Béhar considered many options. The OLPC engineering team and fuseproject decided to incorporate the mechanics behind the display instead of underneath the keyboard, to simplify the wiring so that keyboard and motherboard no longer communicated through a fragile hinge. This, however, made the unit unstable. Two ideas for fixing top to bottom were tested. The first, placing the battery under the keyboard, became impossible after the size of the battery increased twofold. The second, supporting the display by the counterweight of a sturdy handle behind the keyboard, is the version that was developed. All early designs were powered by a hand-crank, but after testing this function on prototypes and finding it exerted too much stress on the hardware, this was abandoned in favour of rechargeable batteries, human power pull-cords and the harnessing of solar power.

In the final design, everything serves a double function: the antennas fold down to shield the USB ports; the handle counterbalances the display and doubles as an attachment for the shoulder strap; and the surrounding coloured bumper seals the unit from dust and integrates the rubber feet. Once all areas of the design had been defined, the PC's ABS main body was injection-moulded in plastic. Three processes were considered; double-shot and insert-moulding were rejected because of their lack of recyclability. The antennas were also injection-moulded but then insert-moulded to add a layer of protective rubber. The rubber keypad was moulded in a single piece, and then glued over the connectors on to a steel plate and mounted on the unit so it reinforces the construction and seals the electrical components from moisture and dust.

The OLPC scheme has received a lot of criticism from for-profit IT industry leaders, as a superficial requirement in areas where many children don't have access to classrooms, let alone computers. Béhar himself sees it as a great democratizer. 'For the kids it is about making projects together, collaborating and communicating,' he says. 'OLPC is the first thing I've seen in many years that is in line with the original goal of the PC: to bring information, communication and education to all.'

ONE LAPTOP PER CHILD XO COMPUTER

YVES BÉHAR/FUSEPROJECT

Manufacturer: Quanta Computer
Concept/engineering: Nicholas Negroponte
H: 24.2cm (9½in) x W: 22.8cm (9in) x D: 3cm (1⅛in)
Design to manufacture: 30 months
Mass-manufactured
www.fuseproject.com/www.quanta.com.tw/
www.laptop.org

Thanks to a transformer
hinge, the OLPC can be used
as a standard laptop, for
e-book reading as well as
for gaming.

1. Exploded perspective. Everything in the design serves a double function, with antennas folding down to shield the USB ports.

2–4. Fuseproject starts a commission by strategizing before beginning on sketches (2), rough mock-ups in foam (3), 3D modelling studies (4) and prototypes (40 were created in total).

5–6. Two early prototypes were presented to Media Lab. Yellow was propped up by a sturdy handle behind the keyboard (5). Blue had a battery beneath the keyboard to give an ergonomic tilt (6). Both counterbalanced the display that concealed the electronics and were thus top-heavy. Both prototypes were generated using a hand-held crank. This function was rejected because of the need for longevity and the reliability of the overall unit.

7. The laptop consumes five to ten times less power than a standard laptop and can be recharged by human power. This is advantageous for children in areas where there is no electricity. Power solutions include rechargeable batteries, foot pedals, solar power, and the human-powered yo-yo, conceived and engineered by Squid Lab.

8–9. CAD drawings were used to finalize details of the design.

10. The body was injection-moulded. Double-shot and insert-moulding were rejected because the mixing of two materials would make the laptops unrecyclable.

11. Image of the cavity tool taken during the Electrical Discharge Machining (EDM) process for the upper handle plastic part of the laptop.

12. Copper EDM tool used to apply texture to the upper handle cover, along with the pre-texture handle-cover plastic part.

13. Core tool for the injection-moulded plastic part that forms the underside of the upper handle.

14. After the materials were tested, and the unit submitted to various performance assessments such as drop testing, splash-proofing and resistance to ultraviolet, examples were sent out to be used by schools in Nigeria and Uruguay. Design improvements were then made.

15. A system was developed so that the children could recognize their own laptops; 400 different colour combinations of the XO logo were added to the designs.

The Bombay Sapphire Foundation was set up in 2001 with the aim of supporting the best in contemporary glass design. Each year, the £20,000 Bombay Sapphire Prize recognizes the outstanding achievements of international artists, designers and architects working in that medium. In 2006, for the first time they allocated a further £5,000 to be awarded to the best newcomer. The accolade went to Laura Birdsall, a young British glass designer fresh out of London's Royal College of Art. The judges recognized in the series of vases, Interior Landscape, an inspiring contemporary approach to the age-old technique of glass-forming and blowing.

Birdsall studied 3D dimensional design at Buckinghamshire College of Higher Education and received an MA in glass design from the Royal College of Art. She has always had a hands-on attitude to her work and is accomplished in the ancient art of glass-blowing. The physical process of making an object, in manipulating the glass and recognizing its intrinsic fluid qualities, is as important to Birdsall as the design itself.

The vases are informed by a journey into interior space. 'I am interested in a child's ability to see a whole universe in something very small. It is this sense of wonder, invention, and the unexpected that I want to convey,' says Birdsall. 'The interior spaces of my work suggest a microscopic world of dimly illuminated caves. They are imagined spaces inhabited by strange and curious organisms.

They are a fantastic voyage through awe-inspiring landscapes and miniature worlds.' Her inspiration came from looking at microscopic photography; from the 1966 science fiction film Fantastic Voyage, in which shrunken doctors in a mini-submarine are injected into the body of a dying Czech scientist; and Verner Panton's organic, womb-like foam-rubber interior environment Phantasy Landscape (1970). 'I wanted the viewer to look inside the vases and find something unexpected,' comments Birdsall.

For Birdsall, the important attribute of glass is that, when molten, it is a soft and pliable material that she can manipulate at will. When she started her training she felt dictated to by its mercurial properties, but with experience came the confidence to harness these same characteristics to her own ends. In Interior Landscape, Birdsall wanted to express the depth of colour that is possible in hand-made glass and explore the way light could be made to move through the material even when opaque.

The design was worked out using 3D models made quickly in clay, then in glass, and refined in a series of abstract drawings. The work was hand-blown and formed without the use of a mould. The shape was achieved by rolling and pushing three layers of glass over one another on a steel marver: first coloured, then white, and finally translucent. The ball was blown and fashioned by hand using wooden blocks and a pad of

dampened newspaper. Each vase has slight variations. A simple tool – a metal rod – was then used to create the indents.

Getting the temperature correct was crucial to the procedure. The outer transparent layer is stretched through the two colours on the inside, giving a sense of illumination. The vases were allowed to cool overnight before the cold work began.

The hardest part of the concept was to achieve the optimum opening. It was necessary for the viewer to see just enough of the interior to draw them in, but if the aperture was made too big then all sense of magic would be lost. Birdsall started by drawing a line for the rim and carefully cutting it using a diamond saw, but found the effect too contrived. After experimenting she decided to cut through each vase independently, judging where the line should fall based on the first indent and then slicing through it so that the form dictated the opening in each case. This gave a much freer line and each piece became unique. Various wheels, diamond and emery-coated, were employed to give a smooth finish to the vases, which were finally sand-blasted on the outside to achieve a matte appearance.

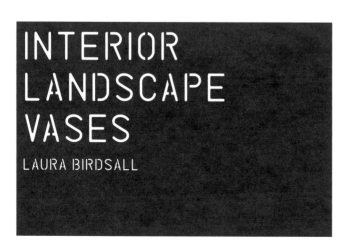

INTERIOR LANDSCAPE VASES

LAURA BIRDSALL

Production: Laura Birdsall
Hand-blown glass
H: 40cm (15¾in) x Dia: 16cm (6¼in)
Design to production: 12 months
Limited batch
www.laurabirdsall.com

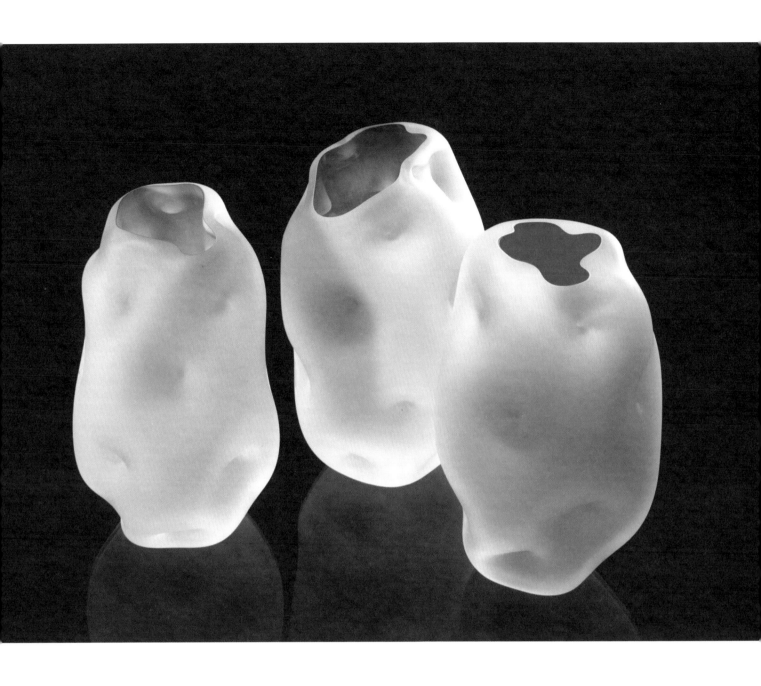

Each Interior Landscape vase
is hand-blown in three layers
of glass to give it more depth
and intensity.

1. The Interior Landscapes series was inspired by Laura Birdsall's fascination with looking inside and finding something hidden. She quotes Verner Panton's 1970 <u>Phantasy Landscape</u> as one of the greatest influences for the vases.

2. The viewer is tempted to look inside the vases through the asymmetrical openings to discover the unexpected; a landscape of strangely glowing protuberances.

3–4. Birdsall worked up the design using 3D clay models (3) that are quick and easy to create, followed by glass models (4).

5. Abstract drawings were also made to move the concept forward.

6. The coloured glass was added to the blowpipe.

7. A white layer of glass was laid over the coloured glass and rolled on the steel marver.

8–9. The layers of glass were formed using dampened newspaper (8) and wooden blocks (9).

10–11. The vases were blown to size (10). Each shape is judged by eye and every piece is individual (11).

12. The indents were created by pushing a steel rod into the glass while still malleable, stretching the transparent layer through the white and finally into the coloured glass.

13. Keeping the temperature correct is important to this procedure.

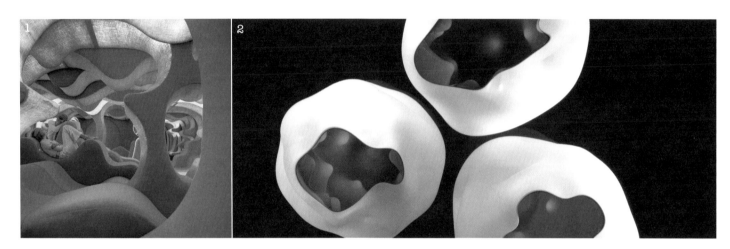

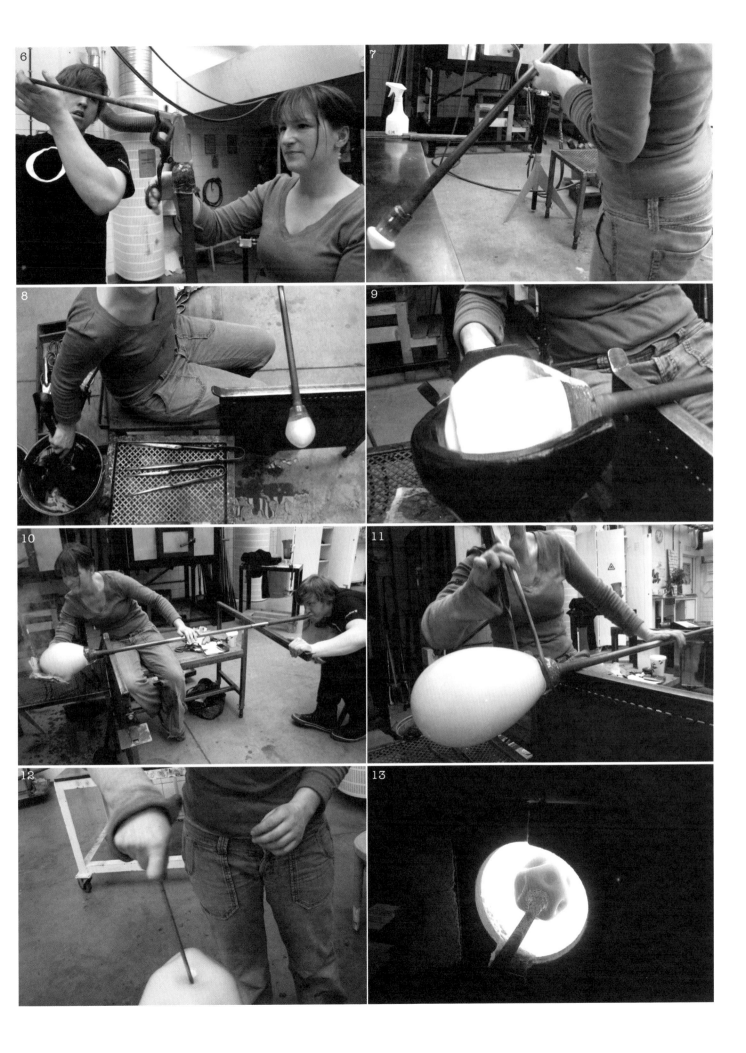

Since their discovery in 1997 by Giulio Cappellini, founder of the eponymous Italian manufacturing company, Ronan and Erwan Bouroullec have built up an international reputation, with a monograph published by Phaidon Press in 2003 and major solo exhibitions at the Design Museum, London (2002), the Museum of Contemporary Art in Los Angeles (2004), and the Boijmans Museum of Art in Rotterdam (2004). Their functional and unpretentious work places them at the forefront of contemporary design.

The Bouroullecs are great admirers of British designer Jasper Morrison, who in turn has championed the pair from the beginning, describing their work as 'thoughtful and disciplined with a real spirit and poetry'. The brothers are hesitant to define their style, but what all their pieces appear to have in common is a concern with the needs of today's consumer. They have the ability to reinvent traditional types of furniture or products by recreating them in a way that is peculiarly appropriate to our generation. Their creativity lies not in technical or technological innovation, but in an examination of the peripatetic and flexible living requirements of modern society. From the Lit Clos (a modern, practical way to create private sleeping space in open-plan apartments) to the Joyn office system (consisting of broad, communal desks that the user customizes with slot-on partitions), and the Algue modular clipping system (which snaps into place without tools to create

walls that can be constructed and deconstructed following the various life changes of the inhabitants), the brothers' work is multi-functional and conceived to be adapted and personalized by the consumer.

The Steelwood chair was originally commissioned by Eugenio Perazza, the owner of manufacturer Magis, who requested an inexpensive wooden chair with simple joints in pressed metal. As the junction of parts in wooden objects is the most complex element to their design, Perazza thought straightforward stamped metal parts would result in a relatively cheap chair, easy to assemble, to collapse and transport. The brothers were taken to a stamping factory, and it was then that they started to think of a more mixed chair, with metal and wood used in more-or-less equal proportions. They wanted to create a piece that would compete in cost with a plastic chair but would have a long shelf-life and throughout the years increase in character as the metal takes on a patina and the wood wears.

The design was developed through sketches, 3D modelling and the creation of CAD drawings using Rhinoceros® to give concrete shape to the drawings and refine the form and assemblage points. The construction of prototypes helped in the understanding of proportions and the physical aspects of the chair. The pair then reverted to modelling and drawing to examine details of shape, comfort and finish. Finally, a new set of CAD files was developed from which the stamping factory created the moulds.

After a long and interesting initial drawing process, the chair was already very precise; the maquettes, prototyping and rendering stages were aimed at making the final result as close as possible to the last set of sketches. Eight successive versions of the final prototype were produced. These were then modified, millimetre by millimetre, to get the end version correct.

In total, nine tools gradually curve and shear the metal in sequence. The complex pressing and bending technique was difficult to achieve. What appears to be a simple form is the result of a series of complex deformations, and the initial tooling investment was high. Once set up, however, the level of mechanization of the process meant that the units were produced at a price competitive to an iconic plastic chair. The screw holes were added during the cutting and bending, welding was carried out by robot, and the basic beech seat and legs cut and then shaped using a numerical milling machine. The only hand involvement was in the assembly of metal and wooden parts and the finishing of the wood.

STEELWOOD CHAIR
RONAN & ERWAN BOUROULLEC

Manufacturer: Magis SpA
Steel plate, beech
H: 75cm (29½in) x W: 55cm (21½in) x D: 40cm (15¾in)
Design to manufacture: 29 months
Mass-manufactured
www.bouroullec.com/www.magisdesign.com

The original commission
for the Steelwood chair
was for a wooden seat with
pressed metal junctions. The
Bouroullec brothers developed
the concept using wood and
metal in similar proportions.

1–3. After a long and detailed drawing stage, the first sketches vary little from the end result. The most complicated aspect of the design was to make the final curves resemble the original drawings as closely as possible in spite of the limits of the fabrication process.

4–6. Computer renderings showing how the metal and wooden parts were intended to slot into place.

7–8. A series of prototypes was developed in plastic and wood (7), and metal and wood (8), to help understand the proportions and the physical aspects of the chair. Eight successive versions of the final prototype were produced and modified. The final was then tested by CATAS, the Research and Development Centre, to certificate resistance and load-bearing.

9–10. In total, nine tools were developed to gradually bend, curve and laser-cut the shape of the metal back in sequence, from initial steel plate to final form.

11. The selection of the steel sheet depended on its ability to carry weight: the result was the use of the material, FE MC 355 with a thickness of 20/10.

12–14. Press housing the mould for shearing the flattened metal sheet and incising the holes for the screws, and to attach the steel in the tool (12). Top part of the mould (13). Bottom part of mould (14).

15–16. Mould for coining the perimeter and central part.

17. Mould to fold the perimeter and central part.

18–19. Mould to trim the angles after folding.

20–22. Mould to fold the central part.

23–24. Mould to shear the lateral windows.

25–26. The lateral windows are curved.

27. The production of the Steelwood chair is highly mechanized. The only hand involvement is the assembly of the wood and metal parts, and the finishing.

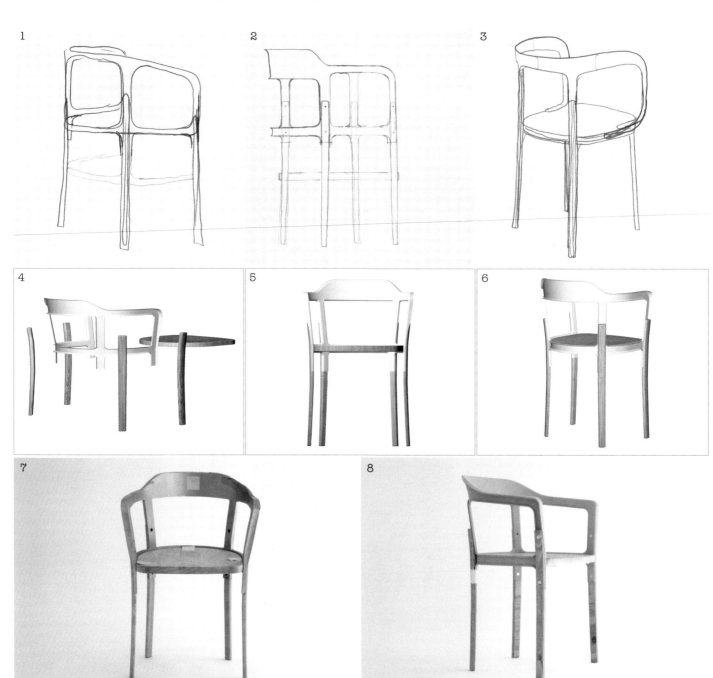

For over a decade, Portugal has been at the centre of a cultural rebirth. Lisbon is one of the top weekend destinations, and the building and infrastructure regeneration that led up to the football extravaganza of Euro 2004 has encouraged international architects to undertake commissions in the country: Rem Koolhaas's Casa da Música was completed in spring 2005, and Frank Gehry's Parque Mayer theatre complex is currently on site. All this activity helps to focus international attention on a country that lies on the western border of Europe with its back to its dominant neighbour, Spain, and facing the Atlantic – a country that has until relatively recently been on the edge looking out. The political isolation imposed by the fascist Salazar regime was lifted following the Sweet Revolution of 1974. The young designers of today are the first generation to grow up without fear of repression; these are designers with an intellectual curiosity, characterized by inventiveness and sensitivity, and with a freshness born from the fact that the discipline was virtually unheard of ten years ago.

Fernando Brizio was born in Angola of Portuguese parents and came to Portugal following the revolution. Today, along with Miguel Vieira Baptista, he is the key figure in the Portuguese product design scene, his work also bearing a passing resemblance to some of the more refined pieces by the highly conceptual Dutch collective, Droog Design. Brizio combines narrative and shared memory in items that function and in forms that are never far from their archetype. To many design purists, Brizio's work might appear too close to that of the artisan. However, this oversimplification would ignore the way in which he mixes ingenuity and technical skill in work that examines how objects interact with one another and with the user on both a functional and emotional level, calling on collective experience and humour. His earlier Painting with Giotto bowl was Brizio's response to the ugly stain that a leaking fountain pen left on his trouser pocket. Taking an unglazed earthenware piece, he attached 95 felt-tipped pens to the rim of the bowl and let them leak their colours into the porous limestone, capturing the kaleidoscopic effect for ever. Brizio's Sound System lamp and jar recreate, in hundreds of stacked steel discs, the physical shape of the sound waves generated by the words 'lamp' and 'jar' as they are recorded into a scientific instrument of sound measurement.

The Viagem tableware is probably Brizio's most thought-provoking project, examining as it does material behaviour and production processes. Most of Brizio's pieces are defined by a moment of serendipity: in the Viagem series the unpredictable informs the aesthetic. The concept was inspired by the collapse of a birthday cake in the back of Brizio's car while he was driving to a party.

Using a series of drawings that outline the generic shape of pots, bottles and water containers, Brizio instructed the potter to create the designs. Several types of ceramic with different drying rates were tested before porcelain was selected. Clay performs in much the same way, having a similar colour and texture to porcelain, but unique to the latter material is the fact that any attempt to correct irregularity prior to firing is useless as the defect returns when the material is heated.

The raw vessels were placed in the back of a jeep and taken on a journey. Brizio chose to develop his concept in the city of Caldas da Rainha, not only for its wealth of good ceramic workshops but because the area is rich in the choice of both urban and rural paths and roads. As the jeep travelled over the tortuous terrain, the pieces were shaped and took on the impressions of every curve and bump, morphing under the speed and braking of the vehicle. The pots were then removed and fired, capturing for ever the memory of their creation.

VIAGEM TABLEWARE

FERNANDO BRIZIO

Production: Fernando Brizio
Porcelain
Various dimensions
Design to production: 7 months
Limited batch
fernandobrizio@cliz.pt

For the Viagem tableware,
porcelain was selected over
other ceramics such as clay
or stoneware because of its
ability to embody memory.

1

2

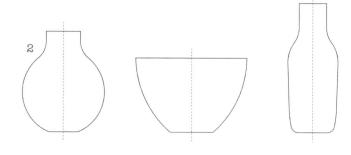

3

1. The inspiration for the Viagem tableware was the collapse of a birthday cake placed in the back of Fernando Brizio's car.

2. Brizio sketched the archetypical shapes of vases, bowls and bottles.

3. The generic forms were given physical form by a potter in porcelain.

4–5. The fresh vessels were placed in the back of a jeep and taken on a journey.

6–7. The city of Caldas da Rainha was chosen not only for its ceramic workshops but because of the varied terrain that surrounds it.

8–9. The deformed pots, which recorded every curve and bump of the journey, were removed and fired.

10. The Painting with Giotto bowl (2005), an earlier work, was created by allowing 95 felt-tipped pens to bleed their colours into a porous limestone bowl. The kaleidoscopic effect is preserved for ever.

11–13. The Sound System lamp and jar (2003) (12–13) is another interesting early project, which recreated, in dozens of stacked steel discs, the physical shape of the sound waves generated by the words 'lamp' and 'jar' as they were recorded into a scientific instrument of sound measurement (11).

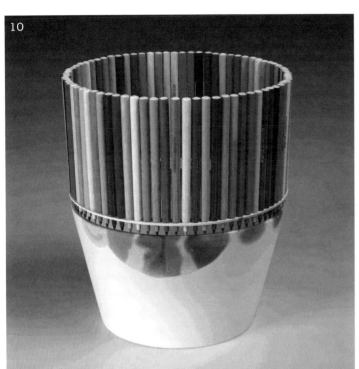

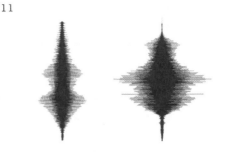

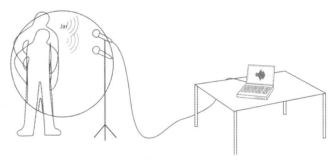

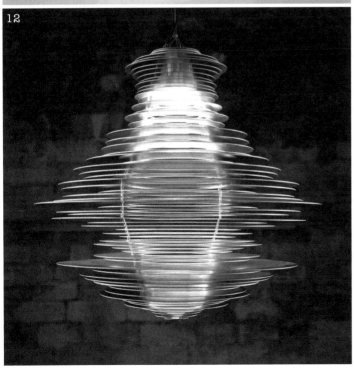

Both the mass-manufactured Part nesting tables and the Handmade range of outdoor 'paper' furniture comprise elements of the same body of research that sees Stephen Burks experiment with ways of folding flat patterns to achieve pyramidal structures – the most efficient form of support. Handmade was inspired by study models left over from the Part tables, which included some shapes that were impossible to create in brake-formed aluminium. Burks used these models as a means to explore the possibility of a paper furniture collection that would allow him to work without the limitations imposed by industrially formed aluminium.

Burks studied architecture at the Illinois Institute of Technology before transferring to the product design programme, from which he graduated in 1992. He formed his own company, Readymade Projects, in 1997 and has collaborated with major European manufacturers: Cappellini, Moroso, Zanotta, Missoni, Covo, Boffi and now B&B Italia. He has been the only African-American designer to work with these companies and has become a role model for young African-Americans in product design. Additionally, through his work with the American non-profit Aid To Artisans in collaboration with home accessories manufacturer Artecnica, Burks has travelled to South Africa and Peru to collaborate with local craftspeople to create objects to be marketed worldwide and unite the contemporary design world with the developing world. His formal

and rigorous training makes him less of a stylist and more interested in how things are crafted and in manufacturing processes, which, he laments, are not concentrated on enough in today's design schools.

Hand sketches are always part of the way Burks works, as are detailed hand drawings and computer drawings that are printed out in full scale and then drawn over and corrected. He uses Form Z and Rhinoceros®; the former as a sketching tool to make illustrative models and the latter for final models and to translate technical data to the engineers. Working with models, preferably at full scale, is critical to Burks' development process as a means of understanding proportion and usability. 'I think everyone responds more immediately to 3D, because it's tangible. Even if it may not be the final material, it can be touched and analysed as a real thing,' he says.

The Part collection of nesting tables was commissioned on the basis of 1:10 scale study models. The project was made from laser-cut flat sheets of 4mm (⅙in)-thick aluminium to limit the weight of the final pieces. The flat triangular patterns were developed to be cut, brake-formed in three places and continuously TIG (tungsten inert gas)-welded along one seam on the underside of the part; this process allows for greater control and a thinner, cleaner weld. The pieces were then cleaned and sprayed with a rubberized (soft-touch) paint finish that subtly expresses the material quality of the aluminium.

Early prototypes were created, but as brake-forming aluminium is an unforgiving process (the metal is bent over a large tool forcing the sheet material into the shape of the die and is then further formed at an angle determined by the operator), a lot of work was carried out by hand in the factory to develop the correct shapes and the prototyping phase was extended into the manufacture.

Handmade, a range of outdoor furniture, is formed from flat patterns cut from 5mm (⅛in) foamboard sheets that are then creased and folded into three-dimensional forms and the open edge welded with hot glue. The original concept was to only use paper; Burks is currently experimenting with additive materials to make this possible, and to achieve a more organic finish to better reflect the initial idea and bring out the aesthetic of the material. At the time of going to press, epoxy resin is poured on to the chairs, stools and tables and brushed evenly until dry. Several coats are applied to the outside surface, and the inner is lined with woven fibreglass to add strength. Both are sanded smooth using a hand-held rotational sander.

PART TABLES
STEPHEN BURKS

HANDMADE FURNITURE
STEPHEN BURKS

Manufacturer: B&B Italia SpA
Aluminium, soft-touch paint
Various dimensions
Design to manufacture: 11 months
Mass-manufactured

Production: Readymade Projects
Paper, foamboard sheet, epoxy resin, woven fibreglass
Various dimensions
Design to manufacture: work in progress
Prototypes
www.readymadeprojects.com/www.bebitalia.it

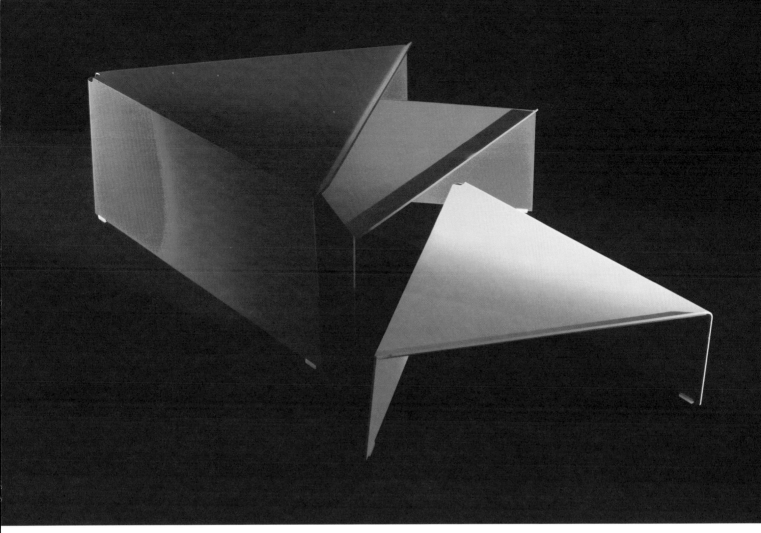

The Handmade range of
outdoor 'paper' furniture
(left) is a studio project
that was born from the mass-
manufactured Part nesting
tables (above), created in
brake-formed aluminium.

1. Early sketch working out the possible forms for the Part nesting tables.

2. A sequential series of hand-drawn, annotated sketches working out the pattern to brake-form the sheets of aluminium.

3. Burks uses renders both to test ideas in the studio and present ideas to clients, but enjoys bringing the objects into the real world through models and prototypes.

4. Models in cardboard. Working in 3D is critical for Burks. Whenever possible he works in full scale to translate sketches, technical drawings and renderings.

5. The first three prototypes tried to resolve the open edge once the aluminium had been folded.

6. A close-up of one of the prototypes shows that the edges were not meeting properly. This needed to be rectified and a way of holding them in place developed.

7. Prototype researching the possibility of closing the edges with bolts.

8. A prototype in the factory that has been brake-formed, TIG-welded and polishing on the side seams.

9. Later prototype with painted surface. The soft-touch finish has the tactility of rubber.

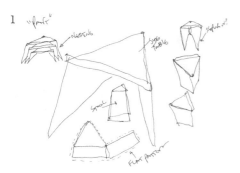

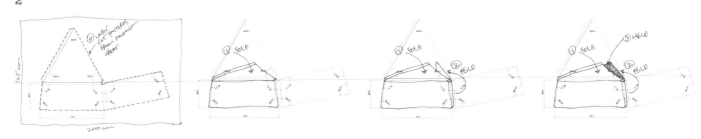

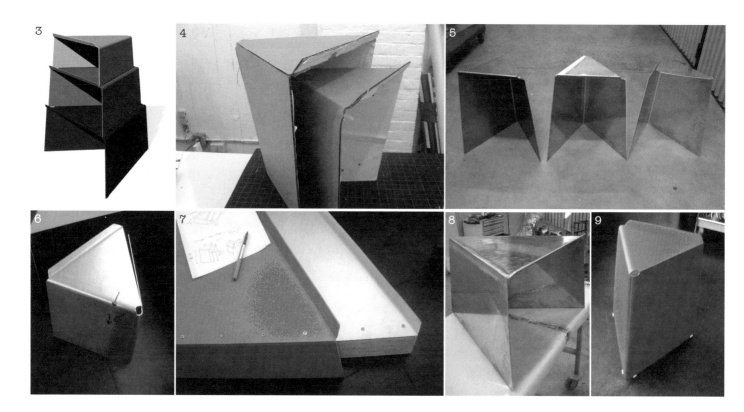

10. The Handmade studio project was inspired by Part. A render for Part shows sides that slope inwards. Despite the technical sophistication of B&B, Burks was unable to develop this shape in brake-formed aluminium.

11–13. Handmade is an ongoing research project so far consisting of a chair (11), a stool (12) and a table (13). Technical drawings of the patterns used to cut the foamboard for each.

14. The goal of the project is to produce outdoor furniture in paper. Burks is currently experimenting with additives to make this possible.

15–20. Once the foamboard is cut (15–16) it is creased (17) and then folded (18) into three-dimensional forms and the open edge was welded with hot glue (19). The outer and inner surfaces are covered in epoxy resin that is brushed into an even coat until dry. Several coats are applied to both surfaces (20).

11

12

13

10

14 15 16

17 18 19 20

Alchemy refers to the earliest investigation of natural phenomena and combines elements of chemistry, physics, metallurgy, astrology and spiritualism. It was prevalent in the ancient world, in classical Greece and Rome and in Europe up to the end of the 19th century: it is now being practised in a small studio in London. Paul Cocksedge may not be in search of the elixir of life, nor is he turning base metal into gold, but what he has the power to do is transform the quotidian into something precious and completely magical.

Cocksedge studied product design at the Royal College of Art, London, under Ron Arad, who has said: 'Paul is one of the best examples we've had of someone who was plucked from the anonymous world of industrial design into being the author of his own work. I don't feel like a mentor to him – absolutely not! The thing about teaching is that normally you're very fast to claim credit for successful students. But I think some people are brilliant and unstoppable not because of us but in spite of us. That's the case with Paul.'

Cocksedge refuses to be typecast, yet his most significant pieces all explore the beauty and emotional qualities of light. For him, light is poetic and goes far beyond a simple illuminating component. His mind is forever enquiring and it's his fascination with materials and processes rarely associated with light that inspires his work. Who would look at a leaf, be reminded of a circuit board and be influenced to create a simple vase of water that

is transformed into a light source when a flower is inserted? (Bulb.) Who would think of invisible messages written in quinine and then make a lamp from gin and tonic that glows an unearthly blue when UV light is shone on to it? (Bombay Sapphire.) A lightning bolt causes him to dream up glass tubes full of natural gas that in daylight appear translucent but when charged with an electric current are flooded by vivid colour (NeON.) Cocksedge sketches with a pencil and produces not only a doodle but a way to connect two points of a circuit to switch on a light. (Watt.) He asks himself the question, 'How do we know that what we see is all that exists?' and uses the 'eye' of the mobile phone or digital camera to allow us to glimpse the world like a reptile that, unlike us, is sensitive to infrared light (Installation for Trussardi, the Italian manufacturer of luxury accessories, during the Milan Furniture Fair 2007).

Cocksedge's latest work, Light as Air, explores the concept of light as sculpture: a lamp that is formed by glass-blowing methods, is made in plastic but looks like ceramic, and, with LEDs that are programmed to be on, off or to gradually fade and brighten, appears to breathe. The concept was born from Cocksedge's desire to make something in glass. He travelled to Murano to study the techniques of the master craftsmen and was so inspired that he wanted to blow his own design. This would have been impossible as the level of expertise is so great it takes a lifetime to perfect.

Knowing the main component of glass to be sand, Cocksedge then investigated other granular substances that are easier to handle: PVC, polypropylene and ABS, to see what would happen if he used glass-making processes on plastic. Choosing PVC for its glossy finish, he placed the bead into a metal pot and heated it. When they reached their melting temperature they became soft and fused, at which point the melt was pushed through a metal ring to make tubes. These were pinched and sealed at one end and blown into at the other using a compressor, or by mouth, exerting approximately 147 psi (pounds per square inch). As the tube began to expand, the areas to remain deflated were cooled with air or cold water to create undulating shapes.

Once the desired form was reached, the ends were gently compressed by hand to cause a horizontal rippling effect similar to that found on ceramics formed on a potter's wheel. The tubes were then cut, the interiors coated with PVC paint to prevent light spilling through the structure's sides, and finally attached to metal bases by way of a simple kettle connector. Each light can be swivelled to cast coloured patterns on to walls.

LIGHT AS AIR LAMPS
PAUL COCKSEDGE

Production: Paul Cocksedge
PVC plastic
Light source: LED
H: 26–90cm (10¼–35½in) x Dia: various
Design to manufacture: 9 months
Limited edition
info@paulcocksedge.co.uk

The Light as Air lamps
investigate light as sculpture,
as they cast magical coloured
patterns on the wall.

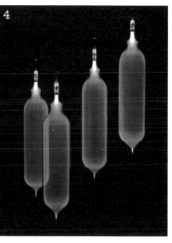

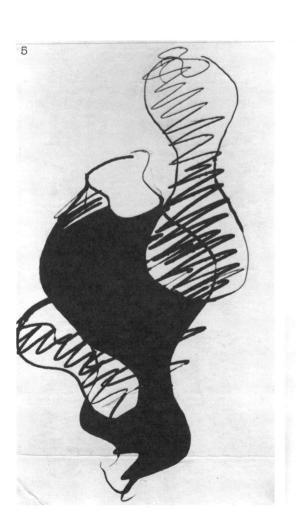

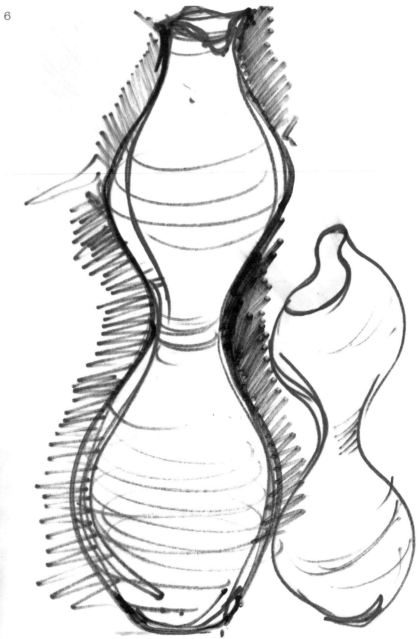

1. Like an alchemist, Paul Cocksedge has the ability to turn the ordinary into something precious and magical. Painting: The Alchymist (1771) by Joseph Wright of Derby.

2–4. The inspiration behind all of Paul Cocksedge's work is his curiosity about materials and processes not normally associated with light, or even electricity. Examples include Bulb (2003), which brings together electricity, water and flower to create a lamp with organic properties. The stem acts as a conductor for the electricity, and switches on a small bulb at the base of vase that is extinguished when the flower dies or is removed

(2). Bombay Sapphire (2004) uses the natural properties of quinine. A bulb-shaped container full of gin and tonic is suspended in a glass sphere. A small light source at the top of the sphere shines UV light on to the liquid, which glows a mysterious blue (3). NeON (2003) consists of hand-made glass vessels filled with natural gas. In daylight they are translucent, but the addition of an electrical charge produces vivid and striking colours in the dark. They were inspired by the scientific explanation of lightning (4).

5–6. Light as Air began as a commission from the Rabih Hage Gallery. They asked Cocksedge for a new piece

of work that would form a range of unique objects. After studying the glass-blowing techniques of Murano craftsmen, Cocksedge decided on a series of lamps blown in PVC. These are initial sketches.

7. PVC bead was heated and fused, then made into a 150cm (5ft) tube. One end was closed and the tube was then blown.

8. The tube was cut into irregular shapes and heights. Some remain individual; others are grouped as families. The rippling effect is similar to the horizontal contours found on ceramic pots cast on a potter's

wheel. They are produced by compressing the tube gently by hand from each end.

9–10. Finished single and group of vases standing on their bases.

In a recent interview Lorenzo Damiani was asked whether he buys a lot of design pieces. His reply that, 'I usually buy cheap and functional objects, the designer of which is not as important as the object itself' reflects the democracy of his own work. Damiani's designs are characterized by their accessibility and functionality, combined with an originality that, although understated, allows his projects to communicate with the user on an emotional and cultural level. 'I think a designer's work should be influenced by observation of what is going on in everyday life: the street, television, simple actions, new attitudes and anything that could make you guess how an object might be designed in a different way.'

Recognizing this approach, IB Rubinetterie, Italy's leading manufacturer of kitchen and bathroom fittings, originally contacted Damiani in 2002 when he was exhibiting projects at the Salon Satellite during the Milan Furniture Fair and asked him to design a series of taps for them. At that early stage in his career, Damiani was mainly attracted to furniture and let the opportunity pass. However, when he was approached a second time during the Fair three years later, he was ready to undertake the task. Following his first meeting with the owner of IB Rubinetterie, Damiani was so enthused that he began to scribble down his initial thoughts on the front and back of his metro ticket.

From the beginning, Damiani's idea was for a mixer that would be simple in both form and function. After some deliberation, he struck on the concept of a joystick. Rough sketches of early solutions were followed by a raw working model using an industrial plastic pipe and adhesive tape, mounted on a wooden support and operated by straightforward mechanical articulation. Damiani inserted a gum irrigation pipe and turned on the water flow. It was the first time he could determine whether the water ran in a uniform manner from the spout and directly into the centre of the washbasin. Damiani presented sketches and computer drawings to IB Rubinetterie, but it was only when he showed them the 3D visualization that they could appreciate how the object interacted with the user.

After the first demonstration, designer and manufacturer collaborated in the initial operative phase. A second model was made of the whole tap, with all the internal components in place. Using stereolithography, a mock-up was constructed in epoxy resin by means of rapid prototyping to evaluate the volumetric aesthetic and to study the water behaviour both inside the tap and during the exit phase. Trial and error eventually determined flow and temperature control, with many tests and simulations being undertaken to achieve a fully functional result.

An element inserted from the front of the tap is made from injection-moulded transparent and coloured polycarbonate. This insulates the water from the brass body of the mixer as well as regulating the flow. The body of the tap is made of moulded brass, and the single hole mixer is available in both cascade and aerator versions that are produced in the same mould – the former with the pipe cut obliquely, and the latter cut perpendicular to the tap's generatrix. Machines were specially designed to test and analyse the successful functioning of the tap after a certain number of cycles: one tests the time duration of the water opening and closing the system, while another verifies the seal of every apparatus. The test carried out with water and air was undertaken to check the tap did not contain micro holes in the internal passageways of both hot and cold water. Each unit was inspected.

The simple and sober shape of OnlyOne belies its technical innovation. The constant diameter of the round section and the gentle curvature allows easily handling. The tap is manoeuvred like a joystick: up and down to open the flow and from left to right to change the thermal variation. Everything is reduced to its essence in a perfect combination of flowing water and movement.

ONLYONE BATHROOM MIXER

LORENZO DAMIANI

Manufacturer: IB Rubinetterie SpA
Chromed brass
H: 195cm (76¾in) x Dia: 40cm (15¾in)
Design to manufacture: 18 months
Mass-manufactured
www.lorenzodamiani.net/www.ibrubinetterie.it

OnlyOne can be easily manoeuvred, up and down to turn the flow on and off and from side to side to change the temperature.

1. The form of the OnlyOne bathroom mixer is based on the movement of a joystick.

2. Lorenzo Damiani's initial jottings on the front and back of the metro ticket he bought on return from his first meeting with the owner of IB Rubinetterie.

3–6. A series of early hand drawn sketches worked out Damiani's idea that the tap should operate in the same way as a joystick.

7–9. An early model, made from an industrial plastic pipe and adhesive tape and mounted on a wooden support, was constructed

(7) using information from the sketches, annotated renderings and from technical drawings (8–9).

10. Damiani made further adjustments that he sketched on to working renderings.

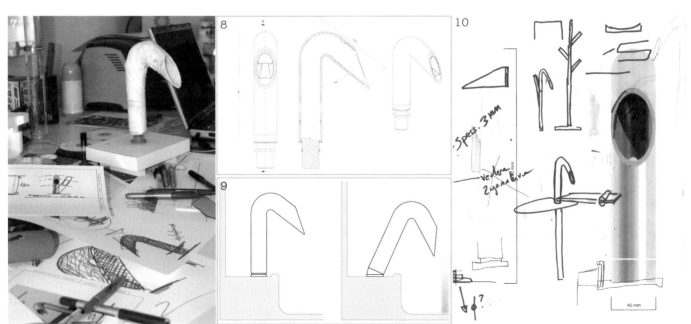

11. Finalized renderings were used to present the tap to the manufacturer.

12. Lorenzo Damiani worked on the early maquette and initial brass mouldings.

13. The work bench for the OnlyOne assembly at IB Rubinetterie.

14. Each unit was tested on specially made machines. Here the mixer is being checked for the air/water seal of the internal chambers of the tap.

15–16. The mould used for the casting of the brass mixers, which are then chromed.

17–18. An injection-moulded polycarbonate insert insulates the water from the brass tap and adjusts the flow coming out of the spout.

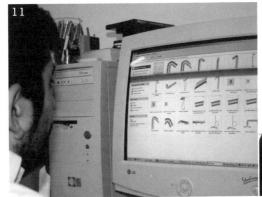

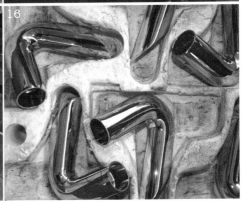

Entropia marks a milestone in digital manufacturing. Although there are many rapid-prototyped designs in the public domain, they are either one-off or limited-edition pieces. At the time of going to press, this small lamp is the first retail design placed on the market by a recognized company, other than a bureau, and is mass-manufactured, albeit in low volume. The complex and amorphous shapes that make up this intriguing sphere defy comprehension, giving no clue as to how the light was designed or made.

Lionel T. Dean and Gregorio Spini, the founder and Creative Director of Kundalini, first met during London Design Week in 2004. Kundalini's philosophy is characterized by an attention to sensation and emotion given physical form in products that use innovative technologies, or traditional methods and materials in a contemporary way. Dean studied automotive design at the Royal College of Art, London, and set up FutureFactories in 2002, researching commercial systems for the creation and marketing of individualized products using 3D printing processes.

Spini was aware of Dean's work and they discussed the possibility of collaborating on a digitally manufactured product. However, at the time the technology was not ready for Kundalini to use commercially, and it was not interested in producing a light that could not reach the mass market. It was a year later that both designer and manufacturer agreed that the

pioneering technique had developed sufficiently to proceed.

Entropia became achievable by employing the prototyping technique of selective laser sintering (SLS) in a production capacity, maximizing the potential of the rapid-prototyping machine to create as many units as possible in one build. Spini's brief to Dean was to embrace the complexity that the technology afforded and not to simply follow the usual mathematical form developed with the aid of a computer. 'The language being used was still that of design for manufacture with repeats and patterns. We wanted to explore a new language of form and push the technology to its limits,' comments Dean.

Taking brain coral as his inspiration, Dean worked directly in CAD, selecting Alias for its high-end surface-modelling capabilities, to develop a structure based on degrees of freedom rather than absolute dimensional values. The concept is a continuous interwoven strand made up of repeated elements that periodically swell and flatten to form 'leaves' and, less frequently, loops with a round, flat, flower-like head. The features were defined by parametric computer models. These were used as templates from which the elements of Entropia were generated through constant iteration and gentle mutation, giving the impression of natural growth.

The lamp was designed to suit the process of rapid prototyping, and its size and form devised to be

economically viable and exploit the potential of the technology. EOS, a well-known manufacturer of rapid-prototyping machinery, was brought into the experiment. This was fundamental to the success of the project, as it gave Spini and Dean confidence in using a new, relatively unproven technology. Once the form had been refined, files were sent electronically from Dean's studio in Lincolnshire, UK, to Italy, where the prototypes were developed.

The irregular chaotic arrangement of the interwoven mesh of leaves and flowers was difficult to assess on screen. The structure required integrity, but the visual mass had to be such that a correct level of light diffusion was achieved. Many adjustments were made between the first prototype and the final design. The leaves were made denser in areas that appeared sparse and the whole made thinner to improve its translucency. Increased links were created so that the flexible nylon sphere would not deform under pressure, giving an appropriate feeling of permanence and quality. This was important for a plastic product competing in price with traditionally manufactured artefacts in materials such as hand-blown glass and ceramic from design-led manufacturers.

ENTROPIA LIGHT
LIONEL T. DEAN

Manufacturer: Kundalini srl
Laser-sintered polyamide
Light source: G9 halogen lamp
Dia: 12cm (4¾in)
Design to manufacture: 3½ months
Mass-manufactured
www.futurefactories.com/www.kundalini.it

(Previous page). Entropia's principal component is a diffuser produced in laser-sintered polyamide. It is available in table, suspension and wall variants.

1. Wireframe images show the geometry underlying the form. From an early stage, a sphere was thought to be the most likely solution as the design needed to be compact and leave a certain clearance around the light source for reasons of temperature.

2. As the design became progressively more complex, it became increasingly difficult to find a way to visualize the model on screen. This wireframe image visually distinguishes the different strings in two colours.

3. A close-up of the flower element and the morphing possible within it.

4. The rendering of the first part built. Again it shows the assembly of separate strings, each depicted in a different colour for identification.

5. A section of the first part built. Digital manufacture allows prototypes to be developed based on sections of the design that are complete. Incomplete sections can be replaced with approximations or simply omitted. Various prototypes were made and adjusted in the development of the design.

6. A computer-generated render produced for visualization when the project was at an advanced stage.

7. Dean's inspiration for the form came from brain coral. 'Gregorio [Spini of Kundalini] wanted my sources of inspiration to show through the design. This has been the guiding principle in the creation of a natural form that seems to have evolved in a completely alien but organic world,' Dean comments.

8–10. The information contained in the CAD drawings produced by Dean was used to rapid-prototype the lamp in SLS nylon. Three images show the formation of layer 555 out of 1,200. The nylon is spread 0.1mm before the laser burns the slice of the design.

11. The best chance of commercial viability was to maximize the potential of the sintering machine. A compact, spherical form meant the build chamber could be filled to capacity and the cost split between the number of components contained within it.

12. The diffusers are extracted by hand from the nylon powder.

13. The laser-sintering machine at work.

Tom Dixon began his career in the 1980s with the formation of Creative Salvage, a company producing one-off sculptures and pieces of furniture from industrial scrap. Since then, he has gone from design maverick to pillar of the community. He was awarded an OBE in 2000 and, as Creative Director of Habitat, injected new life into what had become a moribund business. Today he has his own company producing a line of elegant yet individual products that examine new applications of traditional materials and manufacturing techniques.

Many of Dixon's colleagues were surprised when he entered the establishment world of retailing, but in his collaboration with Habitat Dixon recognized the opportunity to influence consumers and make good design available to everyone.

For the past three years, Dixon has taken over Trafalgar Square during the London Design Festival with the aim of bringing design to the people and raising awareness of environmental issues. In 2006, in collaboration with the EPS Packaging Group, he promoted the advantages of working in expanded polystyrene.

To most people, EPS is just a packaging material. The Group wanted to make the design world aware of the properties that make this under-exploited material so relevant for manufacture in many applications: it is lightweight but strong, shock-absorbent, flexible, suitable for CNC-cutting and moulding and, above all, cheap to produce. In addition, it does not use CFCs, it is inert and innocuous, providing stability in landfill, it is 100% recyclable and, because its composition is 98% air, it has a small carbon footprint. To showcase EPS, the Group was working on the idea for a design competition to be announced at the Festival's 100% East venue when they were put in touch with Tom Dixon, who was looking for an idea for the Trafalgar Square event.

An economical product had to be designed, developed and manufactured within a timeframe of ten weeks from initial sketches to batch production. Dixon came up with an assortment of ideas, including drawings for a geodesic dome. Finally, for reasons of timing and practicality, it was decided to design a chair, and the idea for 'The Grab', an event in which 500 pieces were to be given away absolutely free, was born. Early sketches were inspired by the iconic fan-backed wicker chair, but after discussions between Dixon and the Group's engineers this was rejected as being too difficult to produce in EPS. Various versions were then assessed before the final design was reached: an amalgamation of the previous ideas, retaining something of the original aesthetic but more straightforward and workable.

Presentation drawings were sent from Dixon's office to the manufacturer, who refined them for production. Dixon's first intention was to cast the chair in one piece, but this would have meant a heavy investment in developing a mould with movable slides. Split lines and joints were introduced to produce the chair in two parts, and the struts were increased in size to augment the stability and to facilitate the filling of the chair with polystyrene bead.

Working from templates produced from the drawings, a prototype was form-cut with hot wires from a solid block of polystyrene. This was checked for functionality and sent to Dixon to sign off. CAD drawings were formulated using Pro E and delivered to the tool-maker, who made a resin model to design the reverse mould and sand-cast the aluminium male and female tools. Once the tools were cast they were CNC-cut on the surface for the finish and holes were drilled for the filler guns, vents and ejector rods and pins. A CNC-cut plate was also made to allow information about the event to be embossed on the seat of the chair. The casts were delivered to the factory, and the bead injected, heated (causing them to fuse together), cooled and ejected. The parts were assembled using joints at the four corners and then glued with hot-melt adhesive for extra safety. Fifty pieces were set aside for Dixon, who has since coated them in copper to form an exclusive range from the democratic original.

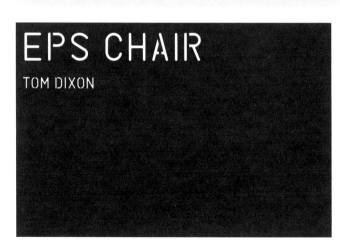

EPS CHAIR
TOM DIXON

Manufacturer: The EPS Packaging Group
Expanded polystyrene
H: 73cm (28¾in) x W: 93cm (36½in) x D: 82.7cm (32½in)
Design to manufacture: 10 weeks
Limited edition of 500
www.tomdixon.net/www.eps.co.uk

(Previous page). The EPS Chair weighs 5.5kg (12lb). The density of the material, 50 grams per litre, means that the chair's marks and deformations become part of its evolving aesthetic, but the chair itself remains strong and resilient.

1. The inspiration for the initial concept was the iconic wicker chair with a fan-shaped back.

2–5. The chair was installed in Trafalgar Square during the London Design Festival in 2006.

6. 'The Chair Grab'. At an appointed time on 21 September 2006, 500 chairs were lined up and given away on a first-come first-served basis.

7. 'EPS is incredibly lightweight and totally versatile – unique amongst plastics; a designer gets the unusual opportunity of working in large solid volumes. Making a polystyrene chair has given me the opportunity to fulfil an ambition to make design available to all; this time literally, by giving away hundreds of these chairs to Londoners – absolutely, no-chains-attached, 100% free.' (Tom Dixon interview.)

8. The chair was also exhibited during the London Design Festival at the 100% East venue on the EPS Packaging Group stand. It was used as the iconic symbol to promote the competition that invited designers to enter concepts for innovative products made in the material.

9. Tom Dixon set aside 50 pieces, which he coated in copper to form an exclusive range from the democratic original.

10. The original concept for the 2006 Trafalgar Square event was a huge geodesic dome fashioned from EPS facets. This was rejected for reasons of time and practicality.

11. Dixon's first sketch was for a chair cast in one piece, but it was too expensive and complicated to tool.

12–17. Series of sketches showing various versions of the chair: two-piece, vertical split (12); two-piece, horizontal split (13); three-piece, horizontal split (14–15); and three-piece jigsaw (16–17).

18. The final design was for a chair in two parts. This was an amalgamation of the aesthetics of the former versions and retained the wide, encompassing back of the original concept. Final drawings were sent to the EPS Group, which refined them for manufacturability.

19. Dixon discussing the construction of the prototype. It was form-cut with hot wires from a solid block of polystyrene using templates made from the drawings.

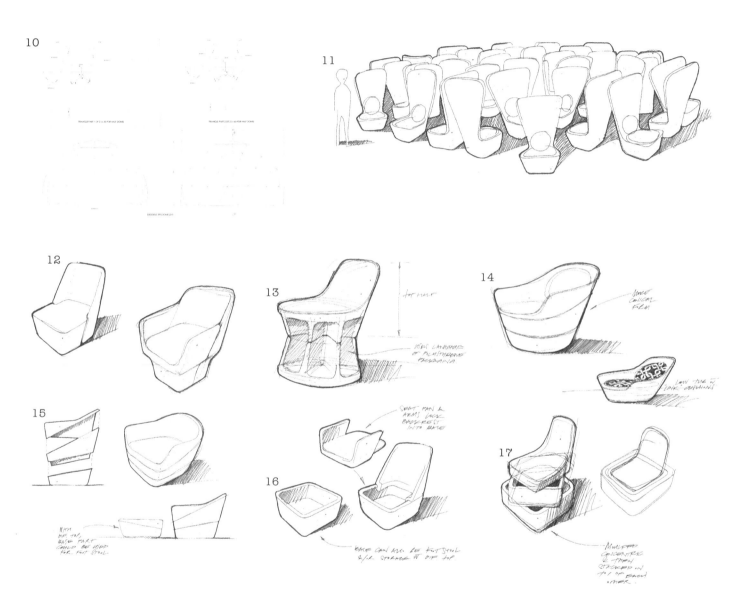

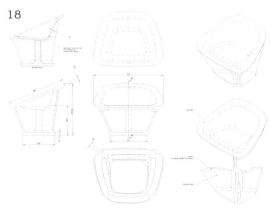

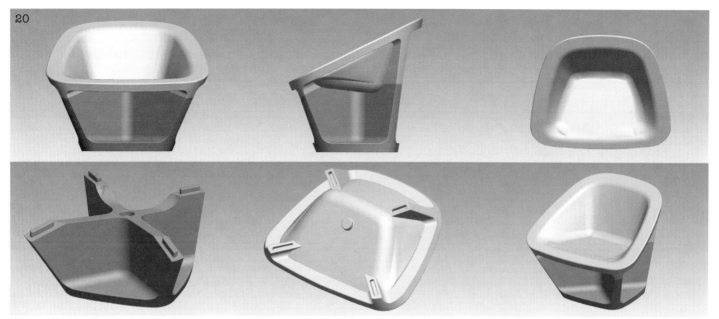

20. A series of CAD drawings were produced in Pro E and delivered to the tool-maker to make the mould.

21. The resin model is layered with sheets of fibreglass and wood. Once the depth of material needed is ascertained, the model is pulled out to create the mould.

22–23. The male and female moulds are sand-cast in aluminium. They have been CNC-cut for finish and to introduce holes for filler guns, vents and ejector rods.

24. A plate was also made so that information about the event could be embossed on the seat of the chair.

25–26. The mould is mounted in the press (25). Polystyrene bead was injected and steam introduced to heat them up and fuse them together. The part is allowed to cool; a process accelerated by the introduction of cold water running through the press behind the mould. Vacuum pressure is then used to

withdraw excess moisture and the parts are ejected (26).

27–29. The parts were assembled using joints at the four corners. They were glued with hot-melt adhesive for extra safety.

Stefano Giovannoni describes himself as an industrial designer. He is primarily interested in making products for mass manufacture, so each of his designs begin with this consideration in mind. The Chair First gas-injected plastic chair will be produced in a quantity of 100,000 per year, with the mould working around the clock, seven days a week to meet the target.

In 1999 Magis commissioned Giovannoni to design a steel chair made in two parts: a metal structure to form the back and rear legs and a simple plastic sheet to create the seat and front legs. He worked on this idea for two years before it was finally rejected for being too heavy and too expensive to tool. Giovannoni then introduced an earlier proposal for a chair moulded in two materials and although Magis' owner, Eugenio Perazza, had initially turned down the concept, he decided to go ahead.

Giovannoni developed the chair's 3D form using Alias/Wavefront software and experimented with various material combinations such as making the back section in plastic and the sheet in wood, leather or aluminium. A clean junction between the different materials proved too complicated to achieve, so he considered making the chair out of two pieces of plastic instead. Following discussions with the plastics supplier it was decided to produce the chair in one piece, using gas-injection moulding, to reduce weight and cost.

Gas-injection moulding allows for a light, hollow structure and, despite a costly initial outlay, the complete chair can be moulded quickly and cheaply. Although gas-injection moulding has long been used in the automotive and electronics industries, it has only recently been adopted by the furniture industry. A gas (azote – a form of nitrogen) is injected simultaneously with the plastic to maintain a consistent wall thickness, creating an empty structure within the shape of the chair. The first chair to utilize this technology was Mario Bellini's Bellini Chair for Heller in 1998, followed by Jasper Morrison's Air-chair for Magis in 2000. In the case of Bellini's chair, the triangular section of the leg led to compromises in the surface quality and weight. Morrison's design optimized the section of the legs and structure, but left the tubular form visible, as if a thin skin had been draped over a chair frame.

After the Air-chair, many companies began using the same technology to produce gas-injected chairs. The innovation of First was to push the technology further by injecting the gas, not only into the empty tubular sections, but also into more complex volumes around the seat and back. This allowed for a more three-dimensional organic form without the visible structures that are seen in other chairs.

Giovannoni's initial idea was to give the back of the chair a shiny finish and the seat surface a rougher, textured finish to prevent slipping. The first prototype was made in polyamide, achieving an exquisite aesthetic result, but after extensive stress-testing it was judged to be too unstable. The structural solution was to mould the chair in polypropylene with added fibreglass for rigidity. This unfortunately made it impossible to retain the glossy finish on the back surface, so in the end it was decided to treat the entire mould with a uniform, textured finish.

All critical points of the chair were studied using structural analysis programs (Abaqus for static load tests and ls-dyna for dynamic load tests), then carefully refined in a continuous exchange between the designer and the manufacturer. Different plastic materials were tested; the balance between solid plastic and hollow spaces where gas entered was optimized; and the injection-moulding machine was adjusted until the right settings were found. The mould itself was made from a block of hardened steel, tilted according to the parting lines of the chair to facilitate extraction from the mould.

CHAIR FIRST
STEFANO GIOVANNONI

Manufacturer: Magis SpA
Reinforced polypropylene
H: 77.6cm (30½in) x W: 50cm (19¾in) x D: 52cm (20½in)
Design to manufacture: 60 months
Mass-manufactured
www.stefanogiovannoni.it/www.magisdesign.com

The final Family First series
includes the mass-produced
Chair First and Table First.

1. The inspiration for the Chair First was an earlier design concept combining two materials, which Giovannoni had presented to Magis in the mid-1990s.

2–3. The concept was rejected in favour of a steel chair made in two parts – a metal structure to form the back and rear legs and a simple plastic sheet for the seat and front legs (2). This too was rejected for being too heavy and too expensive to tool, especially the mould for the back part (3).

4. Giovannoni eventually developed the 3D form for the present chair using Alias/Wavefront software.

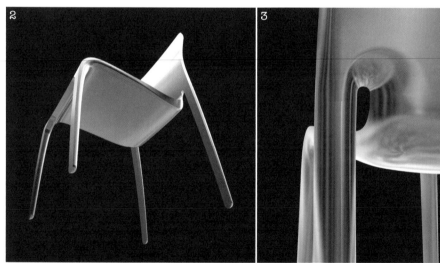

5. Prototypes were developed to test various materials such as wood, leather or aluminium for the sheet in combination with a plastic back section. A clean juncture between the different materials proved too complicated to achieve.

6. Giovannoni's idea was to give the back of the chair a shiny surface and the seat texture to prevent slipping. A prototype was developed in polyamide.

7. After stress-testing, however, the prototype was judged to be too unstable for manufacture.

8. The 8.5-tonne mould is made from a block of hardened steel in male and female parts (female mould shown here mounted in the press). It took two months to tool from the final aesthetic 3D data, resolving technical issues such as draw, cooling, flash, gas channels and plastic flow.

9. Male mould. The mould was tilted according to the parting lines of the chair to improve the draft and facilitate extraction.

10. A cross-section of the first moulding test to examine the cavity created by the gas within the chair.

One of the lessons learnt from life is that everything has an antithesis. Natanel Gluska's Long 8 Chair is an object where the design and development, from inspiration to production, can be summed up in a few words.

Natanel Gluska was born in Israel and now lives and works in Zurich. He trained at the Rietveld Academy in Amsterdam, graduating in fine art in 1989. Since then he has built up an international reputation for his playful, roughly hewn, artistic furniture, which he describes as functional but above all sculptural objects. He launched himself on to the design world in the late 1990s courtesy of Milan's SaloneSatellite, the offshoot of the Milan Furniture Fair that showcases the work of emerging talents. In 2007 he was featured in their ten-year retrospective, 'A Dream Come True – SaloneSatellite Projects: from Inception to Production'. The exhibition highlighted the success of designers who have transformed their concepts and prototypes into commercial reality.

Gluska's work is unique, with every item a one-off. The technique he uses to make this hybrid of art and design is as straightforward as it appears. The inspiration for the Long 8 Chair came to him while walking home one evening through his local park and, on discovering the felled trunk of a tree, visualizing the iconic shape of an upholstered armchair. Single-handedly he spent the remaining hours of the night laboriously rolling the trunk to his nearby studio and the next day bought a chainsaw. He had never used one before but insists that it came naturally to him to be able to wield it the way an artist would a pencil, or a sculptor a chisel.

From a series of quickly sketched forms that he kept before him as a blueprint, Gluska marked a rough outline on the trunk. He then attacked it with the chainsaw, cutting away, pausing, reassessing and carving again until he was satisfied with the result. He used a series of chisels, rasps and abrasives to smooth the areas that would come into contact with the body and to give the surface a defined yet coarse finish that displayed the natural beauty of the material used. The result is probably still the piece most closely associated with Gluska and its silhouette appears on his letterhead.

The intervening years have seen a prodigious output that has secured Gluska a niche market. He is collected worldwide, with clients including Ian Schrager, Philippe Starck, Karl Lagerfeld, Donna Karen and the famous Swiss department store, Globus. Today Gluska still works in the same way, but he now has a number of foresters who contact him when they have suitable timber available. He works only in European hardwood; usually oak, beech, chestnut and elm. He needs trunks with at least an 80cm (31½in) diameter. These are transported to his workshop by truck and crane, where he carries out his 50/50% commissioned and personal pieces. He fills notebook after notebook with drawings, releasing their forms from the solid blocks of wood. To keep symmetry in his furniture he uses measurements, but fundamentally relies on his expert eye to create the shapes, believing that beauty comes from slight, almost imperceptible, imperfection. He keeps the finish as simple and natural as possible, adding beeswax only to the pieces intended for outdoor use.

Today there is a situation in the design world where the boundaries between art and design are blurring; this is a movement into which Gluska's work sits comfortably. Design is no longer only about problem-solving but about expression and having personality. In limited-edition collectors' items, inhibitions, whether creative or market-led, can be shed, allowing for a freedom missing in mass production. The fact that Gluska works in wood rather than any other massive material lets his craftsmanship prevail and prevents his work slipping into gimmickry or parody. He underlines the importance on the culture of design of individuals who still make by hand and whose small but significant business initiatives have found success.

THE LONG 8 CHAIR
NATANEL GLUSKA

Production: Natanel Gluska
Oak
H: 70cm (27½in) x W: 55cm (21¾in) x L: 188cm (74in)
Design to manufacture: 1 month
One-off
www.natanelgluska.com

Natanel Gluska fashions
a hybrid of sculpture and
functional item from one
piece of wood (above). After
the initial sketch, he attacks
a virgin tree trunk with a
chainsaw (overleaf). He is now
working on an alternative,
sculpted from a solid block
of Styrofoam coated in
fibreglass that is intended for
commercial manufacture (left).

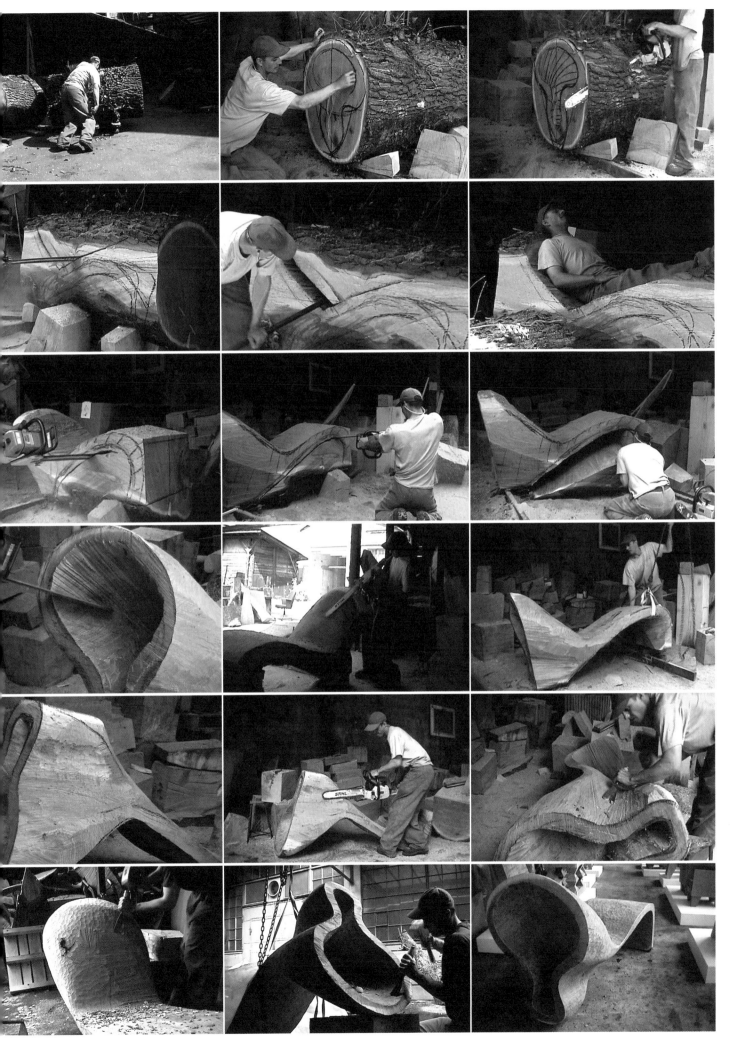

It is impossible for Konstantin Grcic to talk about the development of the Miura stool without referring to chair_ONE, which he produced in die-cast aluminium and developed for Magis in 2003. For him this was a personal breakthrough in terms of technology and expression; a work that showed very distinct traces of using the computer in the design process. The commission from the manufacturer Plank to produce a monoblock barstool in plastic created the perfect opportunity for Grcic to take things one step further.

While chair_ONE is just a naked structure, a bare skeleton, Miura is a structure with a computer-modelled skin. Grcic's approach to the stool was therefore less pragmatic and more sculptural. Like the chair, however, it originates from a structural working method. Although Grcic uses the computer almost from the outset of a project, his principal approach is not digital but physical. He uses sketches, sometimes expressively, but generally as tools to explain details to his assistants. He initially designs on the computer, but very primitively to sort out basic principles of volumes and form. He then quickly produces 1:1 scale models in various materials, depending on what is being tested. He considers it a privilege to be able to work in this hands-on way.

Grcic is an intuitive designer. Once he has made a model he can assess its form and aesthetic straight away; whether it has potential or is feasible, and where the design could

lead. He compares this stage to a game of chess where the master may not always be in control of his opponent's moves, but his skill and experience direct his own moves to find successful solutions which in turn lead to new consequences. It is the most intriguing stage for him. One of the greatest arguments for Miura is that it stacks, but it was not conceived this way. It was only after creating a built structure that Grcic could see it would take a very slight adjustment to the geometry of the stool to add this important functional feature.

The computer came into the development process for modelling the complex free-form surfaces of Miura once Grcic had established the overall geometry. During this phase, heavy use was made of rapid-prototyping facilities. CAD data was fed directly into a laser-sintering machine, making it possible to produce a series of life-size models of the stool, or parts, in order to transform digital reality into physical reality.

Grcic develops prototypes from an early stage; first to check proportion and then as ergonomic, structural and aesthetic tests. Software may appear to model a form perfectly, but it is only when it is viewed in 1:1 scale that physical problems become apparent. This was particularly the case with Miura, whose structural complexity, soft surfaces and refined curves made it difficult to judge accurately on the computer. The proportions of the first prototype were not correct, as viewing the CAD drawings

had given the team the wrong perspective. The viewpoint on the screen tends to be rather low down and the modelling seemed okay. However, it was only once the full-size model was created that the stool was judged top-heavy from a normal viewpoint, which is from above.

Parallel to the design process, CAD files were forwarded to the structural engineers; they used a stress analysis program to perform both static and dynamic stress simulation to test that the stool was statically safe.

After one year of development, Miura was defined enough to enter the production phase. Initially, it was thought the stool would have to be gas-injection moulded as the thicker sections, such as the legs, needed to be hollow. This would have involved constructing a very expensive mould. After further consultation, an alternative plastics engineer was found who maintained he could inject the plastic solid. It was a risk as so much plastic, once ejected from the mould, could distort during cooling. The radical injection technique needed fine adjustment and a lot of pressure, but eventually succeeded in cutting production costs down considerably.

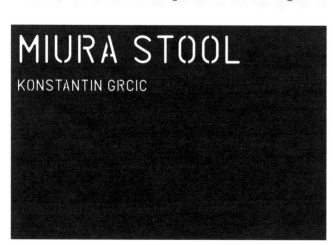

MIURA STOOL
KONSTANTIN GRCIC

Manufacturer: Plank Collezioni srl
Reinforced polypropylene
H: 81cm (32in) x W: 55cm (21½in) x D: 53cm (21in)
Design to manufacture: 30 months
Mass-manufactured
www.konstantin-grcic.com/www.plank.it

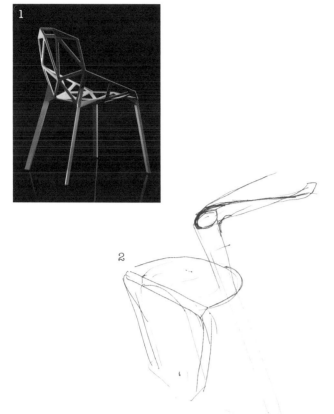

(Previous page). Konstantin Grcic (front right) and assistants, including the project designer, Sami Ayadi (middle back), standing on the first production pieces of the Miura stool.

1. Chair_ONE is the inspiration behind the Miura stool. For Grcic this design was seminal as its aesthetic and technology referred directly to the use of the computer in the design process.

2. Early sketch. Grcic develops a very rough concept of a product on the computer but uses sketches to communicate with his assistants.

3. After the initial volume and shape was determined on the computer Grcic quickly moved on to producing a series of hand-made models to assess form and aesthetics. Here, Martin Plank and Sami Ayadi discuss the first mock-up.

4. Ayadi working on an early model. It was at this stage that Grcic discovered that a change in the leg configuration and the footrest could make the stool stackable.

5. Early models were made in a variety of materials depending on what is being tested. Here the frame is milled from high-density foam and the seat made from craft-paper ribs simulating its three-dimensional shape.

6. Martin Plank, founder of Plank Collezioni (right), his design director, Biagio Cisotti (left) and one of Grcic's assistants, Benoit Steenackers (centre), hold a development meeting. Chair_ONE can be seen in the background.

7-8. Konstantin Grcic tries out the comfort of an early prototype. This was made using rapid prototyping in a plastic-like material (7) from a series of detailed CAD drawings (8).

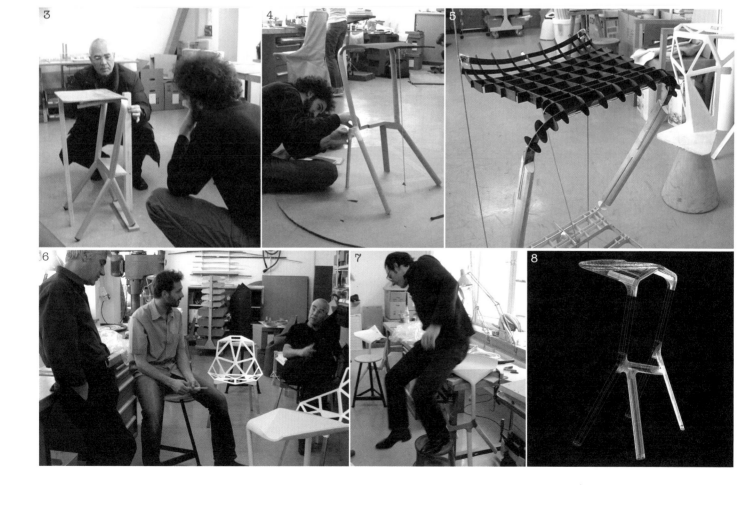

9. Sequence of mock-ups and prototypes illustrating Miura's line of development.

10. An engineer works on a CAD drawing to construct the tool.

11–12. The Miura tool is made from steel in five parts to cast the complex geometry of the stool. The draft and draw are calculated to facilitate easy ejection of the parts.

13–14. Miura is injected solid instead of gas-injected, thereby greatly reducing the expense of the mould. Compared to other industries, furniture production levels are low. Miura's manufacture is innovative as it produces a technologically advanced design using the most economical means.

15. Sami Ayadi (right) and Benoit Steenackers discuss the first off-tool sample of Miura on the phone with the mould-maker.

16. One of the most important features of Miura is that it stacks. This is good not only for the consumer but for cutting down on transport costs and carbon footprinting.

Commenting on Alfredo Häberli's flamboyant yet contemplative character, his close friend and fellow designer, Konstantin Grcic, describes him as a unique mix of rationality and emotion. 'He has two opposites inside him in many different ways. He can be extremely introverted, very serious and reflexive, thinking sometimes too hard about things. And then the next moment he's like a firecracker.' This duality informs Häberli's work, which appears, if not minimal, simple; yet has a playfulness and a poetry that gives it soul.

Häberli was born in Argentina but moved to Switzerland when he was 13. He readily admits that his openness to people, projects and themes derives from his South American heritage, while his courage for complexity, his clarity and ability to analyse comes from his Swiss schooling. He studied industrial design at the Höhere Schule für Gestaltung before opening his own studio in Zurich in 1993. 'I seek simplicity with an added value,' he says. 'I look for a certain flair, a twist, a new function. I cross boundaries, moving between the worlds of discovery and recollection, boldness and naïveté; a need to innovate but still have a respect for traditions.'

Häberli is a strong believer that design often arrives at a point of innovation: this is the case with the Segesta chair. Originally commissioned by Alias to design an upholstered dining chair with an aluminium-structured base, it was only when he stripped away the textile to reveal the beauty of the shell that the concept for the chair, as we know it, was born. The true innovation came in Häberli's search for a material to capture the sinuous lines of the base. He didn't want to produce yet another plastic chair to add to the plethora that exist in the design world today and, along with Alias, researched polymers that had the quality of traditional plastic but a much richer visual appeal. HiREK™, a multi-layered techno-polymer composite made from polyolefine and polyester, is relatively new on the market. With a variable density, a dynamic internal structure that is honeycombed and an outer aesthetic skin, it feels like Corian® but behaves like plywood.

Häberli has a close personal and working relationship with Renato Stauffacher, the CEO of Alias, and designs often develop in a series of informal meetings together over dinner. Stauffacher recognizes in Häberli a designer who is able to think conceptually and who enjoys solving complex problems; dealing with many elements to create a well-functioning product. In turn, Häberli admires Alias' willingness to take on a challenge. Segesta not only uses a new plastic technology but is unusual as it has arms yet stacks. The curved backrest is drawn out of the seat in a continuous line and, because of its distinctive cut-out shape and the flexibility of the material, it reacts like a cantilever chair.

Once Häberli had an idea of Segesta in mind, he started to make the form visually lighter. With his youthful love of racing cars, it's hardly surprising that he drew on the evolution of the Aston Martin grille as an inspiration to make a cut in the backrest and reduce the materiality of the chair. Starting with a few sketches to set out the basic parameters of the piece, the studio then worked on a series of small-scale models in polyurethane foam to define the shape. The information was transferred to the computer and both 2D and 3D drawings rendered using Form-Z software. Although Häberli is aware of the importance of the computer, he prefers to continue to work on 1:1 scale drawings, which he then turns into full-scale maquettes. In collaboration with Alias' technicians several were made in various materials, depending on the function of the mock-up; some to test ergonomics, stability and practicality and others to refine the aesthetic and form. Once all areas of the design were finalized, final CAD drawings were developed by Alias and a prototype was created using rapid prototyping to check that everything was correct for production. The CAD files were then used to develop the mould. Given the complexity of the cut-out and the varying thicknesses of the shell, this was remarkable for being developed in only two parts (male and female). The structure was injection-moulded in one piece, with the injection point on the under-surface of the seat.

SEGESTA CHAIR
ALFREDO HÄBERLI

Manufacturer: Alias SpA
HiREK™, aluminium
H: 81cm (32in) x W: 59cm (23¼in) x D: 56cm (22in)
Design to manufacture: 24 months
Mass-manufactured
www.alfredo-haeberli.com/www.aliasdesign.it

The chair is part of the
multi-purpose Segesta range,
which includes bar stool
and swivel chair, and was
produced using a new plastic
technology, HiREK™.

1. The inspiration for the distinctive cut-out in the backrest and along the integral armrests was the Aston Martin grille.

2. Alias commissioned an upholstered dining chair with armrests to make it comfortable enough to be used for relaxation. First mock-ups appeared heavy, and it was only when the textile covering was taken away that the beauty of the shell was revealed and the concept for Segesta born.

3. Once Häberli had an idea of Segesta in his mind, he started on a series of hand-drawn sketches to work out a way of making the structure visually lighter by creating a hole in the backrest.

4. From sketches, Häberli likes to work on a series of reduced-scale mock-ups. Here the skinned structure is receiving the first idea for the cut-out.

5. Various models were developed in different materials. The orange model is 15cm (6in) high and made from foam; it was used at a very early stage in the development to assess the shape before information was fed into the computer.

6. Methods of fitting the base to the shell were worked on from an early stage. The first prototype was made from cast aluminium; the concept was the delicate balancing of a tray on a waiter's fingers.

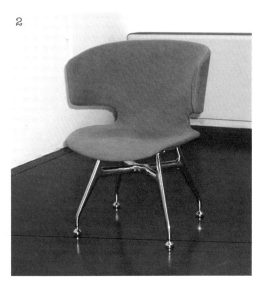

7. Alfredo Häberli at an early stage in the process. Shot in Alias' studio, he is holding the first version of the aluminium cast leg.

8. CAD drawings were made by Alias' technicians using information from Häberli's models and technical 1:1 scale drawings (shown here).

9–10. Prototypes were developed using rapid prototyping to evaluate material performance, and the proportional variation in the thickness of the shell to give support and strength in the seat and a light and springy upper rim. Corrections were marked and adjustments made prior to finalizing the tool.

11. Due to the complexity of the shape of the shell, and its variable thicknesses, it was impressive that the mould was made in only two parts (male and female) and the injection carried out in one piece.

12. The production line.

13. The HiREK™ expanding in the mould. The images were created by stopping the injection after different time intervals and opening the mould.

14. The Segesta chair was designed in 2002, but the range is still being expanded.

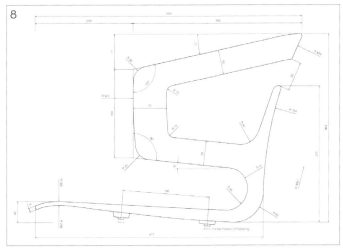

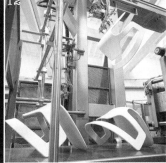

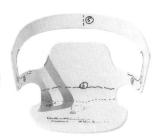

Yoshiki Hishinuma began his career as one of Issey Miyake's assistants, travelling extensively to research new, exotic fabrics, and then returning to translate these materials into fashion items. He set up his own studio in 1992, working only with the most progressive Japanese manufacturers, using modern artificial materials and the most up-to-date machinery. Textile design meets fashion and theatre in Hishinuma's work. His clothes are body-conscious and distinctive in their form and construction, in which haute couture and handicraft are combined.

From the start of his career, Hishinuma has been interested in creating sculptural and architectural clothing, such as his kite-like stage garments, which use light materials like polyester and nylon, and rely on wind to give them their final form. Adapting the triangular shapes, inspired by Buckminster Fuller's philosophy, to fabricate functional clothing on a human scale, he then experimented in making 3D pieces using a shrink process. Three-dimensional shapes were made using blocks and wooden propellers. The material was placed around them and then shrunk to half its size using hot water, causing the garment to take shape over the wooden pattern.

Hishinuma's collection 3D Knit sees him experimenting with knitwear. A visit to Shima Seiki's manufacturing company introduced Hishinuma to the 3D knitting machine, which he uses to make completely seamless, entire garments from beginning to end. This process gives rise to

organic forms and patterns that are no longer constrained by the geometry of squares, circles and straight lines and the haute couture practice of making complicated shapes from cut patterns.

There is nothing new about the 3D knitting machine, which has been used to make mass-produced knitwear since it was introduced in 1995. Hishinuma's intention was to harness its technical possibilities to make complicated designs.

For Hishinuma the possibility of producing intricate forms without seams was an exciting prospect. He likens it to making a one-piece plastic injection-moulded chair. Over a period of three months, and in collaboration with 30 of Shima Seiki's technicians, he started work developing computer programs that would work out the complex shapes of a range of clothing and objects. These included a jumper that takes on the shape of a sitting person, a tailor-made jacket with buttons, collar and pockets integral to the knitted structure, a cardigan where the decoration becomes part of the construction, a 3D handbag, and the Crocodile Scarf, Casablanca Shawl and Knit Body mannequin as featured here.

The Crocodile Scarf was inspired by reptilian scales. The most complicated part of the piece was to create the circular bumps essential to the design. Several attempts were made to produce the effect digitally, but these were hard to assess accurately on the computer as the woollen scarf is made in an enormous size and then felted,

shrinking the piece by 30 to 40%. The first attempts were distorted but a progression of refinement eventually achieved the result that was required.

Knit Body was based on Shiro Kuramata's Homage to Josef Hoffman, Begin to Beguin, in which Kuramata took Hoffman's celebrated bentwood chair, wrapped it in steel rods, welded the joints and set it on fire, burning out the wood and creating what he referred to as 'the glittering aura of a Modernist icon'. The knitted tailor's dummy was made using a complicated process that began with a computer program to make a seamless knitted sock. Then the knit was placed on a Styrofoam form and hardened with resin. The mould was removed by dipping it in a liquid that dissolved the foam and the object was complete.

The Casablanca Shawl was inspired by Ferran Adrià, the world-class chef of El Bulli restaurant in Gerona, Spain, who is famous for his deconstructed dishes. Ingredients are separated, cooked individually and then reassembled in layers, relying on the diner's knowledge of the original to recognize what he or she is eating. To mirror this process, Hishinuma separated a lily into two parts – pistil and petal – and then created computer patterns for each constituent, reforming them to produce a shawl of 3D frills.

3D KNIT
YOSHIKI HISHINUMA

Production: Yoshiki Hishinuma
Wool, polyester, nylon
Various dimensions
Design to production: 3 months
Limited batch
www.yoshikihishinuma.co.jp

Yoshiki Hishinuma, crouching beside Shima Seiki's 3D knitting machines.

1. The scales on the back
of a crocodile inspired the
Crocodile Scarf.

2. The final piece is perfectly
symmetrical.

3. Computer programs were
created in collaboration
with 30 of Shima Seiki's
technicians to develop the
complicated shapes of the
scarf. Here the red diamond
shape makes one of the
crocodile's scales.

4–5. The first attempts at
creating the bumps came out
distorted (4). The scarf is
made on a huge scale and then
shrunk by 30 to 40%. It was
impossible to visualize this on
the computer without a series
of trials and refinements (5).

6. The scarf is felted, a
process caused by heat
and agitation. The garment
was placed in an industrial
washing machine at the
highest temperature to shrink.
'It's very easy to change the
face with heat and boiling,'
says Hishinuma.

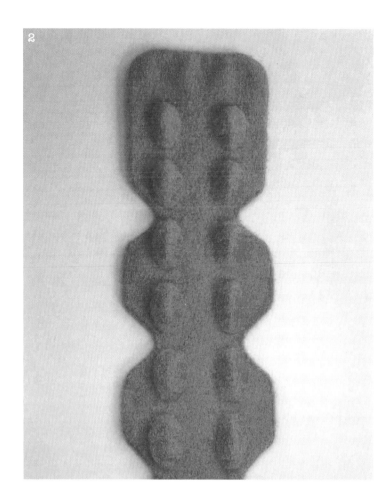

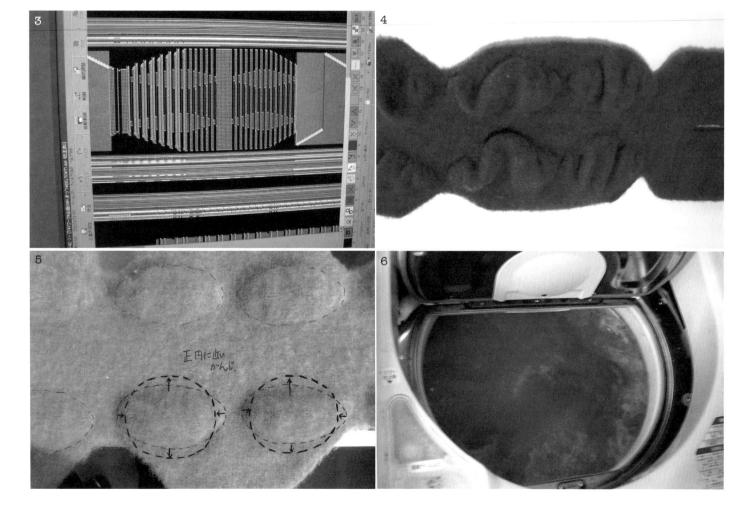

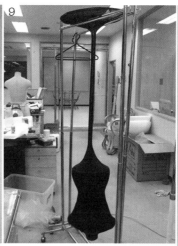

7. Knit Body is based on Shiro Kuramata's Homage to Josef Hoffman, Begin to Beguin. Kuramata wrapped the bentwood Modernist icon in steel rods and set fire to it, burning out the original.

8. Digital design was used to form a sock in polyester.

9. The sock was then stretched over a Styrofoam mould and coated in resin. The foam was dissolved in liquid, leaving the hardened form and finished object.

10. The completed Knit Body.

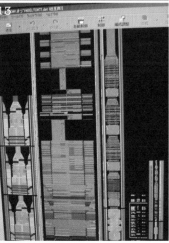

11. The Casablanca Shawl was inspired by the tiramisu of Ferran Adrià, the world-class chef of El Bulli restaurant in Gerona, who is famous for his deconstructed dishes. Ingredients are separated, cooked individually and then reassembled in layers.

12. Hishinuma separated a lily into pistil and petal.

13. A computer program was made for each constituent. The two were combined and the information fed into the 3D knit machine, which produced the intricate three-dimensional frills of the design.

14. The first model: the pistil is in blue and the petal in white.

15. The finished shawl.

Setsu and Shinobu Ito were born and educated in Japan. They moved to Milan 20 and 10 years ago respectively and have worked there ever since. The partners have produced a wide range of work including architecture, furniture and product design, packaging and tableware art, such as the hand-crafted Stardust vases. What unifies this diverse output, regardless of scale, typology, material or technology, is a strong philosophy that originates from their Japanese background. 'What is important to us,' says Setsu, 'is to make cultural comparisons in our work between East and West. The recognition of our heritage is what gives our designs their identity and originality.'

Their work is based on five doctrines (Space Rhythm, Senscape, Emotional Island, Subconscious Polyhedron and Leaf Solid), all linked to the Japanese belief that design does not stand in isolation. 'We do not design objects that have purely aesthetic or functional values; we are interested in exploring the act that unfolds around them, in the rapports between individuals and society and the interaction between user, object and environment. A project has to have a dynamic that changes from place to place, from individual to individual and from situation to situation. It has to be able to transform.' To do this they have to look beyond the design itself. The doctrines all examine the space around a product and its connection to the individual, and to nature. They are based on Japanese traditions such as the Sukiya

architectural style, Shinto religion, origami and the shoji sliding screen.

The Japanese divide space – the interior from the exterior and the private from the public – in a much more nebulous way than Westerners, using folding screens and sliding doors that create a confusion between interspace, and the visible and the invisible. The multi-faceted Stardust vases are based on the concept of the Subconscious Polyhedron; creating elements that are so various and multiple that the memory of an object can be recalled but not its exact form. Like looking at the dappled shadows created by sun shining through leaves, the vases were designed to be seen in multiples so that the surface and the surrounding space become interchangeable.

Shape is recognized by perceiving a combination of two axes: the horizontal and the vertical. The Itos worked on a series of sketches confounding this principle by developing a competition of polyhedral planes and curved surfaces to produce visual puzzlement. These were converted into CAD drawings so the form could be conceived in a 3D way. Technical drawings were then created and printed, and paper models were made from them to understand the dimensions, followed by foam models to assess the surfaces. The Itos first considered using crystal for the vases to accentuate the sharp angles of the design, but this was rejected in favour of ceramic, which is cheaper and easier to work. However, a

skilled ceramicist was needed as porcelain lends itself to organic shapes and, without acute facets, the concept of Stardust would have been lost. Travelling to Sesto Fiorentino, an area outside Florence famous for ceramic artisans, the Itos sourced I+I, the factory of a small Milan-based company specializing in the production of Indian carpets and vases, who could hand-craft the necessary angles and lines.

A series of resin models was made 8% larger than the vases to allow for the shrinkage of the porcelain in drying and sent to the producer to make the female gesso stamp moulds. Liquid ceramic was poured into the moulds, which were shaken to make certain all the surfaces were coated before what remained was emptied out. The moulds were left for a few days to dry, and the vases then removed and sent to the craftsman to hand-finish the angles to perfection using a knife and sandpaper. The vases are dipped in a pool of paint to create an irregular hand-made aesthetic on the interior, but spray-painted on the outside in metallic black and silver to emphasize the angularity of the design. They are then fired.

STARDUST VASES
SETSU & SHINOBU ITO

Manufacturer: I+I srl
Ceramic
Various dimensions
Design to manufacture: 3 months
Small-scale production
www.studioito.com/www.i-and-i.it

The Stardust vases are
named after stellar rocks
that fall to earth and smash
into multi-faceted pieces.
The vases were designed to
be seen in multiples so that
surface and space between
become confused.

1. The vases were inspired by the visual confusion of multi-elements and surfaces such as the dappled shadow of sunlight through leaves.

2. Hand-drawn sketches were created to develop a competition of polyhedral planes and curved surfaces to produce visual puzzlement.

3. Computer renderings gave 3D reality to the sketches.

4. Technical drawings were developed and then printed to make templates to create a series of paper models.

5–6. The paper models were used to assess dimensions.

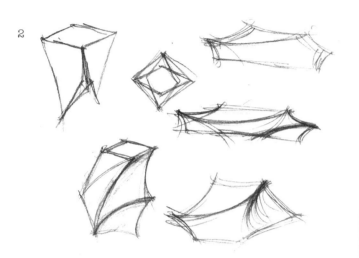

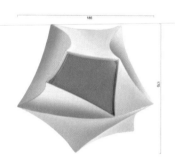

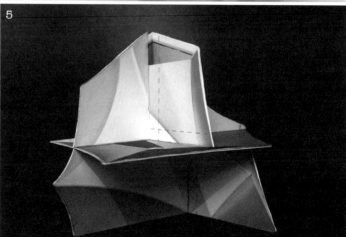

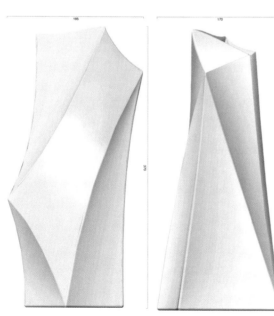

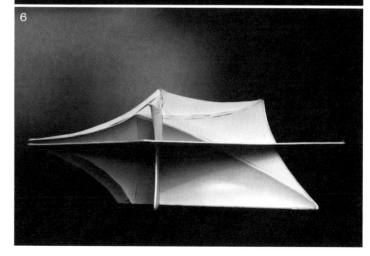

7. Foam models were employed to look at the various surfaces of the design.

8. Once the design had been refined, resin models were created 8% larger than the actual vases to allow for the shrinkage that occurs as the ceramic dries.

9–10. The resin models were sent to the producer who made female stamp moulds in gesso still 8% larger than the actual vases.

11. Liquid ceramic was poured into the moulds.

12. The moulds were shaken to make sure that the ceramic coats all the surfaces and the surplus is poured away.

13. The vase was allowed to dry in the mould for several days and then removed.

14–15. The angles and planes were hand-sharpened and shaped using knives and sandpaper.

16–17. The vase was dipped in a pool of paint to create a hand-finished aesthetic on the interior (16), but spray-painted in metallic black and silver on the exterior to accentuate the angularity of the design (17).

18. The vases were then fired.

Tavs Jørgensen is a craftsman. He trained as a potter and today runs his own design consultancy and lectures on ceramics and glass at London's Royal College of Art. His pioneering research, however, is in the utilization of digital technology by the designer-maker. There is nothing new in craftsmen employing modern production methods, but there is a definite suspicion of the use of IT in their creative processes, largely due to its association with automation and industrialization.

Jørgensen is currently a research fellow at the University College of Falmouth, as a member of the 3D Digital Design Research cluster team, or Autonomatic as they call themselves. (The name is a neologism formed from the words 'automatic' and 'autonomic'. It represents the combination of involuntary, repetitive, machine-like actions with human self-sufficiency, independence and uniqueness.) The group is composed of researchers with skills in many crafts, from metalwork to textiles. They all share the belief that computer-aided design and manufacture, far from being anathema to freedom of expression, offer equal scope for individualism. Their aim is to demystify digital technology and introduce it to the contemporary world of craft and design.

Jørgensen first became involved in computer technology in 2001 after being invited to participate in a rapid-prototyping project. The result was the Contour Cups, a set of digitally designed china bowls using a laminated object manufacture (LOM™) process, which builds up 3D forms by the layering of laser-cut paper. After working on a number of related projects, Jørgensen's focus is now to introduce an element of physicality into CAD: 'I want to use digital tools but utilize them in collaboration with the dexterity of the human hand,' he says.

His first experiments used the Microscribe™ G2 digitizing arm – a point-and-click device for scanning physical objects. By using it as a freehand tool, Jørgensen discovered it could record spontaneous three-dimensional drawings that are fed directly into the computer. Thickening the lines and giving them volume meant they could then be rendered in solid form by using rapid prototyping. Subsequently he worked with the ShapeHand™ motion-capture glove. Originally developed for use in animation and special effects, it is wired to a computer and translates not only hand but also arm and finger movements into digital drawings, thereby introducing a humanizing element to the formal geometry, which can often be the result of designs created via IT-based drawing tools.

The One Liner bowls were designed with the aid of the Microscribe™. They utilize the material properties of molten glass as a medium for the concept. Holding the tip of the Microscribe™, a series of loops were described in mid-air to form the rim of a bowl, and the linear motion digitally recorded via Rhinoceros® 3D software. These lines were extruded in the Z-axis and turned into two-dimensional surfaces by using the software's unroll surface command. Combined with the X-Y dimension (top view), the three-dimensional line could then be represented by two two-dimensional projections. The Z-axis was CNC-cut from bendable 0.5mm stainless steel, and the X-Y axis from 6mm (¼in) MDF. By squeezing the stainless steel into the laser-cut loop in the MDF, accurate models of the three-dimensional splines were achieved. The models were used as kiln moulds to shape the bowls from flat sheets of glass. In order to do this, the stainless steel had to be further supported by casting refractory plaster around it so the flammable MDF could be removed prior to the mould being fired. Circular discs of 6mm (¼in) glass were used to create the shapes of the vessels by using a process called free fall slumping. Under heat the glass will soften and gravity will allow it to 'slump' in the centre, creating the body of the bowl while taking on the form of the stainless-steel edge to develop the rim. After cooling the bowl is removed from the mould and the glass that overhangs the edge can be trimmed or left on for aesthetic effect.

ONE LINER BOWLS

TAVS JØRGENSEN

Production: Tavs Jørgensen
Glass
Various dimensions
Design to production: 2 months
Limited edition
www.oktavius.co.uk

The One Liner bowls were designed with the aid of a Microscribe™ G2 digitizing arm to utilize the material qualities of molten glass.

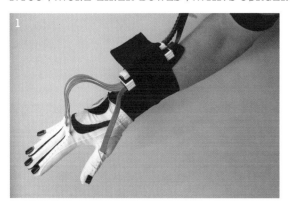

1. Jørgensen uses both the ShapeHand™ motion-capture glove and the Microscribe™ G2 to digitally create his designs. The glove was originally developed for animation and special effects. It captures arm gestures, but unlike the Microscribe™, it also records the dynamics of individual digits. Drawings can be made in mid-air, fed into a computer, manipulated and 3D models subsequently produced.

2. The One Liner bowls were developed using the Microscribe™ G2, which was used as an interactive three-dimensional drawing tool.

3–4. A loop describing the rim of a bowl was drawn freehand using the digitizer (3) and recorded in a Rhinoceros® 3D CAD program (4).

5. The line is extruded and unfolded using Rhinoceros® to convert the three-dimensional information into two two-dimensional representations, one of the Z and the other of the X-Y axis.

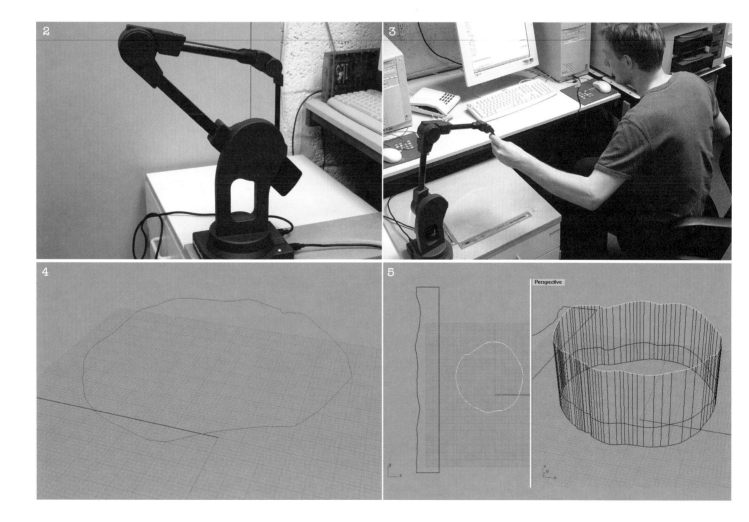

6–7. A CNC machine (6) is used to cut the two-dimensional representations, the Z axis in stainless steel and the X-Y axis in MDF (7), to allow the stainless steel to be supported.

8–9. The two two-dimensional representations are joined together to form a physical model of the three-dimensional line recorded with Microscribe™.

10. A refractory plaster cast is placed around the stainless-steel ring to enable the flammable MDF to be removed before the glass-slumping mould goes to the kiln. The stainless steel is prebent to ease the fitting into the MDF section.

11. Circular glass discs ready to be used with the glass-slumping form.

12. The mould is placed in the kiln with a glass disc placed on top ready to be fired.

13. The slumped glass piece after firing.

14. The rim of the One Liner bowl is the main focal point of the object, providing a physical manifestation of the way it was created. This is particularly evident when the excess glass has been trimmed, leaving the optical qualities of the glass to create a dark edge much like the original computer drawing.

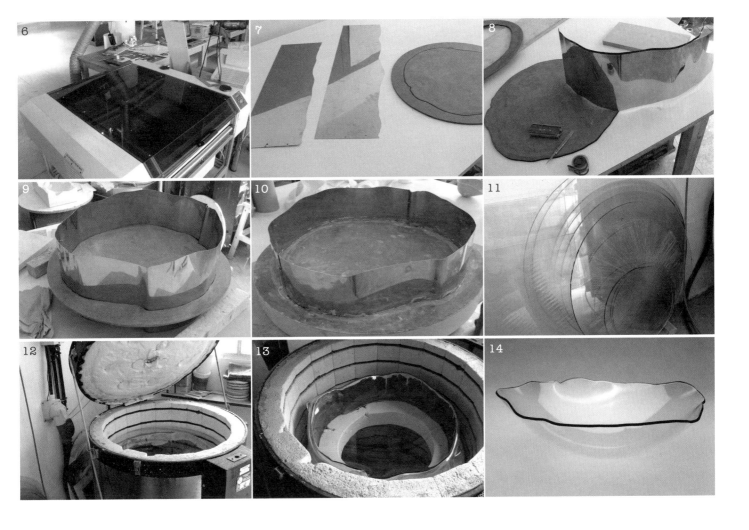

Reed Kram and Clemens Weisshaar's backgrounds are very different. Kram specializes in media design and began by designing video games before founding the Aesthetics and Computation Group led by John Meada. Weisshaar studied product design and was assistant to Konstantin Grcic before setting up his own studio. KRAM/WEISSHAAR was founded in 2002. The company is committed to the philosophy that cutting-edge technology and craftsmanship can liberate potential in traditional manufacturing techniques, which the designers believe is the only way that manufacturing in Europe will be able to compete with the production lines of the Far East. This belief is evident in both the computer-generated aesthetic of the Breeding Tables and the hand-painted digital imagery of tableware series, My Private Sky.

The Breeding Tables were inspired by the designers' disappointment that not enough design companies were using IT and advanced technological manufacturing methods to produce something completely different. The duo began writing software (which they refer to as their digital sweatshop) to create iterations of a simple table. Basic algorithms were used, some dating back to inventions by 19th-century mathematicians, to develop a computer application into which data (table width, height and length as well as typology rules) was input. The algorithmic application then continuously generated infinite three-dimensional structures, each inheriting a set of properties from the mother table.

As in nature, rogue mutations can lead to advantageous results. 'The computer itself is neither intelligent nor creative but rather known for meltdowns and errors, so unpredictable things happen,' says Weisshaar. 'While we craft the computer code there are more surprises than anything else. These are moments we appreciate a lot.'

The software works out a construction surface by triangulating the base geometry that is extracted using angled cutting planes: a digital three-dimensional model of the table is now available. Once this has been computationally tested and is passed suitable for production, the program uses an unrolling facility to produce flat geometrics that make up the cutting pattern for a given table structure. The pattern is transferred into the laser-cutting machine, where it scores the sheet steel. Each leg is incised individually, with the bend and joint information for assembling the table engraved in the table leg itself. The cut-flat leg is then moved to the bending machine, where the technician follows the instructions on the leg, turning each bend the specified number of degrees. The final stages involve joining the table legs together, applying a powder coating that is hand-finished by local craftsmen, and attaching the tempered glass or sheet-metal tops.

Breeding Tables began as a self-financed personal project, later receiving support and becoming the subject of an exhibition, 'Breeding Tables: La Raccolta', first shown during the Milan Furniture Fair 2005, and subsequently acquired by the Pompidou Centre in Paris. While KRAM/WEISSHAAR still produce exclusive, unique copies of the tables for private collectors and museums, the prestigious Italian furniture manufacturer, Moroso, have been given the licence to produce two models, entitled Countach #996 and #525.

Kram and Weisshaar have built up a large network of highly skilled technicians and craftsmen around Munich. Their first tableware series, My Private Sky, was produced in collaboration with Nymphenburg, the famous Bavarian porcelain manufacturer, which is still owned by the Bavarian royal family. The manufacturer continues to use watermills and relies exclusively on hand labour. As with the Breeding Tables, the plates combine sophisticated computer technology with hand-finishing. The duo designed software based on NASA's database of the 500 brightest stars, nebulae, stellar clusters and planets, calculating their position in the night sky on a customer's birthday according to the longitude and latitude of the place of birth as well as the date and hour of delivery. The pattern is then hand-painted on to a series of seven ceramic plates using gold and platinum paint to produce digitally bespoke pieces.

BREEDING TABLES
REED KRAM & CLEMENS WEISSHAAR

MY PRIVATE SKY PLATES
REED KRAM & CLEMENS WEISSHAAR

Production: KRAM/WEISSHAAR
Sheet metal
Various dimensions
Design to manufacture: 8 months
One-off
www.kramweisshaar.com

Manufacturer: Porzellan Manufaktur Nymphenburg
Hand-thrown and hand-painted porcelain
Dia: 32cm (12½in)
Design to manufacture: 9 months
Limited edition
www.nymphenburg.com

My Private Sky plates (left) are hand-made and hand-painted with a digital impression of the position of the constellations at the date and place of birth of the buyer. The Breeding Tables (below) are created from computer iterations of a base table form that generate thousands of unique pieces.

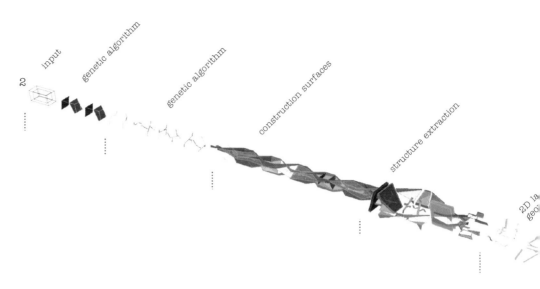

1. The Breeding Tables were inspired by the latent potential of computer-controlled manufacturing machinery, such as that used in car production.

2. 'Production line' of the Breeding Tables from the virtual to the physical.

3–4. Each table is 'bred' according to a set of algorithms that are made usable in a computer environment by the programming of a software application built around them and the addition of specific table data: measurements and defined typology rules. The possibilities are endless.

5. 'It is beautiful to teach a computer to design things,' says Weisshaar. 'Getting it to help you is both thrilling as well as annoying at times. It forces you to reverse-engineer the way you think and extract a logic that has to be crystal-clear.'

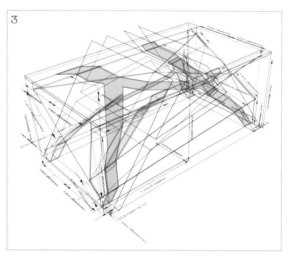

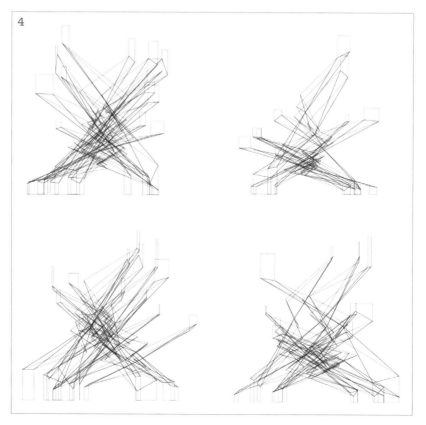

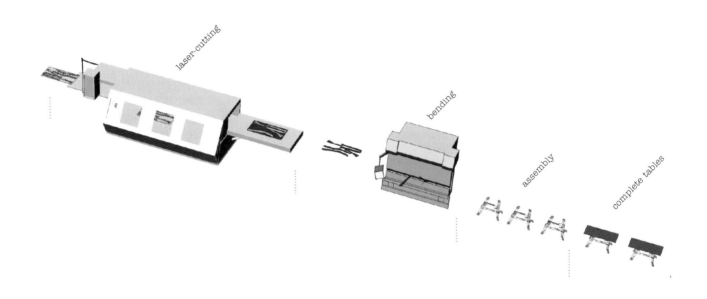

laser-cutting

bending

assembly

complete tables

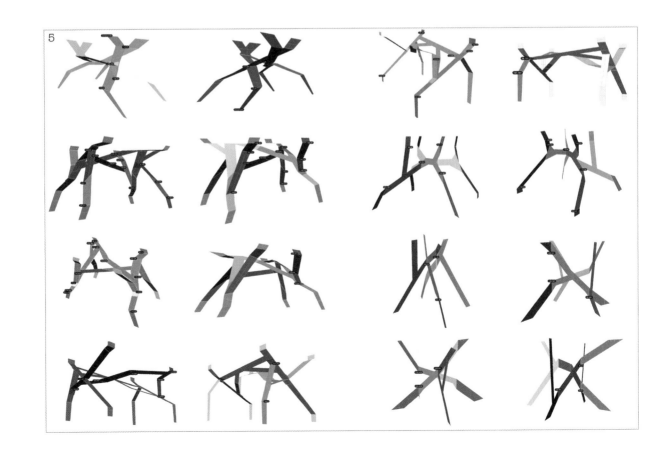

5

6

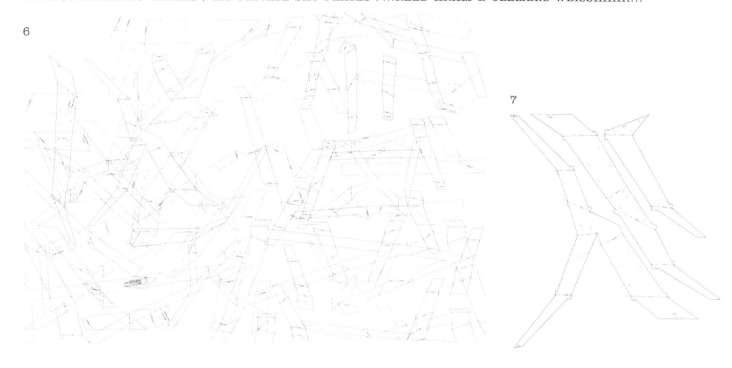

7

6–7. The unrolling facility of the Breeding Table software formed 2D blueprints from 3D volumetric shapes (6), which were then used as cutting patterns for the laser machine (7).

8. The patterns were taken to the CNC laser-cutting machine that manufactures the components of the tables.

9. Components/legs prior to bending. Each part had a set of instructions engraved on

it, which were used by the technicians operating the sheet-metal folding machine to turn each bend the specified number of degrees.

10. CNC-controlled press brake bending machine.

11. The table legs were powder-coated and finished by hand.

13

12

12–13. By designing a
computer program rather
than a single drawing, Kram
and Weisshaar combined the
excellence of master porcelain
painters with the potential of
a custom-developed computer
code that calculated readings
of the night sky.

14–15. The program was
turned into blueprints that
porcelain manufacturer
Nymphenburg's craftsmen use
to hand-paint the plates.

16–17. Nymphenburg has
always been the porcelain
manufacturer of the

Bavarian royal family. The
plates redefine centuries-
old processes into a
contemporary context. The
pigments used are processed
in-house following old and
new – but always secret
– recipes.

Joris Laarman established his own studio in 2004, describing it as a laboratory for 'innovation, aesthetics, curiosity, freedom and more'. He designs objects that are both beautiful and functional and believes that products should have a legitimacy; their forms and aesthetics not created by whim but given reason.

Laarman's Bone furniture imitates the growing patterns of bones, which have a very efficient way of dealing with material and weight. In 2004 Laarman met the German biomechanic Prof Klaus Mattheck, who had developed a computer program based on the fracture behaviour of trees and bones that were being used by German car manufacturer Opel in the design of ultra-light components. In nature, a weakness can be detected and then strengthened by generating material to support it. Bones are hollow and consist of fibrous structures. If a bone is broken and left it will calcify, adding mass to the exterior but taking away material from the interior to control density and gain strength. Similarly, Mattheck's program can detect a structural failure and know where to strengthen a design. The car parts produced by this program have an organic beauty that is lacking in the industrial aesthetics produced by the efficient moulding techniques of the machine age.

Meeting Mattheck was a seminal moment for Laarman; he recognized in Mattheck's work his own desire to give design and manufacture authenticity. Laarman's research into theoretical physics and

biomechanics has resulted in a new aesthetic. His idea is to develop a series of furniture without symmetry and with more constituents bearing weight. The shape remains logical, however, as it derives from a biological process. His aim is to go as far as possible without losing sense of the form. He explains: 'My work is about making functional objects as beautiful as possible. I have found a way to copy the smartest growing principle in nature: bone growth.'

The product started as a personal experiment, but after Laarman was approached by Droog Design and the Barry Freidman Gallery to produce work for the Smart Deco exhibition during Design Miami/Basel 2006 the concept was adopted and received considerable funding. The aluminium chair and polyurethane chaise are just the beginning and are both produced in a limited edition of 12.

Laarman adapted Mattheck's software with the aid of Opel's IT department. Laarman considers the process to be a three-way collaboration between designer, the information fed into the computer and cutting-edge technology. The data given to the program is rationalized. Information for a basic chair, consisting of backrest and seat, large enough to sit on but small enough to cast in one piece, is analysed digitally. The spaces around the shape are filled in by cubes with load-bearing parameters and the computer calculates the stresses and where they will need strengthening. Non-stress material is taken away and

more material added to the parts that bear the weight. The result is skeletal, with every strut having a structural function. The design can be rendered in any material, as the program compensates for the relative strengths and weaknesses and produces different profiles.

Laarman produced sketches and 1:1 blue foam models to work up his ideas. The chair is created using a newly trademarked CAD/casting method produced by Gravotech. The mould is rapid-prototyped in hollow pieces of ceramic that are assembled in the form of a puzzle. Rapid prototyping was used as it recreated the sinuous design produced by the software. This method was innovative as it allowed the structure to be cast rather than prototyped from a CAD drawing. The aluminium chair is cast in one piece and for each chair the mould is broken away. Afterwards, the piece is hand-polished – matte on the struts and mirror on the seat. The chaise is first CNC-cut into a positive first mould. With this a negative mould is created from around 30 pieces of epoxy. The negative mould can be assembled each time for casting in one piece. The chaise is cast in crystal-clear polyurethane with a shore of 90, which is not quite hard and not quite soft. This too is hand-polished, this time into a uniform fine matte finish.

BONE CHAISE
JORIS LAARMAN

BONE CHAIR
JORIS LAARMAN

Production: Joris Laarman
Polyurethane UV-resistant rubber
H: 77.3cm (30½in) x W: 77.3cm (30½in) x L: 148cm (58¼in)
Design to production: 24 months
Limited edition of 12

Production: Joris Laarman
Aluminium
H: 76cm (30in) x W: 45cm (17¾in) x D: 77cm (30¼in)
Design to production: 24 months
Limited edition of 12
www.jorislaarman.com

Joris Laarman seated in
the Bone chaise, a hybrid
of creativity and software
intelligence.

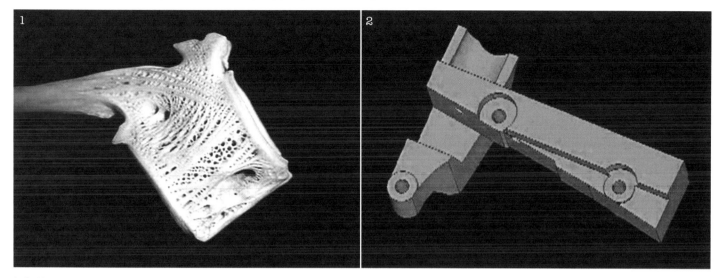

1–2. The Bone furniture was inspired by the work of Prof Klaus Mattheck, whose studies in failure analysis of trees and bones resulted in his development of software currently being used by Opel to produce organic-looking car components.

3–4. With the help of Opel's IT department, Laarman adapted the software to use it as a high-tech sculpting tool. For both the chair (3) and chaise (4) he started with a 3D model, a massive block on which he marked a seat and backrest. The computer took six months to calculate the optimum design for each.

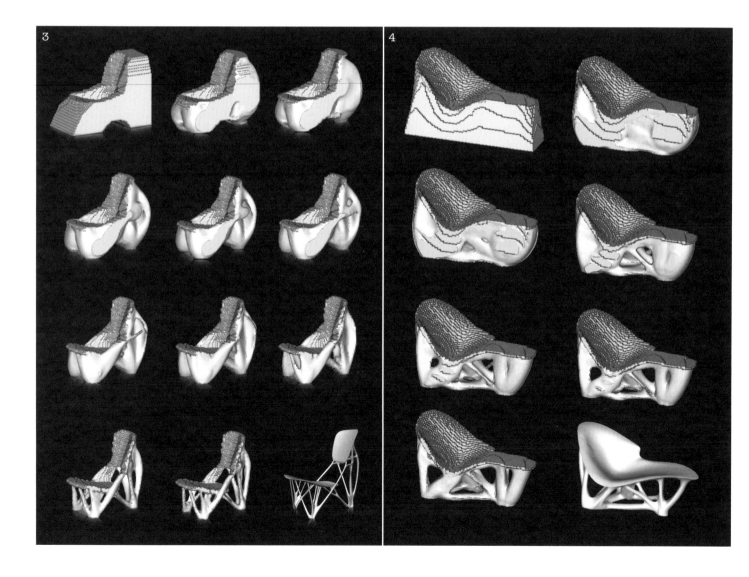

5

5. Laarman inspecting the 1:1
blue foam models of both the
chair and the chaise. He does
not use computer renderings,
believing that full-scale models
are essential for objects that
interact with people.

6. Computer-generated sketches
generate the dimensions for
the chaise.

6

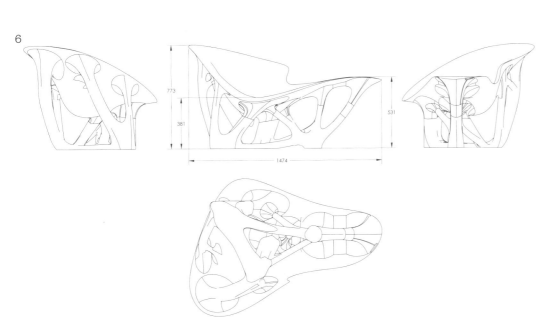

7. The models and the mould for the chair were developed in collaboration with designer Vincent de Rijk from a patented CAD/cast production method pioneered by Gravotech.

8. Molten aluminium is poured into the mould cavity, which is cast in one piece.

9–10. A 3D printer is used to make the ceramic mould for each one of the 12 chairs, and the mould is smashed after each pouring to reveal the finished product.

11. The aluminium is hand-polished; matte on the struts and mirror on the seat surface and backrest.

12. The result is skeletal, with every strut playing a structural function. The more complex the design of the chair, the greater its load-bearing properties.

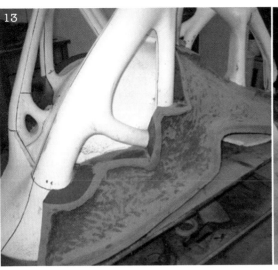

13

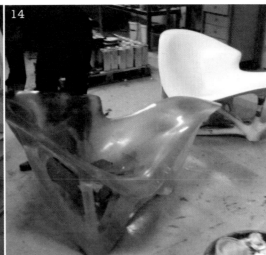

14

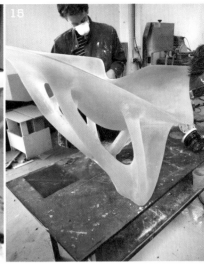

15

13. The negative mould of the chaise is made from around 30 pieces of epoxy, which can be reassembled each time for casting in one piece.

14–15. The chaise is cast in one piece of crystal-clear polyurethane UV-resistant rubber (14). It is then hand-polished to a fine matte finish (15).

16. The aluminium Bone chair in its final form.

17. Designs for Bone furniture can be rendered in any material, as the computer compensates for the relevant strengths and weaknesses. The polyurethane chaise has a more solid profile than the aluminium chair.

16

17

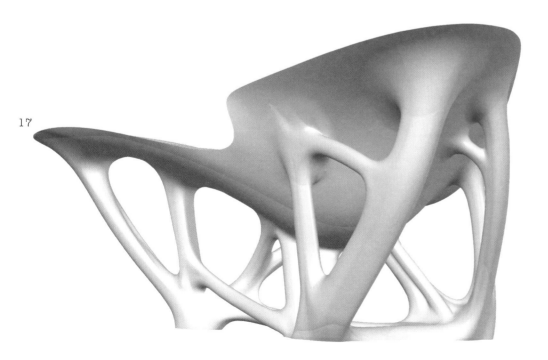

Max Lamb completed his Master's in design products at the Royal College of Art in London in 2007, where he developed his design language, inspired by a desire to explore both traditional and unconventional materials.

The sand-cast Pewter Stool forms part of Max Lamb's Exercises in Seating, a collection that he describes as 'an ongoing project in which the emphasis is more on research and then engagement with a process, rather than on the product itself'. This recent work is focused on exploring the potential of disappearing local skill-based industries and exploiting the inherent qualities of native materials, combining these with high-tech and digital processes. In addition to the Pewter Stool, the series consists of a laser-cut stainless-steel chair; a bomb-proof seat made from carved expanded polystyrene coated in polyurethane rubber; a copper stool 'grown' on to a wax substrate using a sophisticated electro-deposition process similar to electro-plating; and an SLS stool created in laser-sintered polyamide.

Sand-casting is one of the earliest forms of casting. Molten metal is poured into a cavity mould made from green sand. A master of the design is created that is slightly larger than required to allow for the shrinkage of the metal as it cools. A 'sprue' and riser are added to the tool. The moulding box is made in two halves. The sand is compacted in both halves, the tool is placed on the surface of one of the boxes and the two halves pressed together. It is then removed and the negative cavity is ready for the metal, which is poured in and allowed to cool.

Max Lamb was born and brought up in Cornwall, an area famous throughout the 18th and 19th centuries for its copper and tin mining and for its fine, sandy coast, perfect for casting. Exploring this ancient technique Lamb decided to cast a pewter stool using a very primitive method, on the beach where he had played as a child. He chose a location that had a consistent grain, free from shells and small stones, and at a point that was completely covered by the sea at high tide. This ensured that the sand remained compact and damp throughout the casting once the tide had gone out. A portable gas cooker was buried in the sand and then covered with a wooden board to protect the fire from the wind and to raise the temperature. The 1kg (2⅕lb) pewter ingots took about 15 minutes to melt, during which time Lamb experimented with a series of shapes sculpted in the sand. It took three days of trial and error to ascertain which pattern allowed the pewter to flow easily through the mould. In the end, Lamb decided on a three-legged design, which meant the stool would remain stable even if the legs were short shot and cast at slightly different lengths, topped by a triangular seat formed of 16 tessellating triangles to save on the amount of metal used.

Lamb began by marking a 40cm (15¾in) equilateral triangle on the sand with the sides divided into four sections. The points were connected by lines drawn to the corresponding marks on the opposite side, forming 16 smaller triangles. A 1cm (⅜in) diameter rod marked 40cm (15¾in) from the bottom was sunk in turn into each of the three corners of the large triangle to the depth of the marker and was pushed backwards and forwards towards the neighbouring angles until the sand resisted. The movement gave the leg a strengthening natural taper and a V-shaped cross-section. With a knife, Lamb then excavated further V-shaped grooves along each of the interior triangles, carefully carving out the sand from each channel to a depth of 2cm (¾in). The pewter was poured into each of the legs to a level just below the triangular channels. A second pouring was then added to the slightly cooled pewter in the first leg and allowed to flow along the channels until all the triangles were connected and the two remaining legs completely filled. After ten minutes the metal had hardened and the sand was excavated by hand, allowing the stool to be pulled gently away.

PEWTER STOOL
MAX LAMB

Production: Max Lamb
Pewter (92% tin, 6% antimony, 2% copper)
H: 40cm (15¾in) x W: 40cm (15¾in) x D: 40cm (15¾in)
Design to production: 4 days
Limited edition of 6
www.maxlamb.org

The Pewter Stool was cast on
Caerhays beach in Cornwall,
where Max Lamb used to play
as a child.

1–2. The pewter ingots were melted in two saucepans heated over a portable gas cooker buried in a pit in the sand. The hole was covered with a wooden board that protected the flames from wind and raised the temperature.

3–4. Lamb started by etching an equilateral triangle in the sand and then divided it into four sections. The points on the perimeter were joined to form 16 tessellating triangles. The surface had to be continually dampened with water spray to prevent it from crumbling.

5–6. A rod was sunk into the three corners of the large triangle and moved first towards one of the adjacent angles until the sand resisted and then towards the other. The movement gave the leg a natural V-shaped section towards the top of the leg, increasing its strength.

7. One saucepan of molten pewter was poured into each of the three legs. The second saucepan was then added to the slightly cooled metal in the first leg and allowed to run through the channels, slowly connecting all the triangles.

8–9. Once the pewter had hardened, the stool was excavated by hand and gently lifted free of the sand.

10. The surface of the stool is textured by the sand. A three-legged design was selected so that the stool would remain stable even if the legs were cast slightly unevenly. During his experiments Lamb noticed that the water table dropped more slowly than the tide and the pewter didn't always reach the same depth in all the leg holes.

11–12. The Copper stool forms part of Max Lamb's 'Exercises in Seating'. A substrate of wax is sculpted and patterned in hot water (11). It is then coated in a conductive silver solution, wired up to electrodes and submerged in an electro-deposition tank containing an aqueous solution of copper. When charged, the copper clings to the structure, nanocrystal by nanocrystal. Once sufficient deposits have occurred, the stool is removed from the tank and the wax is melted out (12).

13. The completed 'grown' Copper Stool is part of a collection of chairs by Lamb that demonstrates his research into traditional or unconventional materials combined with high-tech production methods.

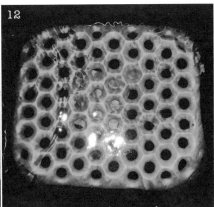

Since the turn of the century, the design industry has been far more accepting of a refreshing pluralism, which has seen a blurring of the boundaries between architecture, design, craft and art. To some, this is anathema. For UK-based Jasper Morrison, who describes his own work as 'simple', designers, along with architects and graphic designers, should be the guardians of the man-made environment; he rejects the adherents to a more conceptual approach to design. Tom Dixon, too, is sceptical of products that he considers 'too close to the art gallery'. However, with the huge popularity of shows such as Design Miami/Basel, and with consumers collecting one-off and limited-edition design objects as if they were pieces of art, there are obviously many who see this cross-over as liberating; craft-based, low-tech, individualistic approaches are enjoying an unprecedented popularity. Clare Lane's work sits within such a context.

Lane trained as an architectural and building surveyor, working in that industry before changing her career to study textile design at Leeds College of Art and Design. She recently completed a two-year residency at Manchester Metropolitan University in the embroidery department and won the Craft Council's Development Award for Creative Industry. While her earlier working life was concerned with the physicality of the built environment, her current textile practice represents the urban habitat in stitch, and combines a mix of photography, pattern design, digital imaging and the expression of outline, texture and relief in a unique form of tapestry.

Lane's wall hangings examine the frenetic, modern city with disturbed sight lines, huge buildings and bold monuments surrounded by a detritus of rubbish, bill posters and graffiti. Her current interest lies in places of transition that are either declining or shifting from a state of dereliction to renewal.

The Bishop's Square textile piece takes inspiration from a prestigious development in the Spitalfields area of London and the extensive photographic records held by Allen & Overy, the international law practice who commissioned the piece. The key theme was to examine both the historic and dynamic setting of Spitalfields, and to include iconic references such as the 18th-century Hawskmoor Christ Church as well as the construction process of the new development. The piece is a combination of photographs and drawings, digitally combined, manipulated and 'painted' on the computer.

Photographs were the primary source of research for Lane, combined with a thorough investigation of the scale, street patterns and dominant views of the area. The size of the piece, 1m x 2.68m (3¼ft x 8¾ft), demanded a panorama. A simple composition, a line drawing painted in with watercolour using a select colour palette, was calculated to scale to form the base of the montage. The sky, painted in blue oil pastel on paper, formed the background and was scanned into a computer at a quarter scale. All the other images were then gathered and overlaid using Photoshop. The base composition, complete with notes, was the first image to be added.

The composition is laboriously refined, and colour added and blended. The finished image is scaled up to full size before printing. The printing process involves colour testing with many samples digitally printed on cotton canvas. The main image is adjusted until the print matches the colours on the screen. The full printed canvas is then backed with an iron-on stiffener in woven fabric to stabilize the stitch work. The basic satin stitch is added on a free-needle sewing machine. As there is no footplate the fabric can be freely moved so that only the desired areas are covered. The stitch width can also be varied from dense and smooth to open, which makes the texture more visible in the end composition. As it is important to achieve a balance between the amount of area filled with stitch and the amount left in flat print, an A4 paper record is constantly referred to. When the stitch work is finished, the canvas is stretched across a timber frame.

URBAN FABRIC
CLARE LANE

Production: Clare Lane
Printed cotton canvas, embroidery cotton, timber frame
H: 1m (3¼ft) x L: 2.68m (8¾ft)
Design to production: 4 months
One-off
www.urban-fabric.co.uk

(Previous page). Clare Lane's wall hangings explore the modern city. Detail from the Bishop's Square textile, shown in its entirety (right).

1. The inspiration came from the huge photographic collection of Allen & Overy and includes images of the development. Lane also researched and photographed the scale, street patterns and dominant views of the area.

2. Lane's Bishop's Square textile in full, which documents the prestigious development of Spitalfields, and includes references to historic landmarks as well as regeneration.

3. The first idea was a rough sketch in oil pastel. Strong verticals divided the panoramic view. Black acted as a foil to the other colours and, when stitched, added depth to the completed work.

4. The base image was of the sky in blue oil pastel on paper, which was scanned into the computer. The next step was to overlay the 'diagram for base composition'.

5. The diagram for base composition worked out line, detail and colour. Reds and oranges predominated; these were based on the colour of the frame, preselected by the interior designers of the boardroom where the commission was exhibited. The notes were used as a tool for the overlaying of the final montage of images.

6. Details of photographs were cut out in Photoshop and overlaid, as were contextual shots. Computer with details to be overlaid.

7. Close-up of one of the details.

8. The final composition was printed out on cotton canvas.

9. The stitching was carried out on a free-needle sewing machine. The absence of a footplate meant the fabric could be easily moved to vary the stitching, and to avoid areas of the print that were to be left unworked. These areas added relief to the texture.

10. The stitching was very dense and pulled the fabric. An embroidery hoop was used to stretch the fabric drum tight. (Illustration is of another commission, for Blackburn Royal Infirmary).

Tomáš Gabzdil Libertiny's beeswax pieces form part of his Masters of Design thesis for the Design Academy, Eindhoven. Examining the dialectic that happiness derives from the fulfilment of desire, his essay critiques consumer society, by examining the transient but precious nature of objects made from this fragrant, colourful, tactile yet fragile substance. Desire informs our need to purchase but the value of an object dissipates with possession. For Libertiny this realization contradicted his preconceived idea of a product as something solid, not only in terms of physicality but also metaphysically. He reasons that an object becomes vulnerable and consequently ephemeral when affection is lost for it – which is all too common in a market that is dominated by excess, accessibility and built-in obsolescence.

Libertiny is inspired by post-minimalism; in particular the work of Guiseppe Penone as well as members of the 1960s Italian art movement, Arte Povera, most notably Wolfgang Laib, who challenged commercialization by pitching nature against culture in the use of natural substances in his work. Talking about a series of pieces comprising mounds of pollen, Laib says, 'These mounds are so precious, so fragile, so small and yet so big, and inaccessible. Today, in our culture everything seems, or has to be accessible, touchable and available. And before, in most cultures, in all "primitive cultures", things were handled with much reverence, many things were too precious to be touched.'

Libertiny's work advocates the importance of time and labour in building on something that is already there. 'For me, the idea of intervention in the growth process is more tempting than the idea of an independent, autonomous creation. Fundamentally, it is about having certain expectations from a process but not completely being able to control its outcome. It is in some way an extension of the idea of growth (design process) that is dependent on already existing natural mechanisms.'

The beeswax pieces connote time and value through the repetitive and laborious work of the honey bee. Taking what is perceived as the negative values of an industrial product – fragility, ephemerality and primitiveness – Libertiny seeks to compete with the consumer standards of durability, functionality and technological innovation by creating unusable objects of desire.

For Libertiny, the most logical product to develop was the vase, as wax comes from flowers and in the form of the vase ends up serving them on their last journey. The object is a combination of natural matter and cultural iconic form. The first objects made were a series of small beeswax vases, cast in plaster moulds that were elegant in their simplicity and surprising in their honey-like scent. This was followed by an amphora: an exhibition piece of exaggerated proportions. A mould was made in wet plaster and the wax poured into it in stages using a series of different qualities from very yellow to brown to give the piece texture and pattern. At every pouring the mould was rotated so that all the surfaces were equally covered. As beeswax shrinks when it cools, the amphora cracked – an imperfection that Libertiny kept as part of the concept of fragility. At this point Libertiny asked himself whether it would be possible to make a product at the place where the material originates: the hive. Could he make the bees construct wax differently from how they normally build their honeycomb?

He started by putting one of his solid beeswax vases in the hive to see if it would be disassembled by the bees and reconstructed; would they make holes in it or destroy it? After two weeks nothing had happened. He then experimented with a construct in traditional vase form made out of preprinted honeycomb. After a week the hive was opened and to Libertiny's amazement the bees had inflated the form, adding their own extensions. Each vase made by the bees is the only one of its kind, a sculptural expression and an object of desire too delicate and precious to be used or touched but with unique symbolic value.

AMPHORA
TOMÁŠ GABZDIL LIBERTINY

MADE BY BEES
HONEYCOMB VASES
TOMÁŠ GABZDIL LIBERTINY

Production: Tomáš Gabzdil Libertiny
Beeswax
H: 130cm (51in) x Dia: 70cm (27½in)
Design to manufacture: 8–9 months
One-off

Production: Apis Mellifera Carnica (honey bees)
Beeswax
Various dimensions
Design to manufacture: bees active April to June
Limited edition
www.studiolibertiny.com

The Amphora (above) was rotationally moulded using varying grades of wax and was exhibited as if it were an archaeological artefact. The Made by Bees Honeycomb Vase (left) was constructed in the hive by honey bees.

1. Screengrab from a short animated film made by Libertiny illustrating that, as wax comes from flowers, a vase (which serves them on their last journey) is the logical product to produce in beeswax.

2–4. Various models of the amphora were developed using different methods and materials. This model was never developed into a mould. It is made out of multiplex boards, cut out by hand and then glued together and roughly milled on a lathe that had to be custom-made because of its large size.

5. The 1:1 model of the final version was developed on the computer. Cross-sections were taken from a CAD drawing and cut from multiplex board using a CNC machine. Multiplex is resistant to moisture and was used to react with the wet plaster. The cross-sections were put together and the gaps three-quarter filled with polystyrene blocks.

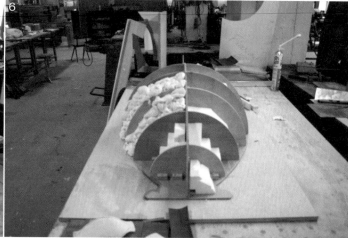

6. Polyurethane foam was sprayed in, completely filling the spaces.

7. The model was covered in plaster using a technique of scraping with a profile. A negative profile was cut (seen here leaning against the table).

8. The profile was attached with hinges to the model. It was then rotated following the same axes as the model. The profile is slightly larger. Plaster was added and then smoothed with the profile to get the perfect shape.

9–10. Handles were made in polyurethane and attached. Template for handle (9).

The model was finished by sanding the wet plaster (10).

11–12. The model (which was produced in symmetrical halves) was coated in a separator and a 5cm (2in) plaster layer gradually built up around it, evenly covering the surface. The layer was left to harden and removed, forming the

two parts of the mould that were later strengthened by the application of epoxy and fibreglass.

13–14. The frame to perform the rotational moulding was built into the plaster mould by embedding it in a fibreglass coating.

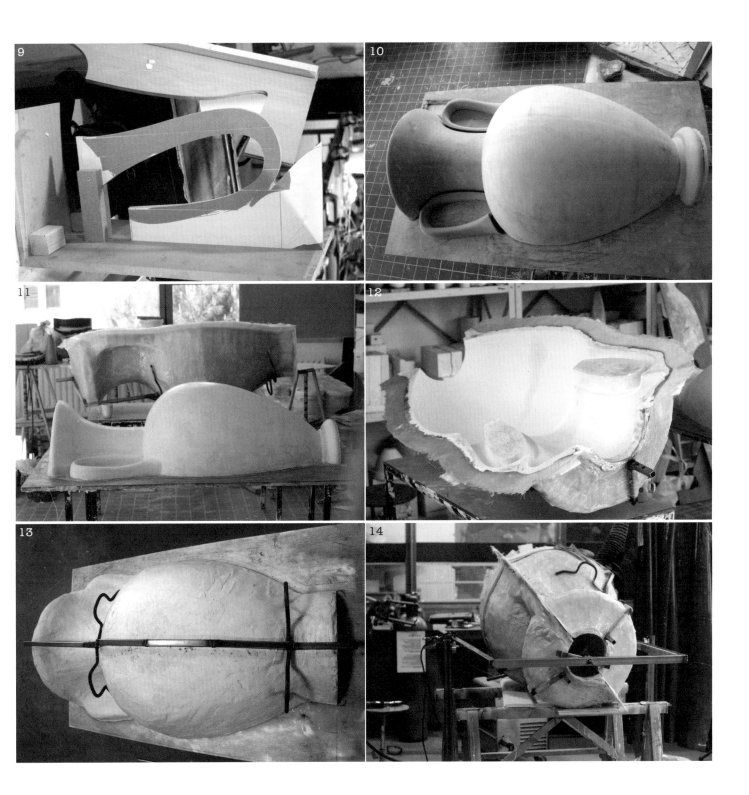

15–17. Different qualities of wax were used from bright yellow to brown to add texture and pattern (15). Each of these was heated (16) to 68°C (154°F) and poured in turn into the mould (17).

18–20. The mould was revolved around two axes at each stage allowing the molten wax to tumble around the inside of the die, where it built up to develop a hollow form. The mould was wet inside, and as water and wax don't mix, the wax solidified as soon as it touched the wet plaster.

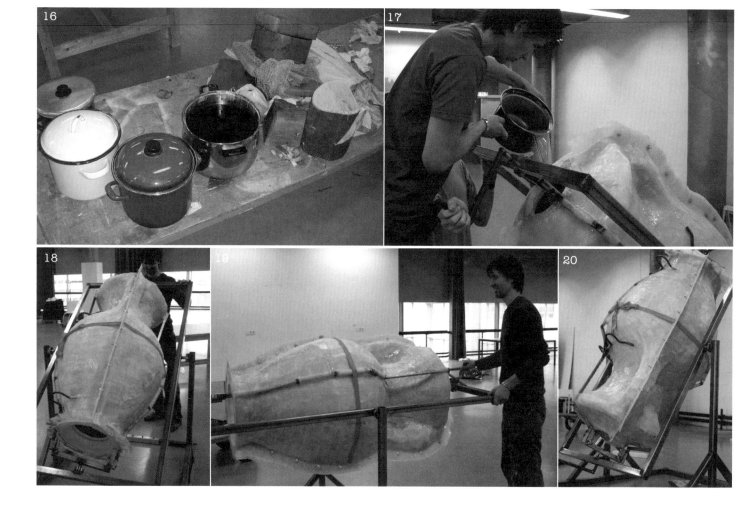

21. The creation of the Made by Bees Honeycomb Vases required a thorough understanding of the life of a bee, its natural behaviour and cycles. Close cooperation with professional beekeepers, Cor Bunthof and Cornelius Blokland, was essential to the project. No bees were hurt in the creation of the vases!

22. The initial idea was to place a solid wax vase in the hive to see if the bees would make holes in an attempt to create something new. After two weeks nothing had happened.

23. A vase made from a honeycomb construct was then employed and the honey bees responded by building up extensions. Sketch of the construct.

24. The vases in the hive. Each time the bees were given the same predesigned form with an embossed hexagonal structure on the surface. This enabled them to build up the comb from ground up – the same way a building raises up from a ground plan.

25–26. Libertiny's drive to push things further led him to manipulate the colour of the honeycomb. After learning

that bees do not see red, a coloured wax construct was made and added to the hive. Amazingly, the result was a corresponding honeycomb vase in each case.

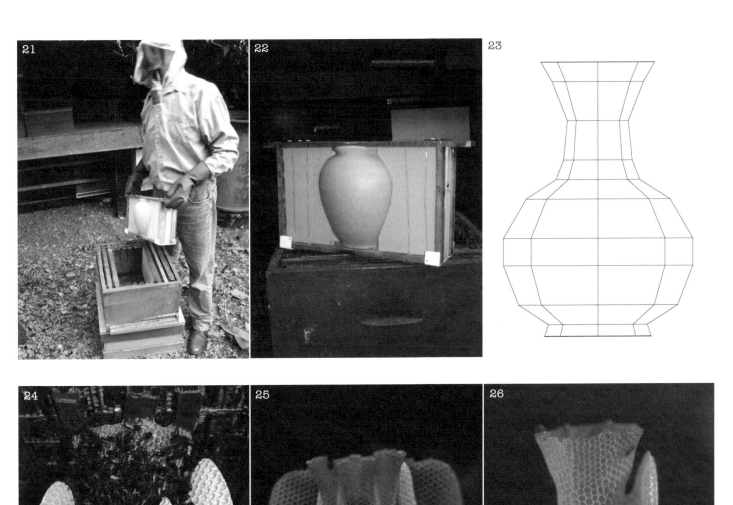

21

22

23

24

25

26

Xavier Lust is recognized as the most talented designer in Belgium; he has become famous for his sculptural furniture, made by bending and shaping single aluminium sheets. He coined the expression '(de)formation of surfaces', and his work has recently been the subject of a solo exhibition at the Grand-Hornu near Mons in Belgium and a monograph written to accompany the show. Lust's timeless furniture combines aesthetic and technical innovation with function.

The S Table started out as a personal project. It was originally intended as a new phase in the working process focused on '(de)formation', examples of which have been manufactured by the likes of De Padova, Extremis and MDF Italia, but always made in collaboration with Liège-based Atelier Georis, the only folder of metal in the world that can reproduce Lust's involved designs.

Lust's work often has a graphic/typographic aesthetic, revealed both in the names he gives to his pieces and their profiles; for example, the PicNik combo-table, which looks like a Chinese character. The S Table's complicated profile links two 'S' shapes joined in a single surface. It has a dynamic that would be difficult to produce by hand, or imagined visually, without the aid of a computer and was developed using Rhinoceros® software. Its form appears curved but is generated by many straight lines that have been unrolled using the software to produce a flat 2D surface from a 3D volumetric

shape. Lust took the concept to Atelier Georis, which tried to develop a prototype using the '(de)formation' technique: cutting aluminium using either laser or water-jet and then cold-folding the sheets. However, the metal-folding machine was found wanting as it could not enter inside the convoluted design to produce the complicated curves of the double-S base. Lust then presented the idea to Bruno Fattorini, the owner of MDF Italia, who accepted the design, and the computer-aided diagrams were discussed with MDF's technicians.

Based on Lust's production instructions, various alterations were made, including an increase in the steadiness of the base by enlarging the S-profiles on the floor to allow larger tabletops to be used. It is no coincidence that the S Table also reads as 'stable'. The idea of using metal was abandoned in favour of Baydur®, a polyurethane resin formed by the combination of two components. The technique used in moulding the Baydur® is traditional. As the mould is made from mixed media and not milled from a stainless-steel cube, it is relatively inexpensive, although, due to the materials used, it has to be remade after a certain number of pieces has been produced. This, however, has the advantage of allowing the manufacturer to make improvements from one series to another.

Before the mould was constructed, a 20% reduced prototype was produced in epoxy using stereolithography. Once this was

assessed, scale models of the mould were created from multiplex wood. It is traditional in Italian manufacturing to produce the necessary models of both the product and the mould as, although computer renderings can present details of the design visually, they cannot express the relationship between the volumes and how the user will interact with the object.

A 1:1 model was made from rigid foam and multiplex wood. After that, a full-scale mould was created and the two components of the resin were mixed and poured into it. The exterior of the mould is made in two parts from welded steel and the interior in four parts: two in fused aluminium and two in mixed media. Once the resin had hardened, which takes 20 minutes, the mould was opened, rotated and the base ejected. Experiments were conducted to find the optimum way of attaching the tabletop to the base. Finally it was decided to make a cross line in the base in which holes were cast. Metallic pegs were fixed under the top, inserted into the holes and finally attached by small screws. This explains why the upper S is 'seriffed'. The latest series of the S Table replaces Baydur® with a bi-component resin called Ekotek that has the appearance and texture of Corian®.

S TABLE
XAVIER LUST

Manufacturer: MDF Italia srl
Baydur® (Ekotek for latest series)
H: 73cm (28¾in) x Dia: 156cm (61½in)
Design to manufacture: 36 months
Mass-manufactured
www.xavierlust.com/www.mdfitalia.it

The S Table's base links two 'S'
shapes joined in a single surface.

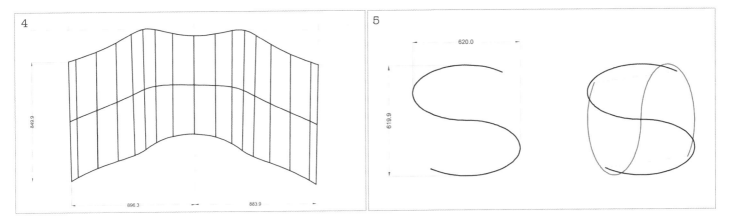

4

849.9

896.3 883.9

5

620.0

619.9

1–2. S Table was originally intended to be an exercise in the bending and shaping of steel sheets, which Lust refers to as the '(de)formation of surfaces'. Previous examples have included Le Banc (1) and the PicNik combo-table (2).

3. A series of CAD drawings shows the complicated shapes of the double-S motif; they would be impossible to create without the use of computer software.

4–5. Computer drawings showing the result of the unrolling of the 3D volumetric shape into a flat 2D surface. The two S shapes are placed to design the rotational geometry.

6. A scaled prototype was made in epoxy using stereolithography (far right).

7. From the prototype, scaled models were made of the mould to verify that the base could be ejected successfully and to understand the correct movement of each part.

8. The white form is the first scaled S Table made in resin, which was poured into the scaled mould.

9. A 1:1 model was made from rigid foam and multiplex wood.

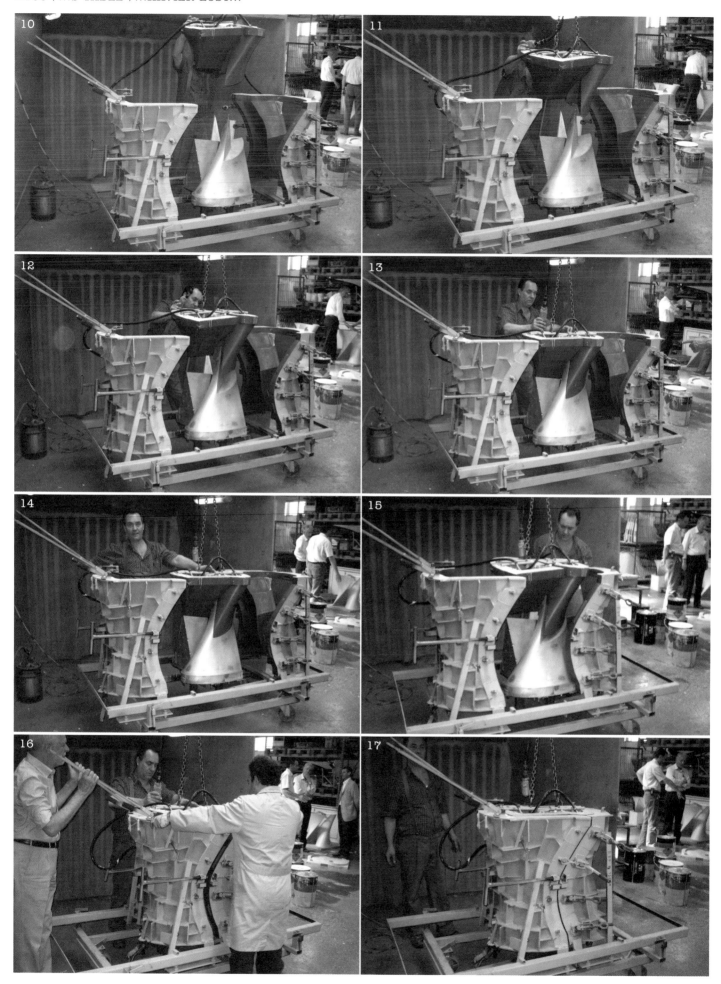

18

19

20

21

22

10–17. Images of the six parts of the full-scale mould (two in aluminium, two in mixed media and resin, and the two external parts constructed from steel and resin), showing all the steps to close it before the pouring begins.

18. The mould is ready for use. Verification of the opening and closing.

19–21. The Baydur® is poured in and left to harden for 20 minutes, then ejected.

22. The upper S of the table's base is seriffed due to the holes cast in the Baydur®, which allow metallic pegs to attach to the glass top.

Marco Maran is well known for seating designs that share flexibility and a lightness of spirit. The technological evolution of a product, and its ultimate accessibility to the consumer, are of utmost importance. He is not concerned with statements and his work is democratic: he never designs in limited editions and wants his projects to be available to all at a reasonable price. Maran's work also has an honesty that derives from his training as an industrial designer and architect. The X3 range of furniture, which includes a bar stool as well as the chair featured here, is an exercise in quality, elegance and versatility, and was created to highlight the innovative technology used in its manufacture.

Experimentation has given rise to seating with a transparent and simple aesthetic made with a new technological procedure for furnishings: the single-piece seat and back is obtained from the bi-injection of two materials, clear polycarbonate and mass-coloured Desmopan™. The design has been patented, as it is the result of a complex moulding technique that has been applied for the first time in this specific sector.

The X3 chair was commissioned by Maxdesign, with whom Maran collaborated on two previous designs: the Ricciolina and So Happy chairs. Inspiration came from Maran's examination of a toothbrush. He noted that the process of bi-injection had been used in small objects but never in anything larger scale. He wondered why this dialogue between hard and soft and transparent and matte had never been applied to furnishings.

The first stage was to give a physical form to Maran's idea of using bi-injection in a chair, using glossy, rigid and transparent polycarbonate for the base and soft and matte Desmopan™ for the lines. Various options were worked out in rough sketches before Maran decided upon the simplest. This resembled an unfolded handkerchief with the surface articulated by the fold lines. The fold/construction lines are in Desmopan™, a thermoplastic polyurethane elastomer combining characteristics of rubber with the strength of polyurethane, outlined against the transparent polycarbonate surface.

Once the aesthetic had been determined, further sketches and detailed drawings were used to construct a prototype that was executed following the same production process suggested for the final chair. A wooden mould was built and then injected with a resin that, when set, gave Maran a physical form to evaluate the shape, proportions, resistances and comfort of the chair. The data was then fed into a computer and CAD drawings created in order to machine the tool.

The manufacturing process was completely new both to Maran and the experts in bi-injection who worked on the production. He remained on hand throughout in case modifications needed to be made, although prior discussions with the technicians had determined the parameters with which they would be forced to work. First, a small mould was created to experiment with the injection of the second material. On a polycarbonate panel a grid of lines was created in different widths and sections to see which combination worked best.

A steel mould in three pieces was realized from the CAD calculations (a normal mould usually has two pieces; hence the name of the chair). The granular polycarbonate was passed through a 'hot chamber' in the plasticator, changing its state from solid to liquid. The melt was then forced through the nozzle at high pressure into the mould, filling the empty spaces and cooling. Once the shell was obtained, the second part of the mould was replaced by the third in a sliding movement. The mould was then closed and the Desmopan™ injected. The material filled the tight channels to generate the lines. Great skill was needed to achieve a balance between temperature and pressure while injecting the second material to achieve thin lines, sharp and precise edges and a good adhesion to the polycarbonate: if the Desmopan™ cooled too quickly it would not fill the grid, and create voids. If injected too forcefully it could break the catches of the mould and cause imperfections.

X3 CHAIR
MARCO MARAN

Manufacturer: Maxdesign srl
Clear polycarbonate, Desmopan™ lattice
H: 77cm (30¼in) x W: 52cm (20½in) x D: 47cm (18½in)
Design to manufacture: 24 months
Mass-manufactured
www.umbrella.it/www.maxdesign.it

The X3 chair has a simple
look but a substantial
design, with countless possible
colour combinations.

1. The inspiration behind the design of the X3 chair is the bi-injected toothbrush.

2. Developed drawings were created from early sketches. This one is annotated in Italian with the words 'transparent' and 'grid – soft colour'. The idea of the project was to be able to 'sit' on the drawing; the aesthetic came from the idea of an unfolded handkerchief.

3–4. A prototype was created by injecting resin into a wooden mould. This gave Maran a physical form to refine the design. His computer experts then translated the data into CAD files.

5. The CAD drawings were used to machine the tool. They show (left to right): the base, the grid, and how the rod frame attaches to the steel legs, all designed in order not to disturb the line of the shell.

6. The first and second parts of the mould used to create the polycarbonate shell. The mould is open and shows the shell.

7. Close-up of the shell in the mould.

8. The second part of the mould creates the lines on the polycarbonate, which will be filled by the Desmopan™.

9. The first part of the mould slides downwards and is positioned in front of the third part of the mould.

10. The first part of the mould is closed on the third part and the second material is injected on the polycarbonate shell.

11. The mould opens and the shell is complete.

12. This shows the shell and grid (first and second materials combined) within the mould. The Desmopan™ not only serves an aesthetic purpose but, due to its soft and gummy texture, is intended to create friction with the body (polycarbonate is very slippery).

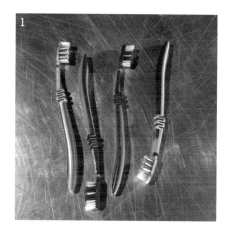

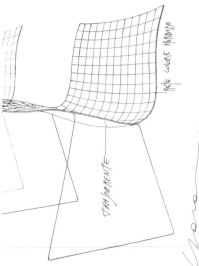

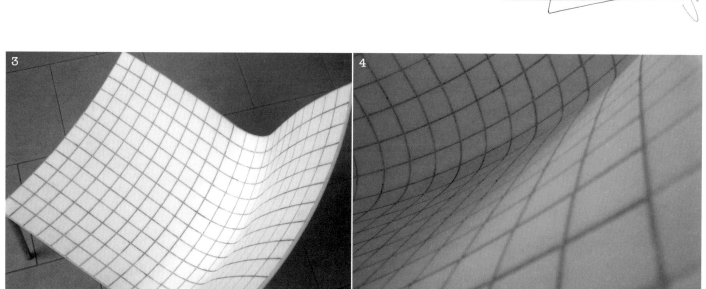

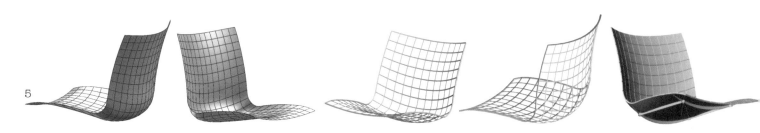

Marc Newson's exhibition at the Gagosian Gallery in New York from January to March 2007 brought together 16 limited editions that are at once visually seductive and technically rigorous. Each piece is created as an experimental exercise in combining advanced technology with the exploitation of traditional materials and craftsmanship. It is the first time that Gagosian has showcased a designer rather than an artist, although it is no departure for Newson to be associated with the exclusivity of the collector's piece. He trained as a jewellery designer and sculptor at the Sydney College of Arts, and made his name in 1986 with the Lockheed Lounge, a fluid hand-made metallic form that he readily admits is 'relatively unusable'. He has exhibited limited editions at the Galerie Kreo in Paris and at the Fondation Cartier also in Paris. Here, in 1995, he created Bucky, a sculptural installation, and in 2003 exhibited Kelvin40, a prototype aircraft.

Nevertheless, Newson remains suspicious of the design industry's current obsession with the art world. For him this is nothing new: he has been working in this way for 20 years. What Newson objects to is the specious designer object and those who have jumped on the bandwagon in search of easy money. Newson may be able to earn a significant amount by the sale of one or two pieces from Galerie Kreo and the Gagosian Gallery, but this is not his primary concern. Today, Newson is one of the most accomplished and influential designers working across all disciplines from industrial to interior design, producing objects as diverse as the Rock Doorstop for Magis and a private jet. In 2006 he was made Creative Director of Qantas Airlines and is currently heavily involved in the aviation industry. He found the experience of exhibiting at the Gagosian Gallery very liberating: 'The thing for me is that this is not how I generate my livelihood,' he comments, 'it's very much something that I need to do.'

As the name suggests, Newson's Micarta chair is made from Micarta, the very first composite material, predating fibreglass by 40 years. It was invented in 1910 as a by-product of the development of Bakelite and, because of its heat-resistance, was used in electrical insulation. It is a strong laminate and behaves like wood but, like most composites, is multi-directional. For Newson it has a bizarre anachronistic quality. Although it is almost synthetic it has an organic substrate of silk, linen or cotton held together by phenolic resin and, as it is not ultraviolet-resistant, its colour constantly changes like a living material. It is a beautiful substance that can be carved and is highly sculptural. The chair is smooth, shiny, wide, low and very heavy, exploiting the luxurious, organic, sympathetic and tactile qualities of Micarta.

Newson comes from a generation that does not work directly on computers. He starts with an idea that he translates into sketches and then uses software – Rhinoceros®, ProEngineer and occasionally his own code – to give the sketches a 3D reality. In the case of Micarta, Newson then produced a prototype using rapid prototyping. From this 1:10 model he made aesthetic and functional alterations. He modified the weight and the way the layers were joined, as well as the orientation of the weave of the material and some minor proportional adjustments. Two artists' proofs were then made to validate the changes so that the next ten pieces would be identical.

The manufacture is straightforward. The hardest part was to obtain the Micarta, which is now produced by only a couple of companies. Once the material was sourced it had to be made to order. Newson chose linen as his substrate because it has a weave that is both subtle and evident, and the composite was fabricated to the thickness he desired. The rest of the process is very similar to woodworking. The sections were CNC-milled from digital data; the layers fitting together with perfect accuracy. They were then bonded together with the same resin found in the composite so that when the piece discoloured it would do so evenly. All the ten pieces of the limited edition were hand-made in the USA.

MICARTA CHAIR
MARC NEWSON

Production: Marc Newson
Micarta
H: 75.9cm (30in) x W: 74.4cm (29¼in) x D: 80cm (31½in)
Design to production: 10 months
Limited edition of 10
www.marc-newson.com

1

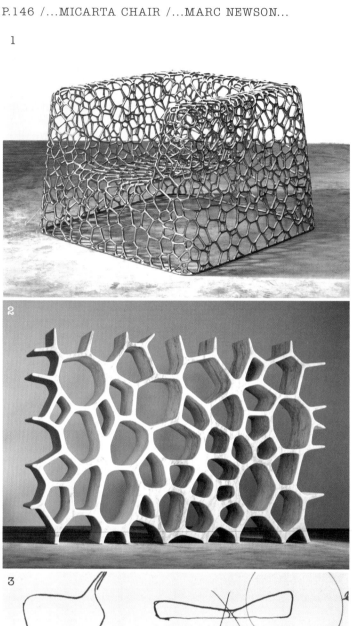

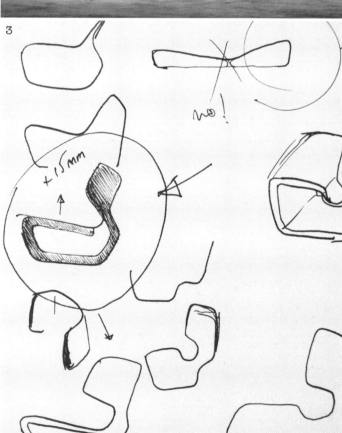

(Previous page). The Micarta chair's solid yet sensual profile.

1. Since becoming Creative Director of Quantas in 2006, Newson has been heavily involved in the aviation industry. Pieces from his recent Gagosian Gallery exhibition reflect this. Random Pak explores electro-forming (the growing of a metallic culture on to surrogate forms), which is normally used to shape the complex manifolds of jet engines.

2. Other Newson pieces link craftsmanship, traditional materials and technology. The Voronoi shelf is made from a solid piece of Carrara marble. Normally marble would be fabricated by joining pieces together; here it has been formed from a single piece.

3. Newson rarely works directly on the computer. He starts with sketches that visualize the ideas he has conceived.

4. The sketches are then fed into a computer to give them a 3D reality and to produce the data from which the chair will be fabricated.

5–7. The layers of Micarta are CNC-milled from the digital data, so they fit together with perfect accuracy.

8–9. A 1:10 model was produced using rapid prototyping from which aesthetic and functional alterations were made in the weight, the layering and orientation of the weave and its proportion.

10. The final chair is sanded and refined to bring out the lustre of the material.

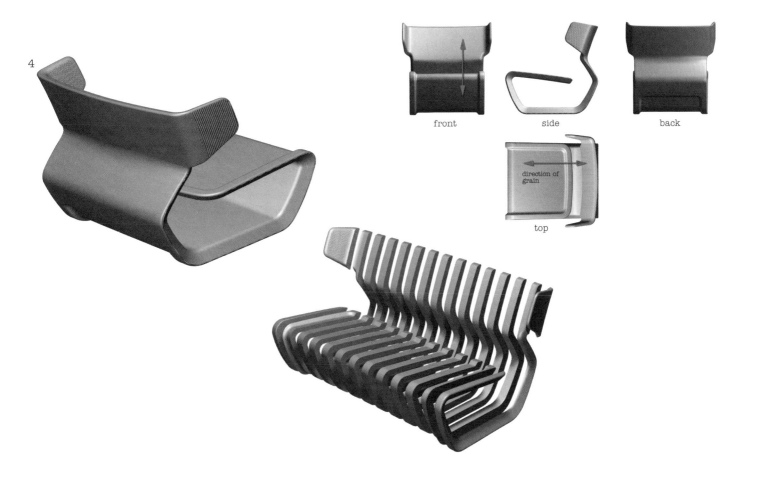

4

front side back

direction of grain

top

5 6 7

8 9 10

Satyendra Pakhalé earned his Bachelor of Engineering and Master of Design degrees in India and later completed a two-year course in advanced product design in Switzerland. He now works in high-tech industry and is acutely aware of the lack of sensorial quality in industrial design. Tactility is often missing in mass-produced design, which has become divorced from the senses and has thus lost its cultural and symbolic meaning. By going back to basics and working with traditional materials and techniques, Pakhalé aims to harness this absent quality to modern technological objects.

The B.M. Horse Chair is made by the bell-metal lost-wax process, which has existed in different areas of the world for many centuries. Pakhalé chose to work with a tribe in central India that has a culture of making art objects. The tribespeople collect beeswax and roll it into spaghetti-like strands, which they wind around a clay mould. The mould is left to dry and then a second layer of clay is added. This is fired in a basic furnace, causing the wax to melt and the clay to harden. Metal is poured into the cavity and allowed to set. When ejected, the metal retains the patterning of the wax strands. By adopting this method in a more refined manner, Pakhalé created a range of contemporary objects that gave him the idea of designing a sculptural chair with a primal horse form; an iconic identity that relates emotionally through symbolic connotation and cultural reference.

The challenge of producing the entire chair in a single piece of seamless casting was to dominate Pakhalé's life for the next eight years. To achieve the desired form and surface quality, Pakhalé hand-sculpted the chair using initial sketches to determine profile and rough dimensions. These were introduced into a computer program to check ergonomics and overall dimensions before a 1:3 model in clay, replicated in plaster, was produced in his Amsterdam studio. It would have been impossible to cast the chair using the facilities available in rural India, so Pakhalé found a sculptor's studio in Nagpur, taking members of the tribe with him to undertake the highly skilled wax spaghetti work. A final full-scale form was made in plaster from which a polyester (fibreglass) mould was produced. A core was cast in a combination of brick powder and plaster, around which the rolled wax strands were wound. From 2000 to 2005 Pakhalé tried four times to cast the chair, but failed each time. To cast an object this big in one piece using such a thin metal wall is challenging, as there have to be enough points for the gases to escape, and the outcome is unknown until the mould is broken apart.

In 2005 Pakhalé moved the exercise to Europe, and started to think of an alternative to be used in place of the natural substance for the patterning. Carrying out a small casting using rubber tube and a silicon mould, he devised a new way to do the wax modelling; then the search was on to find a

foundry that would work with this uncertain technique. After five months an enterprising company in northern Italy took on the challenge. During this time Pakhalé carried out a metallurgical test using 3D scanning and reverse engineering; the digitized version of the chair was carefully studied to examine the metal flow over the highly sculpted surface. A replacement was sought for the wax/rubber piping. A flexible 5mm (⅛in) diameter tube in a plastic composite was needed for the intricate work. Again Pakhalé was lucky to find a company that believed in his research. A manufacturer of all types of tubes for industry fulfilled the bespoke order. The polyester model was skilfully encased in the plastic tubing and was shipped to the foundry. There it was coated in silicon, with a strengthening layer of plaster, and the mould created. From that a hollow wax model was made and the cavity filled with plaster and brick powder. The mould was heated for ten days to slowly harden, and finally fired to melt the wax. The bronze was poured, allowed to set and the cast was broken away. The process had worked. The metal was then chiselled, filed and the patina finished. The finished chair was presented at Design Miami/Basel in 2007. With its mix of craftsmanship and industrial technique, engineering and material research, it was an enormous success.

B.M. HORSE CHAIR

SATYENDRA PAKHALÉ

Production: Satyendra Pakhalé
Client: Designer's Gallery Gabrielle Ammann, Germany
Bronze alloy, recycled bell metal
H: 96cm (37¾in) x W: 55cm (21¾in) x D: 85cm (33½in)
Design to manufacture: 7 years 6 months
Limited edition
www.satyendra-pakhale.com

The B.M. Horse Chair is made
from a unique and innovative
process that combines old and
new materials and technologies.

1–2. In the summer of 1998 Pakhalé created a range of contemporary bell metal objects distinguished by their sensorial quality, refined use of wax patterns and sophisticated designs, finesse and finish. He adapted the lost-wax casting techniques of a tribe in central India that had a specific culture of creating and making art objects.

3. The objects gave Pakhalé the idea of designing a sculptural chair with a primal, iconic horse form. The size of the piece made it impossible to cast in one piece in rural India, so a sculptor's studio was found in the city of Nagpur. Pakhalé needed the specific craft skill of the tribespeople so he took them with him: this was a logistic nightmare, as many had never travelled out of their immediate environment. Four self-financed attempts were made to cast the chair. All of these failed and the exercise was moved to Europe.

4. Pakhalé was encouraged to continue by the positive response he received for a 1:1 model of Horse Chair in flock technique that he designed for Cappellini and exhibited during the Milan Furniture Fair, 2001. He sought to find an alternative method of substituting the natural substance, and rethought the entire process.

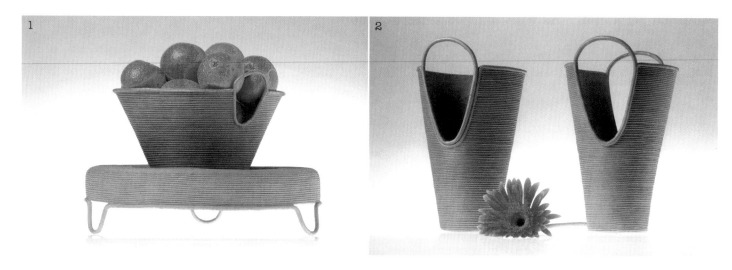

5–6. Pakhalé developed the form using sketches (5) and 1:3 models made from clay, then replicated in plaster (6).

7. Pakhalé creating the polyester (fibreglass) model, which was originally sculpted in clay and then plaster.

8–11. The model is painstakingly covered by the 5mm (⅕in) plastic composite; this is not too stiff and not too flexible, but just right for working with.

12. The skilled operation was of utmost importance to the project, as what is left at this point will be the final appearance of the cast object.

13. The tube being manufactured. The firm that undertook this work made pipes for industry, and its owner was a technical expert who was also culturally interested in design. She took the gamble of closing her factory for two hours to fulfil the order.

14. Packing the model in the Amsterdam studio to send it to the foundry in northern Italy. Pakhalé had sourced an industrial glue used in the automotive industry to stick the plastic tube to the polyester. However, a strict schedule meant there was no time to test the glue and there was a real concern that it might become brittle in the sub-zero temperatures of the plane's hold.

15. Once at the foundry the model was coated in silicon along with a strengthening layer of plaster, and the mould was created.

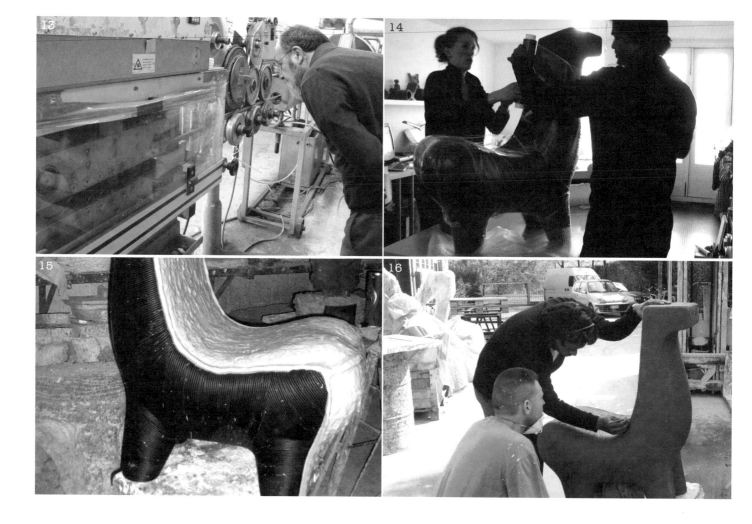

16–17. A hollow wax model was made and then checked by means of a custom-made tool to correct movement and distortion.

18. After the wax model preparation, the real casting work started. The planning of the casting, installing it in the furnace and strategically placing the runners and risers on the wax model are immensely skilled tasks.

19. Once the mould was prepared it was slowly heated for ten days to harden and finally fired so the wax melted. The mould was ready.

20. The bell metal (a combination of bronze and bronze alloy made from broken old utensils) was poured into the cavity and allowed to set. Then the cast was broken.

21. Opening the metal casting. After dedicating eight years of his life to the project, Pakhalé couldn't bear to be present at this point and awaited the news in Amsterdam. Luckily, the process had worked.

22–23. The chair being chiselled, filed and the patina finished.

Satyendra Pakhalé works across many fields, from products to mass-manufactured industrial pieces along with transportation design. For him, design is an exercise in freethinking to be applied across all typologies in different ways. Meander is his first textile piece and took 18 months to develop. The textile design makes conceptual reference to the Scandinavian landscape, and it was launched at the Stockholm Furniture Fair in 2006.

Pakhalé was invited to research and design a fabric for Väveriet, a well-known Swedish textile-manufacturing company established in 1895. The company's aim is to produce the highest quality furniture textiles in the world, using the latest techniques and working with world-renowned Swedish and international designers. Its customers include internationally renowned manufacturers such as Vitra, Cappellini, Cassina, Edra, Moroso, Poltrona Frau, Swedese and Offecct.

The world-famous Swedish team of architects and designers, Claesson Koivisto Rune, are also the artistic directors of Väveriet. They commissioned a select group of designers to produce concepts for contract fabrics, including Satyendra Pakhalé, whose iconic design language they admired.

The brief was to make a pattern that could be used in three directions (which is optimal for upholstery work), and be up- or down-scaled according to the size of the furniture being covered.

The pattern also needed to work monochromatically with several variations of the pattern being created by combining texture and relief developed within the process of weaving itself. This appealed to Pakhalé as he had to go back to basics to produce a pattern with a strong concept to fit with such adaptations.

After familiarizing himself with the way Väveriet makes textiles, Pakhalé wanted to create a textile pattern that not only referred to Swedish textile craft combined with the state-of-the-art technology of weaving, but also alluded to the lovely meanders found in the Scandinavian landscape. He carefully studied how these topographical features are formed, evolving a pattern consistent with his own personal expression. Pakhalé often uses a shape that is a kind of tapering loop; it has almost become an iconographic form for him. It has appeared in several products he has created over the years, including the Akasma tableware for RSVP and the yet-to-be-manufactured series of stools that, inverted, stack together to form a screen for public spaces and conference rooms. Keeping the design brief in view, Pakhalé developed the textile's distinctive pattern, evoking both the memory of the meander as well as a large part of his own work.

Working with his normal intensity, Pakhalé created the basic conceptual sketch and then built a 3D CAD drawing to work out the precise geometry of the pattern. With his technical background combined with careful considerations of detail, he mathematically calculated the right combination of warp and weft to form the design. The drawings were sent to Väveriet, who, in constant dialogue with Pakhalé, adjusted the proportions to work out the correct variations to achieve the required form with the threads. This stage in the design development took considerable time as Pakhalé wanted to achieve the best balance by working out all the possible variations. Wool is a 'living' material, and several trials were needed including washing to ascertain the amount of shrinkage possible. Finally, the right information was fed into the loom, which automatically calculated the ratios. However, to obtain the desired pattern the technical team at Väveriet, along with Pakhalé, had to recalibrate the machines. A selection of colourways was then sent to Pakhalé to consider, from which he chose a range of nine, as well as adding a couple of his own designs for the sole use of Italian manufacturer Cappellini, with whom Pakhalé has a long-standing and close working relationship.

MEANDER ECOLOGICAL TEXTILE

SATYENDRA PAKHALÉ

Manufacturer: Väveriet
92% wool, 8% polyester
W: 150cm (59in)
Design to manufacture: 18 months
Mass-manufactured
www.satyendra-pakhale.com/www.vaveriet.se

(Previous page). The Meander fabric comes in nine monochromatic colourways.

1. The inspiration for the Meander textile is the topographical feature found in abundance throughout Scandinavia.

2–4. Pakhalé made concept sketches (2) from which he developed drawings (3) and renderings (4).

5. Finally, 3D CADs were used to work out the precise geometry of the pattern.

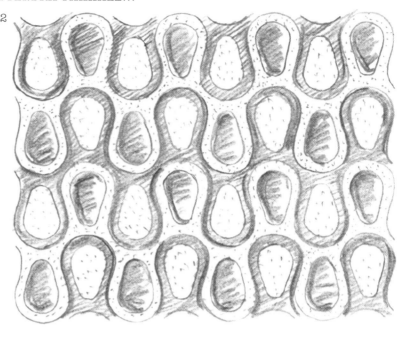

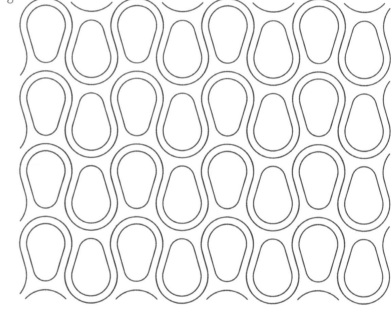

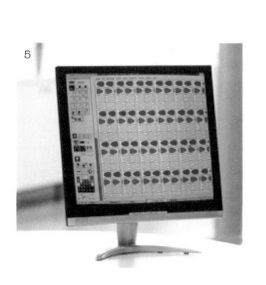

6. Meeting room at Väveriet. Drawings were sent to the manufacturer, who, in constant dialogue with Pakhalé, adjusted the proportions to work out the correct variations to achieve the required form with the threads. The first prototype is on the table.

7. After the correct combination of warp and weft had been mathematically calculated by Pakhalé, and all the variations discussed and thoroughly worked through, the information was fed into the loom, which automatically deliberated the ratios. Then, to obtain the desired pattern the technical team at Väveriet, with Pakhalé, had to recalibrate the machines.

8–11. A series of images showing the weaving of the Meander textile.

Luke Pearson and Tom Lloyd met at the Royal College of Art in London, while studying for their MAs in furniture design and industrial design respectively. They founded their multi-disciplinary company in 1997 and have always been interested in the cross-over between the cultures of furniture and product design. They work within the commercial and industrial realities of mass production, where they believe the challenges and opportunities for the profession are at their most alive. 'We thrive on the restrictions imposed by product type, function, material, process, market, client, and all else that defines the brief. Within this context, our practice is as much to do with observation and collation as with pure invention.'

PearsonLloyd is recognized for its intelligent, controlled and technically innovative designs, which fly in the face of the current prevalence of superficial and self-referential products. The designers do not believe in styles or trends, but rather in the demands of technology and production, which to them are key influences.

The original commission for Soul came from Fritz Hansen, Danish manufacturer of exclusive furniture, whose brief was to develop a new cantilever chair for the 21st century. However, the manufacturer chose not to produce the concept. Instead, PearsonLloyd took the finished prototype to Allermuir, the UK-based furniture designers and manufacturers of contemporary seating and tables, who, recognizing its merits as a universal product, decided to develop it for a wider market and with a different price point to make it more accessible.

Ever since Mart Stam developed the first cantilever chair in 1927 it has become one of the most enduring Modernist pieces of design. Many attempts have been made to reinvent this iconic archetype, but its tubular steel frame has remained. PearsonLloyd wanted to employ technological advances in materials and production methods to address this issue. They studied the form, structure, advantages and qualities of the cantilever and realized that while the tubular steel was still ideal for the lower part of the chair it was no longer needed, or appropriate, above the seat line. Once they had reached this observation, they identified a plastic that would allow them to create the entire top portion of the chair, and built up a sophisticated skeletal frame that, unlike steel, is warm to the touch, flexes and responds to the user's movement. The body was designed to simply plug on to the lower steel frame without the need for holes, screws or welds.

The high-tensile tubular legs flow into progressively slimming planar paddle arms that are bonded to a floating backrest that has a dynamic relationship with the seat, maximizing comfort. As the legs join the main seat frame, a bowled seat loop blends away from the base of the arms and supports a range of seating options: die-cut felt, neoprene or upholstered leather, altering the mood of the chair and making it applicable for a range of different environments. The subtle twist of the planes belies a complex structural analysis but describes the flow of strength around the chair.

PearsonLloyd refer to what they call the 'craft of industrial design', perfecting a product in an ongoing dialogue between cutting-edge computer technology and hand-crafted models and prototypes, integrating aesthetics and engineering to the point where it is difficult to know which is the motivating factor in the design. For Soul, early concept sketches were quickly utilized to make 3D CAD drawings, and models in hard foam. Engineering sketches were used throughout so that no detail occurred purely as an aesthetic ambition. Full-size concept models were created to resolve the massing and spatial complexities of the fluid contours, and were sketched upon and then carved to effect necessary changes. Information was fed back into Pro E CAD software to deliver to the engineers. The design was then refined and the process repeated throughout the development of the chair. Even at the end, hand work was vital in solving final problems before the mould could be constructed. All parts are injection-moulded except the leg frame, which is one piece cut and formed.

SOUL CHAIR
LUKE PEARSON & TOM LLOYD

Manufacturer: Allermuir
Glass-fibre reinforced nylon frame, polypropylene seat, tubular steel legs
H: 79cm (31in) x W: 57cm (22½in) x D: 58cm (23in)
Design to manufacture: 60 months
Mass-manufactured
www.pearsonlloyd.co.uk/www.allermuir.com

The Soul cantilever chair
is a reductive but beautiful
structure – with a rich yet
economic design.

1. The brief for the Soul chair was to develop a 21st-century version of the iconic 1927 cantilever chair by Mart Stam.

2–4. Early concept sketches (2) were utilized to make models in 3D from hard foam (3) and mirrored models to examine the form (4).

5. Only detail sketches were used during the design development. All other work was carried out on the computer or on models.

6. Development engineering sketches were made at every stage to ensure that no detail occurred purely for aesthetic reasons.

7–8. Full-scale models of the whole chair and details were made as early as possible, as computer sketching could not resolve the complex and fluid profile of the chair.

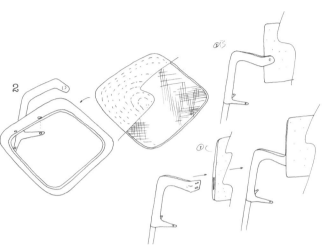

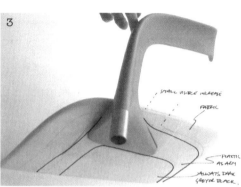

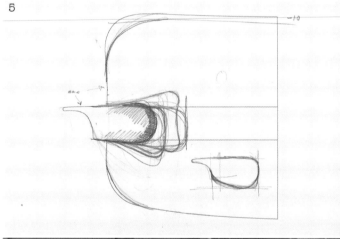

9. The designers found it more accurate, and faster, to sketch and then carve directly on the models to effect necessary changes.

10–11. The necessity to refine meant that CAD was used to machine parts that were then examined and hand-worked until a satisfactory solution was achieved (10). The data was fed back into the computer to be manipulated in detail (11).

12. Throughout the development, meetings were held with the client and their engineers. Here, Luke Pearson (centre) discusses an early model with Fritz Hansen, before the chair was further developed with Allermuir.

13. First structural model.

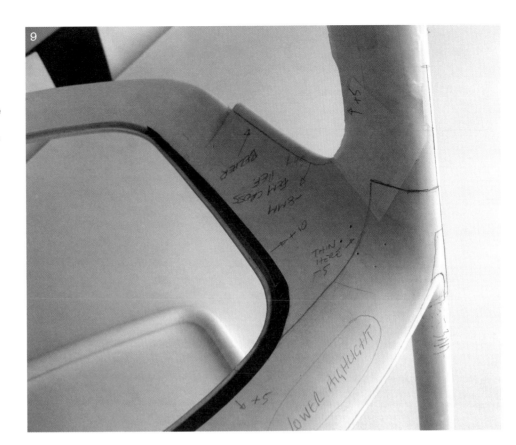

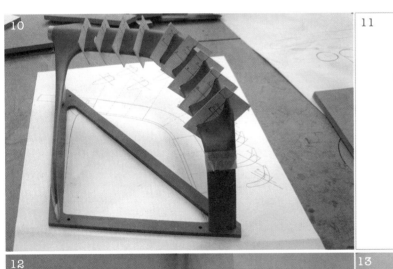

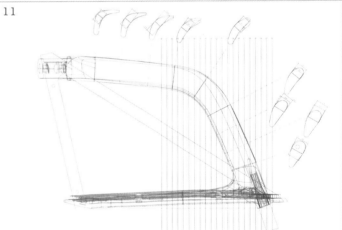

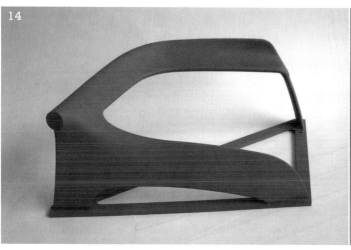

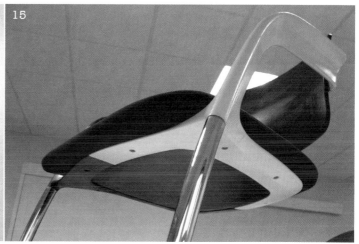

14. A CNC-machined test part.

15. A scale model was produced using SLS.

16–19. Pro E CAD builds graphic images of how the chair will perform under loading. Here they show the surface analysis of various components (16); the pressure each curve exerts on the model (17); an analysis of the surface using zebra curves (18); and an FEA stress analysis to understand the impact of changing sections on the chair to optimize plastic usage (19).

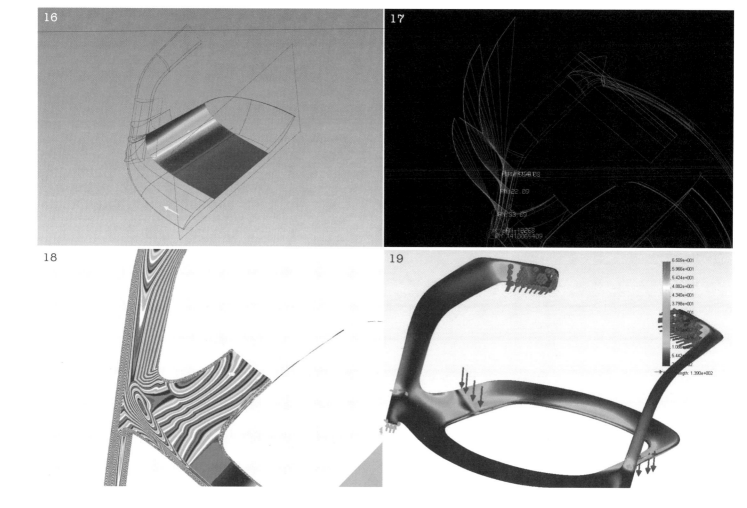

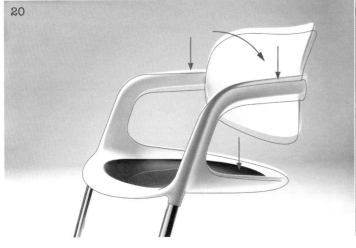

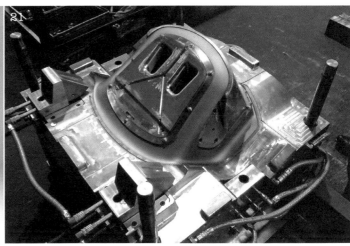

20. Ergonomic studies.
This image shows how Soul
flexes in use to accommodate
changes for good posture; a
unique feature of the chair.

21. The main chair frame is
injection-moulded using one
tool with male and female
parts. The other parts have
their own tools and use
different plastics.

22. Soul is submitted to cycle
testing. Heavy weights are
used to pound, bend and flex
the chair through thousands
of cycles to see how long it
will take to fail.

23–25. Soul has many
structural benefits. As the
content of steel is less than in
a normal cantilever, it is light
and easy to lift, it stacks (23)

and can be placed on the table
so only clean surfaces touch
(24). As it disassembles, it
can be easily and cheaply
shipped, with several
chairs to a box, cutting
down on transportation and
waste of resources –
a determining factor in
the original concept (25).

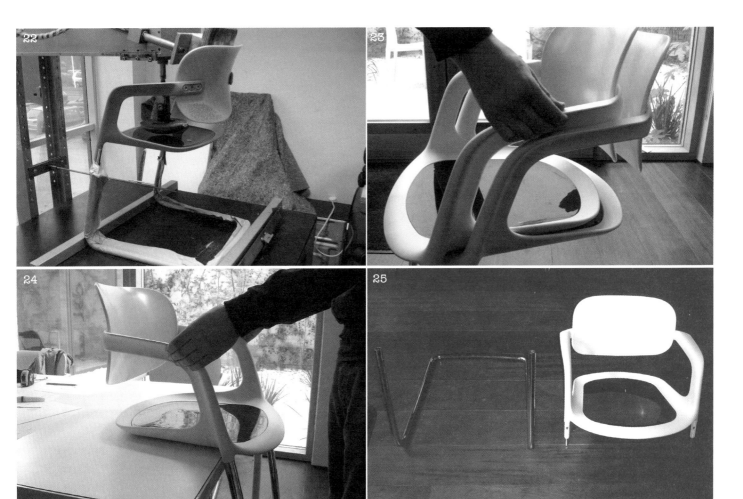

Gaetano Pesce was born in La Spezia, Italy, in 1939 and studied architecture and industrial design at the Università IUAV di Venezia. Since 1981 he has lived and worked in New York, where he heads Pesce Ltd. He began designing in the early 1960s, moving away from the cool, Modernist Italian approach of that period towards the conceptual anti-design, avant-garde movements associated with Ugo La Pietra, Gruppo Strum, UFO, ArchiZoom and SuperStudio. Despite this background, and the reputation he has for making Italian manufacturers go beyond their comfort zones in the production of pieces that challenge preconceptions of 'good taste', he does not believe himself to be a radical. Speaking recently of his work, he says: 'Architecture and design of the recent past has mostly produced cold, authoritarian, anonymous, monolithic, antiseptic, standardized results that are uninspiring. I have tried to communicate feelings of surprise, discovery, optimism, stimulation, sensuality, generosity, joy and femininity.'

Pesce maintains that society has been governed, for a long time, by the masculine side of the brain, with value placed on coherence, strength, monumentalism, dogmatism, seriousness and inflexibility. Throughout his career he has sought to engage with the other side of his brain; the feminine, which is multi-disciplinary, full of feeling, elastic, 'soft', sensual and friendly to the human body. Perhaps Pesce's most recognizable and iconic piece is the UP chair, which he conceived in 1969 and which was reissued by

B&B Italia in 2000. Taking design beyond the functional into the realm of political statement, this resin sponge sphere, attached to a smaller footrest by an elasticated cord (a ball and chain) represents woman's domination by man.

Pesce is probably best known for his work in coloured resin, as utilized in Il Cestello restaurant in Florence, his house in Brazil, where he uses resin tiles, the Sansone tables for Cassina (the colours of which were selected by the factory workers according to their taste) and the Nobody's Perfect range of furniture and lighting for Zerodisegno that gives objects the right to be different and have flaws. Because the materials and processes Pesce uses often do not allow for mechanization, much of his output is produced in small-scale runs, which results in each object being similar but not the same. It has also been described as ugly or badly done with mistakes. 'This is the time of non-homogeneous production. And it doesn't only make economic sense but political sense also – democracy is a system that guarantees to maintain difference. When you say my work is ugly, it's true, because in the human being there is beauty and ugliness, and large and small, but what is really beautiful is what is different.'

Tavolone, a sensuous and expressive resin table, is the latest in a long line of unique, exuberant design that is rich in colour and unconstrained in form. The production technique is straightforward but the piece is as much the result of Pesce's design philosophy as it is of process. The table's human profile, its tactility,

even its smell, give the piece an emotional dimension and reject regularity. Employing all the design values eschewed by Modernism, it embraces irony, kitsch and distortions of scale to undermine the purely functional value of an object and question our concepts of taste.

'Finding new ways to work has been important to me historically. I suggest how to manufacture each piece so it looks unique. I approached Meritalia with the idea of making a table with a certain process, like making a biscuit, and showed them a small model with a soft surface,' he explains. The concept appealed to the manufacturers: tooling was unnecessary, the production, although largely manual, did not involve a large workforce, and as resin hardens naturally, unlike a biscuit, no oven was necessary, meaning that the financial outlay for Meritalia would remain relatively small. The following images describe the process involved in the fabrication of one piece overseen by Pesce himself. The table is destined for a minority market. Unique variations can be made, but Meritalia have adapted the technique for small-scale production.

TAVOLONE TABLE
GAETANO PESCE

Manufacturer: Meritalia SpA
Resin, iron grid, resin-coated particleboard legs
Various dimensions
Design to manufacture: 38 months
Small-scale production
www.gaetanopesce.com/www.meritalia.it

The Tavolone table was
presented along with another
Pesce design, Shadow chairs,
by Meritalia during the Milan
Furniture Fair in 2007.

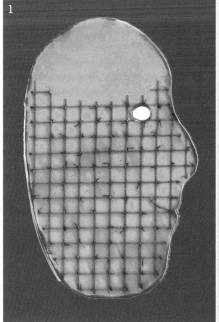

1–2. The computer renderings were developed in 2004 by Pesce as a personal experiment (1) and turned into a small model made from the same material as the full-scale table (2). This was presented to Meritalia the same year and put into production 36 months later. The idea was for a table with a soft surface. The profile was the inspiration. Pesce wanted to make an object with emotion as well as functionality. The intended use of resin, with its tactility and smell, gives the table a human dimension. Practically, soft edges are better than rigid ones: if there is an accident neither product nor user will be harmed.

3–5. The only tooling necessary was the production of a negative mould in wood to make the silicon extrusion used to form the shape of the profile and to contain the poured resin (3). The profile is placed on a clean, smooth and flat surface (4–5).

6. The eye is formed with a piece of silicon that is pressed into the right position on the surface of the mould, so stopping the resin pouring on that part. When removed, a hole is formed.

7. Gaetano Pesce pours an edging of dark resin that will give definition to the profile in the completed object.

8–10. The edge is allowed to harden slightly before the rest of the resin is poured.

11–14. Because the surface is soft, the table needs a rigid structure; this takes the form of a prefabricated, plastic-coated iron grid that holds the top horizontally (11–12). The plastic is added to soften the hard edges and to protect the iron (13–14).

15–17. After the resin has hardened overnight, the silicon rim and iron supports are removed, 'capturing' the grid.

18–20. The legs, hollow rotating volumes, are made in particleboard covered in silicon. On the superior part of each leg there is a metallic fixture that attaches to the iron grid, allowing it to swivel. Each leg has wheels at the bottom so that the user can decide the position of the table as he or she wishes. The legs double as containers for household objects.

Neil Poulton's deceptively simple-looking mass-produced objects belie their technical innovation. He studied industrial design in Scotland and received a Masters in design from the Domus Academy. Poulton is best known for his lighting and electronic projects, which have received international recognition over the years. Most recently his Firewire speakers were awarded the Janus de L'Industrie by the French Institute of Design, and six of his products were put on permanent exhibition at the Pompidou Centre.

In 2006, the Talak light was awarded Red Dot's Best of the Best award and was described by the judges as 'a light with a reduced, delicate and unfamiliar yet also clear language of form'. The original project was personal. Poulton wanted a light that would flood the length of his work surface rather than cast a spot. He had been developing a mechanism for an articulated arm that would support the extra length needed in the head, using the traditional methods employed in the iconic Anglepoise lamp. The required stability could not be achieved: the light either toppled over or the arm moved involuntarily.

After months of development, Poulton had reached a stage where he could present his deliberations to Ernesto Gismondi, the owner of Artemide, a company with whom Poulton has collaborated for over a decade. The evening before, while he was working on this design, Poulton suddenly had the idea of dispensing with Talak's articulated

arm. Taking a football rattle as his inspiration, he spent the rest of the night producing a working prototype from material he had to hand in his workshop. The idea was now for a long encased fluorescent tube cantilevered from a thin stem clamped on to the worktop. The revision was shown to Gismondi, who agreed to develop the concept.

Poulton's initial idea was to fabricate the lamp in metal extrusion with end caps; the same technique used for his task light, Talo, manufactured by Artemide four years previously. Gismondi insisted, however, that the head be produced in plastic to limit the risk of it being copied. The cost of tooling for the large plastic part would be expensive enough to be prohibitive to plagiarism, whereas the extruded metal version could be reproduced easily, as a die and small tool for the end caps are all that is needed. Between Poulton and Artemide's engineers the design was refined using sketches, further prototypes and CAD drawings. During the development the head became 30% larger to meet the requirements of European and international standards and to protect the electronic ballast from overheating. A method to stop the light sliding up and down the stem was also worked on. Holes on the upper and lower surface of the head are offset, causing it to become blocked by its own weight and movement. An internal sheet-steel spring ensures the lamp does not cascade down the support.

The head was injection-moulded in one piece in glass fibre-filled white

polyester resin and then painted. Because of its length and thinness the casting was difficult, as the plastic cooled unevenly, causing twisting. The first batch was deformed, although at 7mm (¼in) along the 86cm (34in) length of the head, the defect was not noticeable to the naked eye. To rectify subsequent editions, a mould with chill zones (which results in the plastic cooling evenly and at the same temperature) was used. As plastic is not totally solid when ejected from a mould, the heads were initially enclosed in metal frames until they had completely hardened to prevent further contortions. Subsequently, the size of the internal components has been reduced to allow for internal ribbing and the frames are no longer necessary. As standard tube was not rigid enough, the 10mm (½in) steel tubing was extruded with a 2.6mm (¹⁄₁₀in) wall section (a heavy section for this diameter). The base is die-cast Zamac to ensure stability.

All horizontal elements are painted in white and the vertical ones in shiny chrome; this catches reflections, dematerializing the support and making the head appear to float.

TALAK LIGHT
NEIL POULTON

Manufacturer: Artemide SpA
Glass fibre-filled white polyester resin, chrome support
Light source: T2 FM fluorescent tube
H: 69cm (27in) x W: 86cm (34in) x D: 16.4cm (6½in)
Design to manufacture: 31 months
Mass-manufactured
www.neilpoulton.com/www.artemide.com

The Talak light uses the
new T2 FM fluorescent tube,
which is only 7mm (¼in) in
diameter, energy-efficient and
environmentally friendly.

1. The inspiration for the Talak light was the way the horizontal arms of a football rattle attach to the support.

2. As all the working parts, including the electronic ballast, are based in the head, it can be removed and used separately.

3. The first deliberations were for a light that would give a uniform illumination, based on the working mechanism of the Anglepoise lamp.

4. Poulton dispensed with the articulated arm and produced a rough prototype using lengths of aluminium extrusions, a new T2 FM fluorescent light source, an electronic ballast, cardboard, lengths of steel tube and an old vice/clamp.

5–8. During the design development, Poulton collaborated with Artemide's engineers to refine the design using sketches (5), CAD drawings (Poulton worked with Rhinoceros® and Artemide with SolidWorks) (6), and further prototypes (7). The method to stop the head sliding up and down the stem was also readdressed (8).

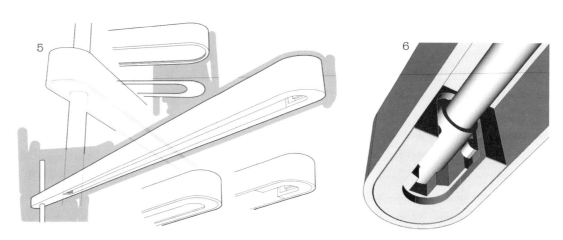

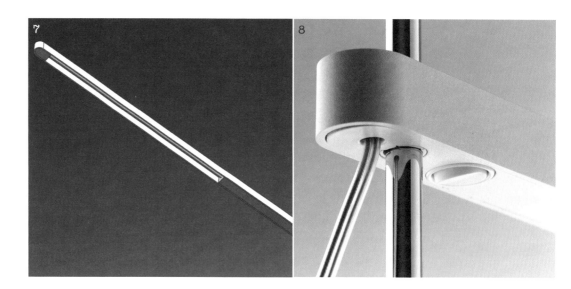

9
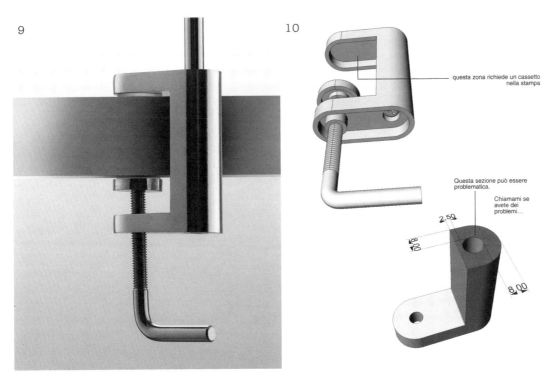

10

questa zona richiede un cassetto
nella stampa

Questa sezione può essere
problematica.

Chiamami se
avete dei
problemi…

2.50

8.00

8.00

9–10. The original prototype was presented to Artemide attached to the desk by an industrial vice. Not realizing that the clamp was being used as a stand-in, Gismondi's (owner of Artemide) only reservation was that he thought that part of the product needed more refinement. He wanted to use a standard clamp, but Poulton fought to design a bespoke version. The annotated technical drawing (10) shows instructions for the engineer.

11. Poulton's Talo light was designed for Artemide in 2002. It was his original intention to have Talak fabricated in the same way in metal extrusion with end caps. Artemide insisted on injection-moulded plastic to help prevent copying.

12–14. The Talak is produced as a suspension (12), wall (13) and table (14) light. The latter is either clamped to a surface or free-standing on a Zamac base (see opener).

11

12

13

14
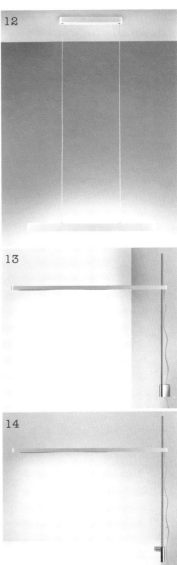

Propeller is one of the foremost design agencies in Scandinavia. Based in Stockholm, it is responsible for many of the most innovative products in the field of Swedish industrial design and its projects are as various as they are challenging: from lights, taps, and kitchen appliances to a condom holder with graphics aimed at the teenage market and a whole new concept in saddle design made from thermo-moulded carbonfibre, expanded PVC and titanium. Its products communicate function, boost a brand name and seduce the intended target group.

The Kapsel Media Center is conceived for the design-minded. Instead of imitating the looks of traditional home entertainment centres, it is designed to be positioned horizontally, vertically or on the wall. It has a minimal, sleek, disc-like profile that sits like an ornament in the living room. The intention was to increase the humanistic appeal and defuse the technical appearance, emphasizing the contrast with the use of colour (black inside and white on the outside) and material (hard and soft). The refined aesthetic is not at the expense of functionality. It is among the most powerful centres on the market, being one of the first to use an Intel Viiv platform, powered by dual-core processors, ensuring the user makes the most of their broadband connection and their Plasma/LCD TV.

Kapsel is Swedish for 'seed pod' and Propeller devised a simple, iconic shape to reflect the fact that this small unit contains all the technology and services needed for a full media/entertainment programme. The unit's appeal is strongly connected to lifestyle and dictated by its environment, so the team came up with moodboards to reflect the different objects, materials and colours found in the upmarket living room of a person totally at home and relaxed with the use of technology.

Propeller's designers use rough, hand-drawn sketches as a fast and efficient way of generating a variety of ideas. They then move on to 3D models at an early stage to make sure that the idea, form and concept are transferable from 2D to physical reality. They work with polyurethane foam from early sketch to final model, although the very last is created in high-density PUR to achieve a good finish when spray-painted. Using models is essential for Propeller in communicating with the client, especially project leaders and managers. For Kapsel, five models were made. The final mock-up was scanned and transferred into the CAID (computer aided industrial design) system, Alias Studio, and the drawings were employed to interface with Kapsel's engineers, who use SolidWorks software for the construction. The designers' CAID files were also employed to produce a working prototype, which looked much like the finished object. The working prototype is an important stage: Propeller can gauge whether the initial design can be preserved, and the client has a physical, functioning object to show to its engineers and focus groups. Renderings are used to try out design solutions without having to build further 3D models, and to determine finishes and colouring. The information is then transferred to the final prototype.

The inner casing, which holds the components, is die-cut and bent from a steel sheet. The outer shells for the first 20 Kapsels were cut from a solid block of aluminium using a CNC-milling machine to check the overall functionality of the product before production started. The final Kapsels are die-cast in aluminium and the shells treated and spray-painted. The large-surface aluminium shells are important in the cooling of the system. The shells are connected to processors that transport the heat out through the material, which is an excellent conductor. The front part (black) in polyurethane is injection-moulded in a steel tool.

Kapsel has achieved a lot of attention in the press and on the web for its low-tech look; it takes a totally new design approach to home media centres that has caught the market's attention.

KAPSEL MEDIA CENTER
PROPELLER

Manufacturer: Kapsel Multimedia AB
Die-cast aluminium, polyurethane, steel
H: 27cm (10½in) x W: 23cm (9in) x D: 10cm (4in)
Design to manufacture: 24 months
Mass-manufactured
www.propeller.se/www.kapsel.com

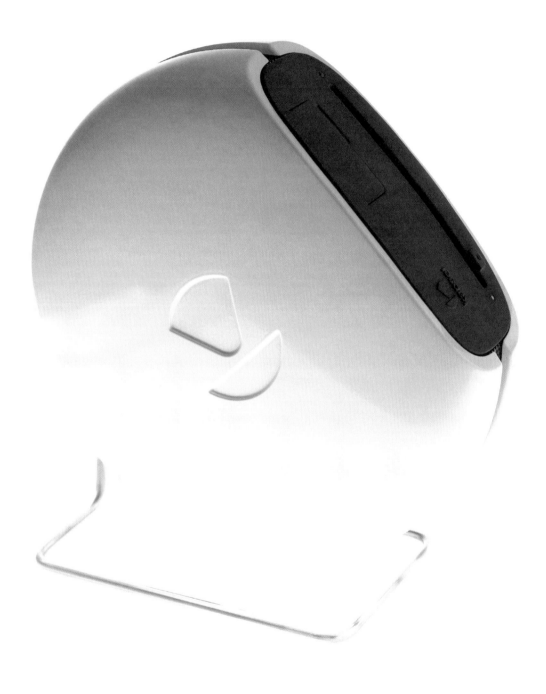

Kapsel was created as a
luxury accessory, a piece of
art or a valued ornament
that has appeal even when
not in use.

1

1. Kapsel is Swedish for 'seed pod'. Propeller devised an iconic shape that promoted the idea of containment.

2. Hand-drawn sketches were the first step in developing the concept.

3–4. Propeller quickly moved on to a series of mock-ups in polyurethane foam (3). The final model (4) is in high-density polyurethane to obtain a good finish when spray-painted.

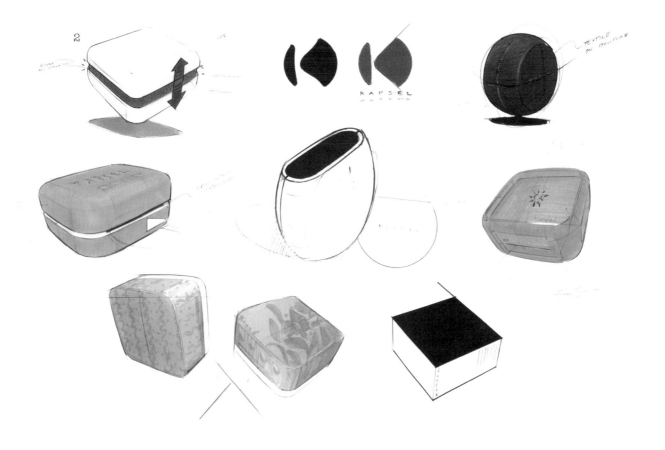

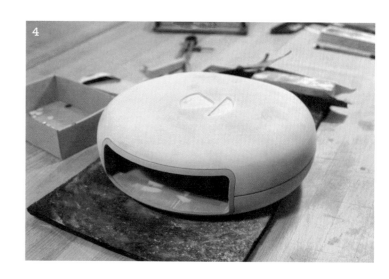

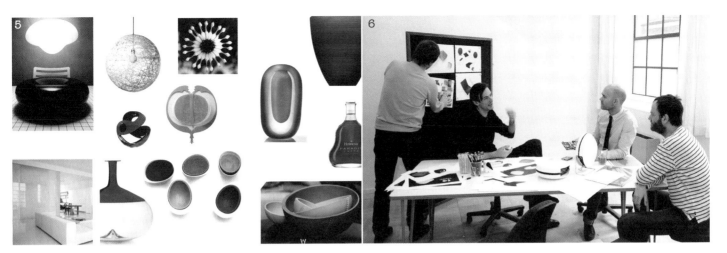

5. Propeller created moodboards to reflect the kinds of object that could be found in the living environment of the upmarket, style-aware consumer, as a way of beginning the aesthetic concept for Kapsel.

6. The team discuss the final working prototype, referring back to the moodboards.

7. Propeller uses renderings as a presentation tool but also as a way to work out finishes and colourings, and to try out last minute design solutions without having to create further 3D models.

8. Information was fed into an Alias software program and CAD drawings were produced to communicate with Kapsel's engineers and determine a working prototype.

9. The construction of the final working prototype.

The inner casing was die-cut and bent from steel sheet metal. The outer shells were cut from a solid block of aluminium using a CNC-milling machine.

10. One half of the tool used for die-casting the aluminium case of the final product. Since the two shells in Kapsel are the same, only one tool was needed, consisting of two steel parts.

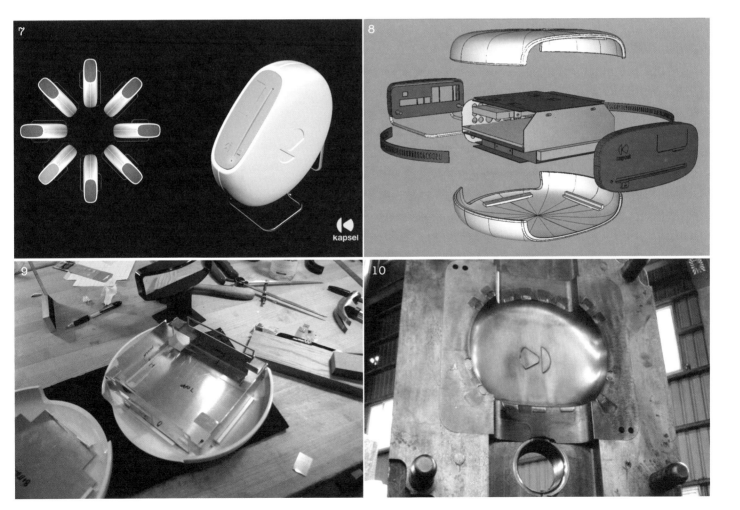

In 2007 Open.Box was awarded Red Dot's Best of the Best title in the lighting and lamps category. Interviewed by the prestigious organization shortly after the award was announced, the designers of Propeller, one of the foremost design agencies in Scandinavia, were quick to point out that in today's changing technological world it is not enough to be able to work with new materials and manufacturing processes; the designer also has to consider the needs and demands of a consumer who is not merely seeking an object that functions well but one that delivers an experience: 'Design is about creating a product experience that meets and supersedes the consumer's expectations, and to be able to handle this increasing complexity the designer needs new approaches in the design process such as working in a multi-disciplinary way.'

Propeller was commissioned by Fagerhult, the Swedish light manufacturer, early in 2005 with a limited brief to produce something that 'breathed' the brand. Propeller started by examining the lighting market to see what was available in the pendant sector. They discovered that there was a preponderance of visually heavy, closed boxes with a very technical aesthetic. They decided to go in the opposite direction and produce a piece that was light and airy with a 'human' appeal and with the luminescence describing the form. The team researched other product areas such as consumer electronics, furniture, new

materials, colours and architecture to gain inspiration. The key words that would inform their design were 'sensual', 'harmonic', 'airy', 'friendly' and 'iconic'. Moodboards were created to act as a working reference throughout the design development period.

Fagerhult's method of assessing a design diverges from normal industrial design practice. Rather than having the designer work up a concept to a highly finished state, it takes early sketches and produces a working prototype from which designer and manufacturer collaborate on detailing and production processes. Propeller worked out their original theory using a series of coloured, hand-drawn sketches and selected the material. Plastic would not take the heat produced without expanding and making too much noise. Aluminium was chosen for its great cooling properties, strength and malleability.

The initial idea did not change greatly throughout the rest of the design, development and production. The pendant uses two different 'housings' that are visually separated from one another but joined by the frame. The lower part has an efficient louvre for direct and glare-free lighting, while the upper part emits soft and indirect light on to the ceiling. For the viewer it is at first impossible to see where the light is coming from, as the centre of the box is open and transparent, and magically illuminated by the lower fluorescent tube.

The working prototype was made in the final material with Propeller delivering only overall dimensions and proportions. It was evaluated by both Propeller and Fagerhult over the following 18 months and changes were gradually made to improve the concept and meet the demands from production. CAD drawings were developed using Alias and Pro E, and 3D mock-ups were made in various methods – CNC-milling, laser-sintering and aluminium extrusions – to give reality to the complex, advanced shapes and detailing generated by the software. The adjustments were fairly minor, although the pendant increased in size by 10–15%.

The sides of the pendant are formed by extruding aluminium; this is the best and most economical way of producing long strips with the same profile. The end caps are moulded using die-casting. Aluminium is not very reflective, so the louvre has a thin layer of metal placed on top. The process is patented and secret. The parts were powder-coated separately so a clear distinction of colour could be maintained. They were then assembled.

OPEN BOX LIGHT

PROPELLER

Manufacturer: AB Fagerhult
Extruded aluminium, sheet steel
Light source: T5 fluorescent tube
H: 13.2cm (5¼in) x L: 124cm (48¾in) x D: 12cm (4¾in)
Design to manufacture: 24 months
Mass-manufactured
www.propeller.se/www.fagerhult.com

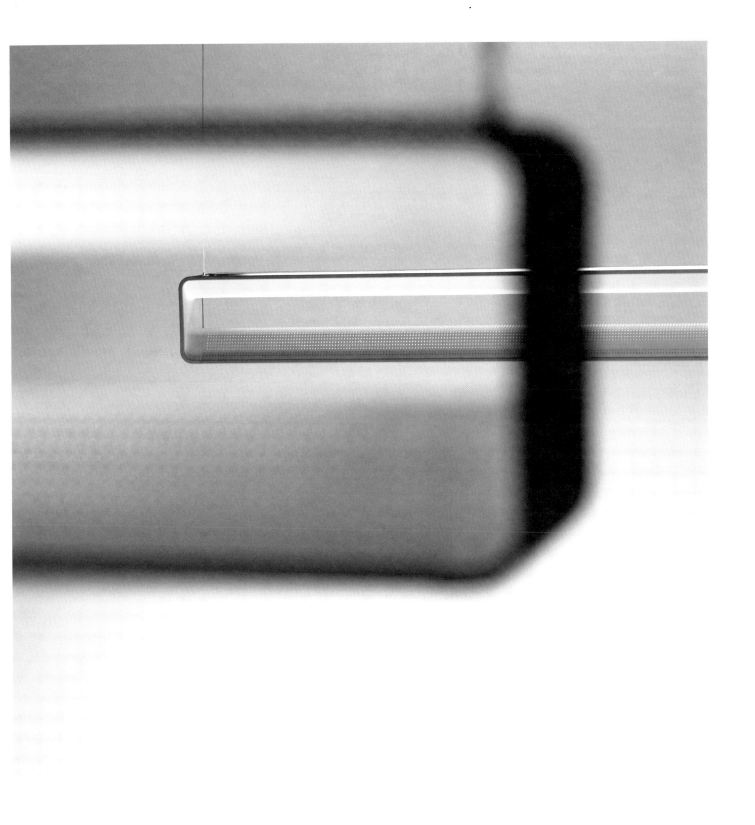

Open Box's lower long side
is perforated so that light
penetrates to illuminate the
interior. This has the effect
of drawing the eye away
from the light source and
into space.

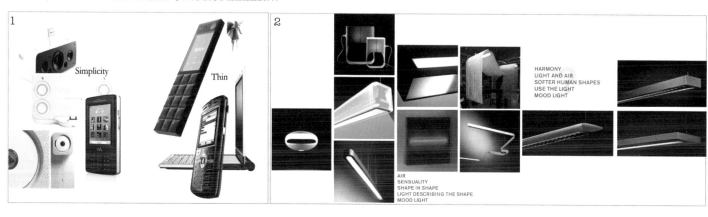

1

Simplicity

Thin

2

HARMONY
LIGHT AND AIR
SOFTER HUMAN SHAPES
USE THE LIGHT
MOOD LIGHT

AIR
SENSUALITY
SHAPE IN SHAPE
LIGHT DESCRIBING THE SHAPE
MOOD LIGHT

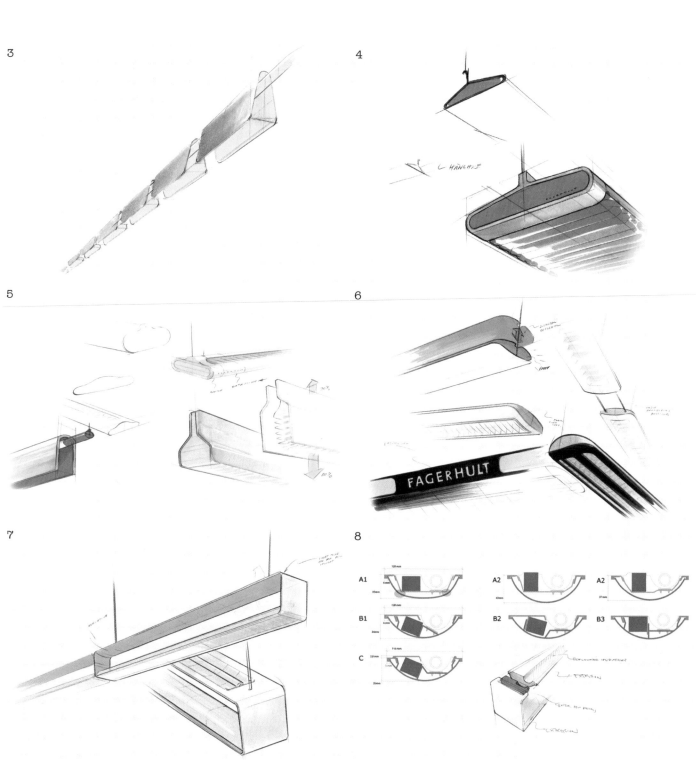

3

4

5

6

FAGERHULT

7

8

A1   A2   A2

B1   B2   B3

C

1. Propeller looked at different areas of product design, such as consumer electronics, for sources of inspiration.

2. The designers also researched what was available in the pendant luminaire sector, before coming up with a list of key words that would inform their design.

3–6. Fagerhult's brief was to design a pendant that 'breathed' the brand. A series of ideas was developed using hand-drawn coloured drawings.

7–8. The final concept (7) was delivered to the manufacturer along with overall dimensions and proportions (8).

9. From the sketches, Fagerhult made a working prototype using the materials chosen by the designers. As the prototype got Propeller's approval from an early stage it was used as a reference during the following 18 months.

10–11. One problem encountered was in the belly.

In the original prototype (10) it was quite shallow; this was aesthetically pleasing but did not allow the components on the top to fit properly. A subsequent CNC-milled model (11) had to find a balance between increasing the belly and not making the pendant too visually heavy.

12–13. CAD drawings developed the detailing and the way in which the electronic components would be accommodated.

14. The extruded aluminium frame and die-cast moulded end caps are fitted together. The frame is slightly tilted to achieve better working ergonomics, while the parts are mounted.

15. The unit is placed on a table and the electronics are placed in it in a process called 'free frame'.

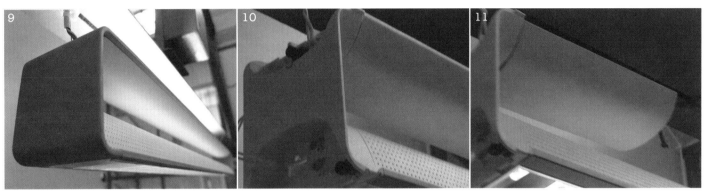

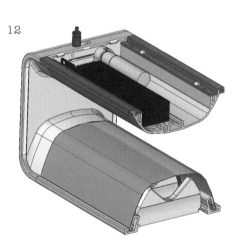

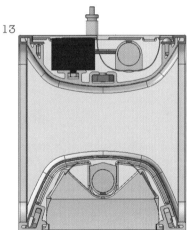

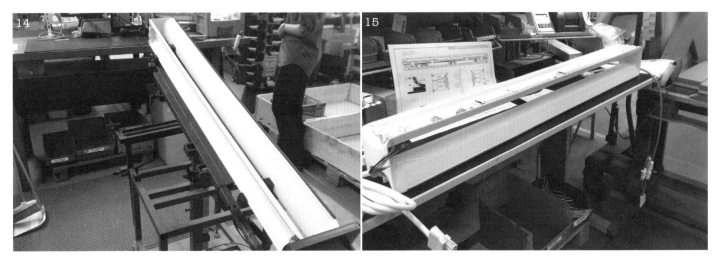

rAndom International is a young design company and creative technology consultancy founded by Hannes Koch, Florian Ortkrass and Stuart Wood, former students at the Royal College of Arts, London. The company uses innovative product design to generate brand-new uses for existing technologies. This inspiration is derived from research into new processes, and the interface between the various products the company is developing.

rAndom's first product, the Watch Paper (which uses heat-reactive technology to show a moving graphic of a digital clock embedded within wallpaper), won the team an iF Design Award and a grant from NESTA's (National Endowment for Science Technology and Arts) Creative Pioneering Academy to evolve a business model for its new company. Since then, rAndom have experimented with several scenarios for challenging the 'pixel craze'. Increasingly, the design and art industry is taking on the pixel as content for its work and the trio has been seeking to work with pixilation to bring an inherently digital (and two-dimensional) concept into the world of analogue and form. Although rAndom is best known for its PixelRoller, all of its digital projects – LightRoller, Temporary Printing Machine, Pixelshades and Temporary Graffiti – borrow their aesthetics from easy-to-understand sources such as the mechanical paint roller, the marker pen, the 1950s lampshade and the spraycan. 'For us as designers/artists, it's crucial to be able to work with, and update,

the meaning of generic shape and form,' says Hannes Koch.

rAndom's digital projects have their origin in the concept of applying a digital image in one stroke to a surface and examining the best possible way of doing this. They are all based on the PixelRoller, which 'paints' digital images on to large surfaces by linking a computer to electro-mechanical solenoid valves in the head of the roller. The software program supplies the valves with data to create the image as well as controlling the amount of paint through the nozzles, and calibrates the tracking of the roller. The roller was first presented as an MA graduation project in 2005; it won grants from the Helen Hamlyn Research Centre and the Audi Design Foundation and earned a second iF Design Award.

The LightRoller replaces the PixelRoller's head with LEDs and visualizes the process by printing with light (instead of ink) on photo-sensitive materials that change their graphic properties under exposure to light. The LightRoller was initially developed as a less messy prototype to test the software and tracking technologies of PixelRoller, but quickly became a product in its own right used to create an entire body of performances and installations. Client-related opportunities then allowed the company to develop its earlier works. A commission from the world-famous London department store, Selfridges, asked for a product based on the LightRoller, and the Temporary

Printing Machine was born. The adaptation works on a different light-sensitive material that temporarily changes contrast under exposure to ultraviolet light and creates ever-changing images. The latest concept is Temporary Graffiti, in which modified spraycans with ultraviolet-LED in the cap are used to create images, again on light-sensitive surfaces.

All the projects shown here are related to and based on the PixelRoller, and the physical process behind their development is the same. Rough sketches are developed as a private language between Koch, Ortkrass and Wood to instruct each of their individual tasks. First models are produced in LEGO® or cardboard and early computer drawings are made in Code software. Breadboards, prototypes of the final printed circuit boards (PCBs), are used to determine the circuitry. CAD drawings are developed in RapidForm and used to interface with the electronic software and the manufacturers of the parts as well as to rapid-prototype sophisticated models. Detailed parts of the engineering are sent out to specialists: PCB-etching is used for the circuitry, CNC-bending and laser-cutting for the sheet-metal parts, and water-jet cutting for the components. The parts are delivered to rAndom's studio and hand-assembled and finished by the team.

DIGITAL PROJECTS
RANDOM INTERNATIONAL

Production: rAndom International
Various materials
Various measurements
Design to manufacture: work in progress
www.random-international.com

(Previous page). PixelRoller is based on a paint roller but 'paints' digital images on to large surfaces by linking a computer (supplied with the data to create the image) to electro-mechanical solenoid valves in the head of the roller which control the paint flow.

1–2. Many of rAndom's digital projects have evolved from the PixelRoller. The LightRoller works like its predecessor but uses a computer-controlled fillet of ultraviolet light diodes to print out any pixel-based digital imagery and text on to a phosphorescent surface. The earliest image of the LightRoller (1). Later version (2).

3–4. A portrait of Ingo Maurer, the German designer of innovative and artistic lights in full (3) and detail (4), was the first permanent image produced with the LightRoller printing on photographic paper. The process has a random element to it as the image is hand-printed in total darkness. The result is only evident once the image is developed. Every version is different as each is rolled by hand.

5–7. The Temporary Printing Machine is based on the LightRoller. The adaptation works on a light-sensitive material that changes contrast under exposure to UV light, creating ever-changing images.

8–9. Pixelshades, the stationary version of the LightRoller, are essentially large 360-degree screens. They continually renew themselves and can temporarily 'print out' any kind of digital information on the large phosphorescent shades.

10–11. Temporary Graffiti is rAndom's latest concept. It allows drawings and words to be etched on to phosphorescent surfaces. The series includes spraycans (10) and light pens (11) modified with ultraviolet-LED. The concept is currently being developed into a toy kit.

12. All the projects are related and developed using the same processes employed for PixelRoller. First models are produced in LEGO® and used to develop concept and software. LEGO® is used to make it easy to change parts of the technology quickly, as for this early LightRoller model.

13–15. Development drawings work out details such as paint supply (13), valve design (14) and print-head detailing (15).

16. Annotated computer drawings refine the printed circuit boards (PCBs).

17. Prototypes of PixelRoller. The first Mark I was produced in 2005 (below right); Mark II in 2006 (left); and Mark III in 2007 (above).

18. All prototypes were produced using rapid prototyping, shown here in the Mark II version.

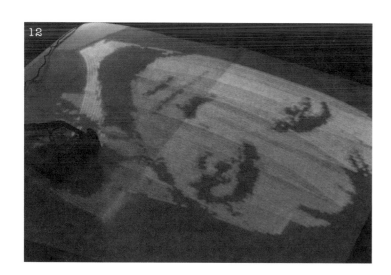

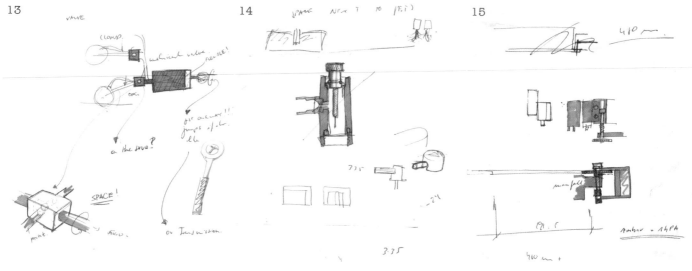

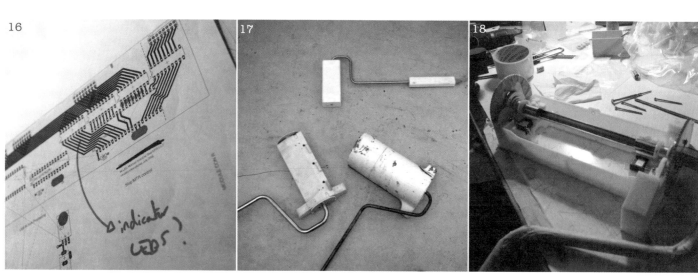

19–21. The parts for Mark II are assembled. Close-up of the nozzle (20).

22. It is rAndom's intention to develop a PixelRoller using spraycans instead of the stamp version. The unit has an open prototyping platform to accommodate different technologies in the same housing as financing becomes available.

23. Resolution tests (here for Mark II) on the print head are constantly undertaken.

24. The tests are normally carried out with a comparison object. The coin acts as a reference to visualize the width of one pixel line.

25. Similar tests are carried out for the spraycan version.

26. Testing of different ink and pigment formulations for the nozzle and valve.

27. The design of the valves was thoroughly altered in the course of the development. Early prototyping phase for Mark IV.

28. Breadboards, prototypes of the final PCBs, were constantly developed and refined. Early Mark II version.

29. Stuart Wood testing Mark II at the Royal College of Art in 2006.

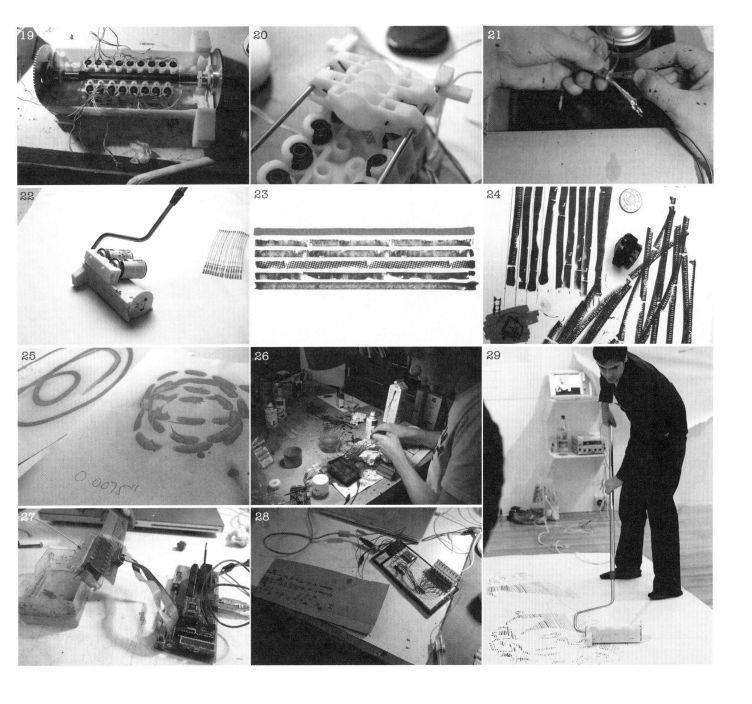

Karim Rashid and Kundalini have collaborated for many years. Both designer and Milan-based manufacturer share the same attitude in their search for a universal language that reflects the zeitgeist. Moving into the 21st century – the 'zeroes', as Karim calls it – demands new forms, materials and styles to reflect the digital age.

Karim has coined the expression 'sensual minimalism' to describe his style, which has an emotional appeal while remaining minimal. For him, soft and tactile forms are more human, signifying comfort and pleasure. The 'blob' has become Karim's trademark and gives physical form to his philosophy. His designs are accessible, and as such it is easy to overlook the fact that they are born from a rigorous understanding of technical advances in both computer software and modern production techniques. These processes have allowed him to liberate biomorphic shapes from his mind and into the marketplace. His products are sensuous to the eye as well as experimental.

Bokka is a personal proposition of Karim's. The concept was to take the notion of 'blobism' to a more complex level, exploring the relationship between volume and surface through optical permeability. Karim produced a series of freehand sketches that gave some idea of the possible dimensions and typologies of the lamp. Early discussions with Kundalini investigated various materials and manufacturing technologies, with preliminary 3D computer studies being undertaken using Rhinoceros® software to refine the lamp's form. From these early CAD drawings, two models were CNC-cut in polyurethane; one with hole tracks and one without. Further modifications on a series of CAD files and models were undertaken before the result was sent to the mould-maker.

Alternative technologies such as rotational moulding, blow moulding and fibre layering were discussed, along with the various materials that would best suit the proposed techniques. As with many of the products manufactured by Kundalini, the choice of material eventually dictated the end result. It was decided to produce the lamp in glass and the most unpredictable and innovative process was eventually chosen.

Water-jet cutting produces fine incisions by forcing a very slender jet of water through a nozzle under incredible pressure and at high velocities. As the cutter works like a plotting machine or a CNC router, very delicate and intricate shapes can be produced. With this in mind, Kundalini commissioned an expert technician to work on the basic software of a five-axis water-jet machine. New software was created that set the machine from cutting metal to cutting glass in 3D. This was a ground-breaking development; never before had anything but a two-axis machine been used on glass, and then only to incise complicated outlines on flat surfaces.

At this point, the mould was cast from the CNC-cut model and the piece was blown using the most traditional, highly skilled methods of the Murano-based master-craftsmen. Once the piece was blown in triple glass layers it went straight to the water-jet cutter and, with the use of custom-made tools, was accurately positioned in the water basin ready to initiate the process. The first glass diffuser came out almost perfectly but further refinements were needed to ensure that the cuts were as smooth as possible and that the jets did not move from their original course to cause refractions and deformation in the surfaces.

The creation of Bokka is important to Karim Rashid and to Kundalini as it dared to do the impossible in cutting glass in a way never attempted before. The lamp combines the most traditional of glass-blowing craftsmanship with state-of-the-art technology.

BOKKA LAMP
KARIM RASHID

Manufacturer: Kundalini srl
Triple glass diffuser, chromed metal base, touch dimmer
Light source: 1 x E27 (E26US) Globolux Max 150W
Table lamp: H: 60cm (23½in) (suspension 52cm/ 20½in) x Dia: 38cm (15in)
Design to manufacture: 9 months
Mass-manufactured
www.karimrashid.com/www.kundalini.it

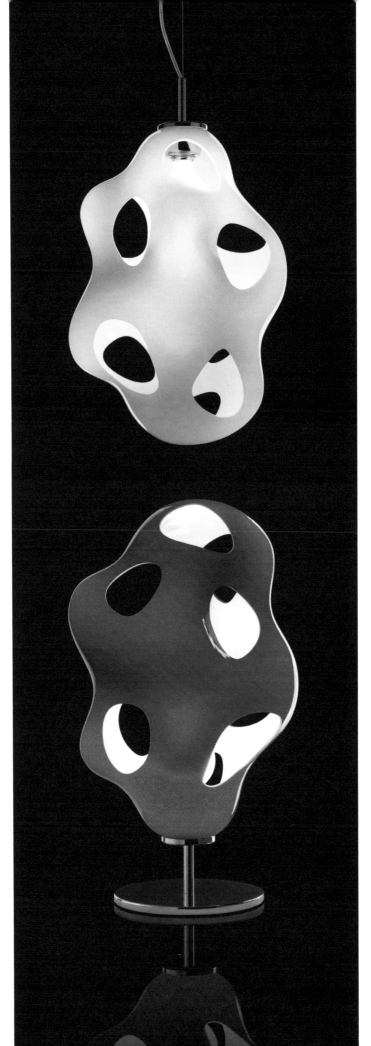

Bokka comes as both a suspension and a table lamp. The inner layer of the triple-layered diffuser is always white to ensure that the light given off is white and not tinted by the coloured outer surface.

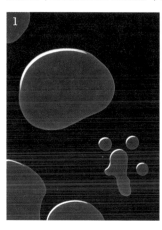

1. A generic 'blob' shape is the source of inspiration for many of Karim Rashid's designs, giving them their distinctly organic feel.

2. Karim Rashid's hand-drawn sketches were an early attempt to come up with shapes and typologies for the Bokka lamp.

3. A series of wireframe CADs were produced, from which two models were CNC-cut in polyurethane. These were refined and the information fed back into the computer. Then the CADs were amended and sent to the factory to create the mould.

4–5. The mould is heated (4) ready to receive the molten glass glob, which has been hand-rolled (5).

6–8. Using traditional Murano techniques, the recognizable Bokka shape is formed in triple glass layers by blowing in the mould (6). It is then liberated (7) and fired (8).

9. The diffuser is placed in the water basin ready to be incised by the five-axis water-jet cutter. This is an innovative technique. Although glass has been cut by water jet, this has only ever been attempted on a flat surface using a two-axis machine.

10. The cuts are located on a very complex 3D shape, their outlines traced and then incised in all directions.

11. The finished diffuser is lifted from the basin.

2

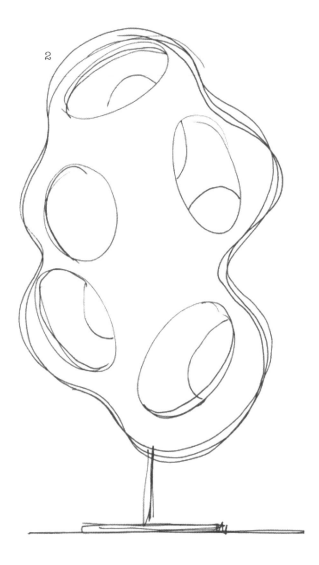

3

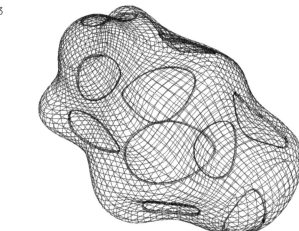

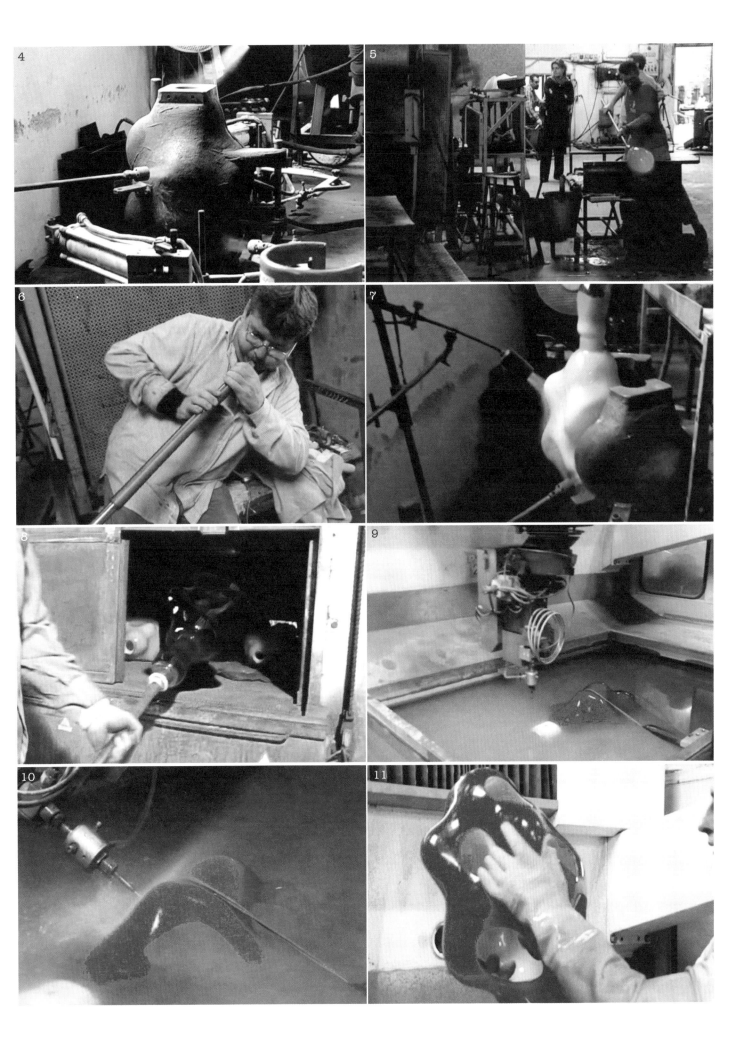

Toshihiko Sakai is primarily an electronic designer but has also worked in the fields of furniture and interior design. His polymath approach has resulted in technologically advanced products that are accessible and share a sense of lightness and clarity in their aesthetic.

Sakai's inspiration always comes from words. Once he is given a commission he thinks up key expressions to describe the function and the form of a piece. He then considers all aspects of the product, from the identity of the client and market trends to styling, taking into account consumers' behaviour and aspirations in order to create an overall picture.

Sakai starts by sketching the general profile, and some of the details, as soon as he has conceptualized the product. The styling comes from considering the drawings and visualizing their 3D forms. Models in polystyrene foam are used to verify size and detailing. Data is fed into the computer to form the CAD drawings to machine the tools. Prototypes are produced to clarify and modify problematic areas, which are then trimmed and adjusted. Renderings are also created and employed to present Sakai's work to the client, along with colour and material samples. He works in Century 3D and Think Design software, making use of their refined fillet commands, which are capable of generating a radius that changes gradually on a curved line or at a complicated intersection of surfaces. Sakai remains involved in the design

process until limited batch production. Up until this point he can address problems, such as inner electronic parts not fitting, or practical deficiencies in the strength or functioning of materials.

BODiBEAT is unique as it is intended solely for use by a jogger. Unlike the iPod or any Nike MP3 player, it senses the pulse rate of a runner and plays music with a tempo best suited to the aerobic exercise being undertaken. This has a positive effect on the efficiency of a training session.

Sakai's key words in this case were 'euphoria' and 'one second's silence'. He developed a mental picture of the user operating the player attached to his or her upper arm in the early morning sunshine before starting to jog. He chose a transparent material, feeling it was necessary to create beautiful reflections to capture the essence of excitement. He then defined his market and the function of the unit: the product would be a completely new category in the field and not intended to compete with the market; the sensors required meant BODiBEAT could not be the same size as a normal portable player; the area of usage would be limited as it is necessary to read the pulse rate via the ear lobe and attach the player to the upper arm; and – as the player was intended for outdoor, athletic use – it had to be waterproof and impact- and UV-resistant. The concept was for a gadget that would become part of the ritual of exercise and an iconic fashion accessory, as well as a scientific instrument to measure

and record the body condition of the person using it.

The design was developed using Sakai's normal working methods (see captions). Styling elements were changed for cost reasons and also to fit better within the American market.

The main body is double-injection rather than insert-moulded. Reinforced transparent polycarbonate and black polycarbonate were moulded at the same time; this was a difficult process to perfect as the inner surface of the black material had a tendency to leak into the transparent outer layer. Also the restricted gate to inject the inner layer had to be specially cut and positioned in a limited space in order to achieve the best flow of the second resin. The moulding machine was developed to meet the specification by rotating the core side to fit the two different cavities. The earphone was injection-moulded. To create the complex shape a slide mould was used in three parts. The armband was planed by sandwiching polypropylene between a layer of Velcro and non-lead PVC, which were bonded together using ultraviolet light.

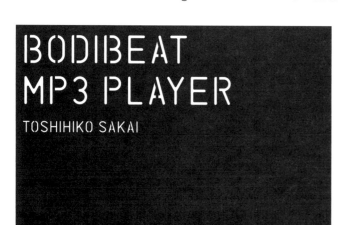

BODIBEAT
MP3 PLAYER
TOSHIHIKO SAKAI

Manufacturer: Yamaha, Japan
Transparent polycarbonate with glass fibre, black polycarbonate, ABS earphones with PVC body
H: 2.5cm (1in) x W: 3.9cm (1½in) x L: 7.5cm (3in)
Design to manufacture: 17 months
Mass-manufactured
www.sakaidesign.com/www.yamaha.com

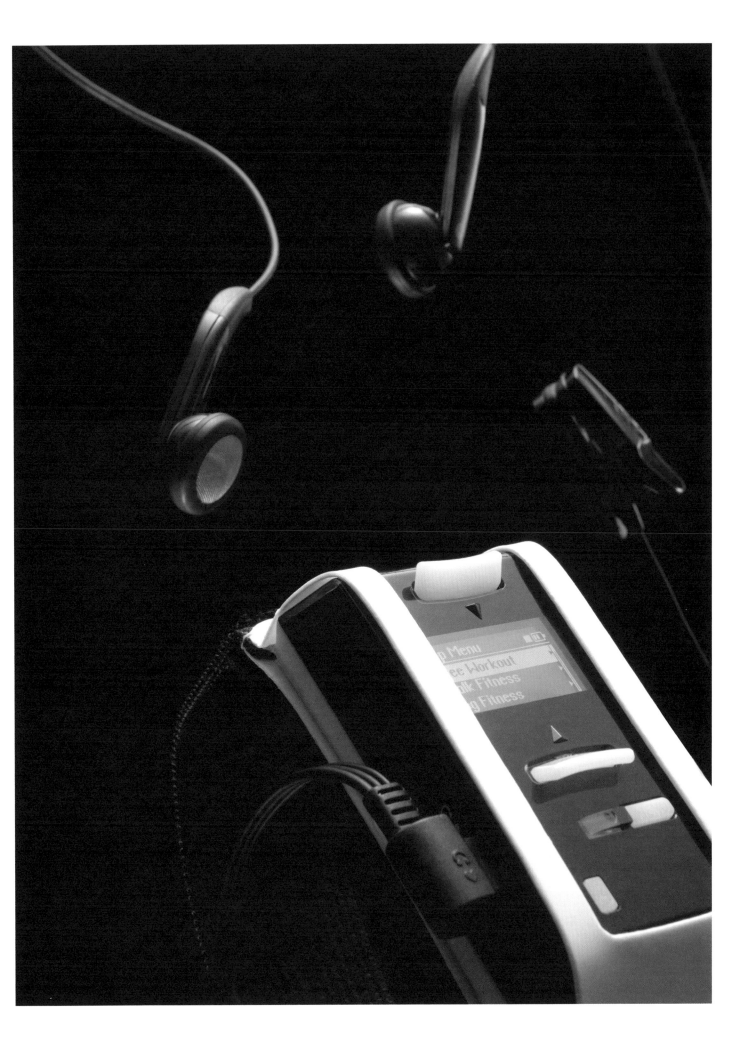

1

装着する高揚感

高揚感 一瞬の静寂

(Previous page). The BODiBEAT MP3 is intended for joggers. It senses the pulse rate and plays music appropriate to the level of aerobic exercise.

1. Sakai's inspiration comes from the words he chooses to express the essence of a design. For BODiBEAT he selected 'euphoria' and 'one second's silence'.

2. Sakai worked on ways of attaching the player to the body that would create a sense of tension and excitement and make the unit a part of the ritual of exercise.

3. The player is intended to be an iconic fashion accessory. It was Sakai's intention to collaborate with fashion and graphic designers to update the design of the belt periodically, to maintain the product's appeal without excessive changes to the model.

4. Sketches were developed to see whether the unit could be attached to other parts of the body. At this stage the acceleration sensor didn't activate well at the waist. However, technological development in the sensor now means that a waist-worn version is soon to appear on the market.

5–6. Polystyrene models were created to test the ergonomics of the design of the earpiece (5) and main body (6).

7. Nylon and ABS armband models were developed. ABS was too stiff, but the nylon version fitted much better.

8–10. A wing-type button that moves in and out of the upper part of the main body (8) and L-shaped earphones (9) were selected and the styling of the armband defined (10). CAD drawings were then created.

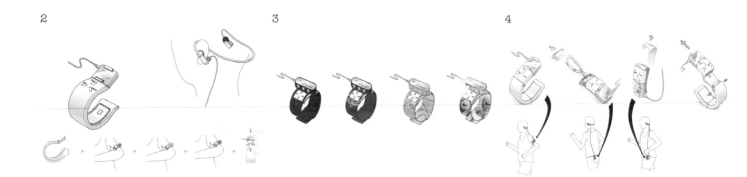

2

3

4

5

6

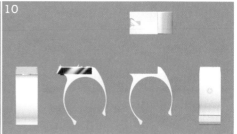

7

8

9

10

11–12. CAD investigation into how the main body could be attached to the armband (11) and a proposal for the internal mechanisms in the body (12).

13–14. Design models of the body, armband (13) and earpiece (14) were produced from CADs.

15. After reviewing the model, changes were made: the earphone and heartbeat sensor, which had been in one piece, were separated to adapt to different ear shapes, and the headphones were then connected to reduce the possibility of them falling off.

16. The armband was changed to a Velcro belt to cut down on costs and because of the opinions of the American sales department, thus losing one of the main initial concepts for the design.

17. The final body was decided and finished in computer graphics.

18. At the very last moment, the earphone returned to a less expensive single piece to reduce costs. Adjustments were made so it fitted more snugly than the earlier one-piece version.

19. Image of the die used to create the upper parts of the earpiece.

20. All the various models of the main body, from early polystyrene to first product.

21–22. A limited batch of the product was made and put through various tests without being displayed in shops. The batch was used for promotional purposes and to iron out any problems with the production processes.

Spider 1 and 2 are the first hard-disk DVD recorders capable of automatically prerecording all eight terrestrial broadcasting channels in Tokyo for a week at a time. They were produced by a small IT company, PTP (Power to the People). Budget restrictions prohibited the use of expensive casting, and the units were manufactured in collaboration with an aluminium factory using cutting-edge finishing techniques.

The interior parts of both recorders make use of existing technology and match predetermined inner layouts with the exterior design. For Spider 1, a non-working prototype in aluminium, ABS and acrylic was made to verify the form. More height was needed so Sakai raised the upper acrylic display area, increasing the overall transparency of the unit.

The aluminium front body was laser-cut and bent in a pressing machine, and the texture applied by sand-blasting the surface with fine grains of metal; this is a difficult finish to achieve at this scale and in a light tone without discoloration. Colour was then added and the finish anodized. The steel body was punched and then bent before being finished. The acrylic parts were cut to shape and submitted to a 'secret' process to increase transparency. The light receiver for the remote control is injection-moulded.

Spider 2 was developed one year later, thanks to a technological advance that had seen the inner parts reduced considerably. Sakai was given the commission in late July with instructions that the product had to be available for the Christmas market. This was a demanding schedule even though the internal layout had been predetermined: drawings had to be presented within ten days. As Spider 2 was a diffusion project, the budget was massively scaled down. The brief required a styling that would link the unit aesthetically with Spider 1. Sakai decided to concentrate on a high quality of finish to visually link the two recorders, and on making the front face as small as possible. Hand-drawn sketches of various possibilities were scanned into a computer, coloured with a Wacom® pen tablet and presented to the client, who decided to adopt a version that had a tilted front panel set back at an angle, thereby reducing the projected area visually and physically. Sakai presented a 3D computer diagram a week later. A prototype was developed in aluminium and the final exterior analysed. Small adjustments were made to the radius of the strengthening frame.

The manufacturing processes and finishing techniques had to be as economical as possible. The front panel was extruded in aluminium from a single die at lengths of 2m (6ft 6in) and then cut to size. Necessary apertures were CNC-cut. Tests to determine surface treatment were carried out. A hairline texture was chosen that was dyed using a dye/anodizing technique, and coated with transparent urethane resin to give a mirror-like finish. The bottom and top steel panels were cut and bent, and holes opened using a pressing machine. The lower part was galvanized to prevent rusting and the upper case treated with a melamine resin finish, which is highly durable.

Both Spider 1 and 2 share the same remote control. The concept was to minimize the size and number of control buttons and to make the unit small enough to fit in one hand. Mock-ups in expanded polystyrene were made to gauge the tactility of the product. CAD drawings passed backwards and forwards between Sakai and the client's engineers to address the manufacturing processes and to refine the design. The controls invite the user to play with them. Sakai's design has what he refers to as an 'afterglow', with the resin buttons taking time to softly come back into position. A prototype was machined in ABS, aluminium and transparent silicon resin. This was used to correct the texture of the silicon controls and aluminium cover. The finished item was produced by precision-pressing using eight separate dies. The surface of the aluminium body was then given a hairline texture, dyed and anodized.

SPIDER 1 & 2 HARD-DISK DVD RECORDERS

TOSHIHIKO SAKAI

Manufacturer: PTP, Japan
Aluminium, steel, acrylic
Spider 1 – H: 34cm (13½in) x W: 59cm (23¼in) x D: 15cm (6in)
Design to manufacture: 26 months
Mass-manufactured

Spider 2 – H: 11.5cm (4½in) x W: 40cm (15¾in) x D: 36.9cm (14½in)
Design to manufacture: 6 months
Mass-manufactured
www.sakaidesign.com/www.ptp.co.jp

Spider 1 (above) and
Spider 2 (below) share the
same custom-made remote
control (centre).

1

静寂
自律的な
緻密

1. Sakai starts any design
project by thinking up
inspirational words.
For Spider 1 he selected
'tranquillity', 'independence'
and 'elaboration'.

2–3. Various exterior designs
were developed to fit the
internal configurations of the
electronic parts.

4. The L shape that Sakai
originally envisioned changed
to an oblong to fit the internal
machinery, which had
increased in size. The plugs
were moved from the back to
the surface to allow the unit
to fit snugly to the wall.

5. The light movement in
the recorder's controls had
to be designed so as not to
be too intrusive at night but
still visible in the daylight. A
number of trial models with
different transmittance levels
and paints were created, and
were tested by placing them in
front of the LEDs.

6. The investor changed and
more money was available
for the exterior design. Sakai
created more height by raising
the upper acrylic display area,
thereby increasing the overall
transparency of the unit.

7–8. A non-working prototype
(7) was created from which
changes were made in the
DVD-loading cover and
the acrylic base. Working
prototypes (8) were developed
and the inner contents settled.

9. Surface treatment of the
front panel. The part was put
in a tank with liquid chemicals
and electrified. Many trials
were carried out as a light
finish was required. This
depended on finely assessing
the amount of electricity
added and the length of
time the panel was left in
the chemicals.

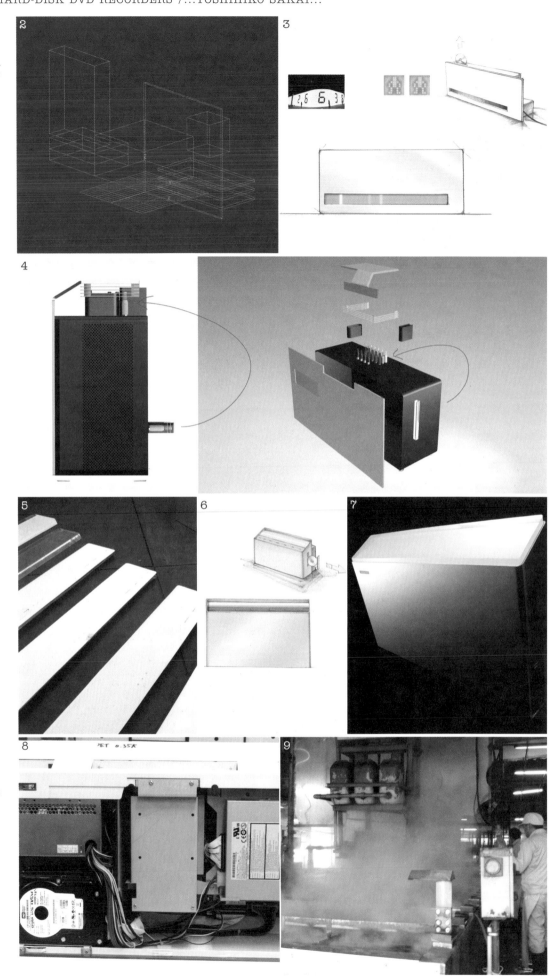

守られる内包物

自律

10. The inspiration words for Spider 2 were 'protection', 'inclusion' and 'independence'.

11. Hand-drawn coloured sketches of various versions were produced using a Wacom® pen.

12. CAD drawings of Type 4 in white and black were developed within a week. Black was chosen to match the mainstream colour of television frames.

13. The front panel is in extruded aluminium. After it had been extruded from the die it was cut in 2m (6ft 6in) lengths and transferred to the processing plant.

14–15. The bottom part of the body is in bent steel and galvanized (14). The top was produced in the same way and coated with a melamine resin (15).

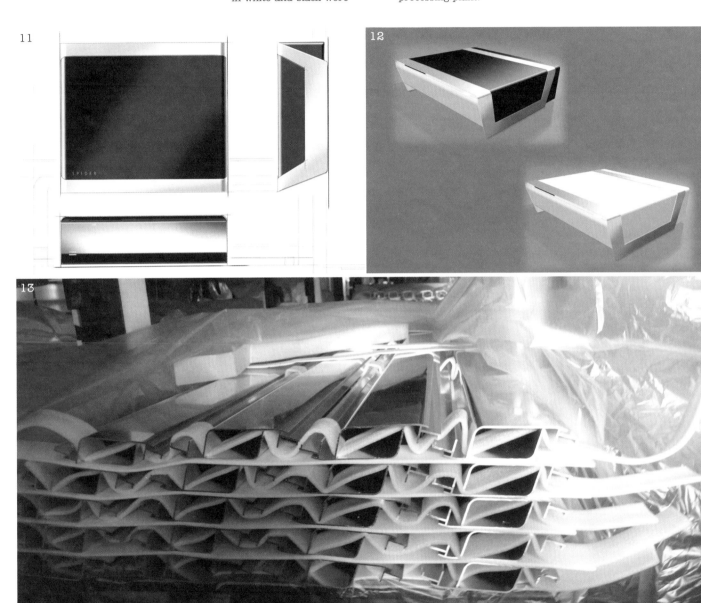

11

12

13

14

15

16–17. A hairline finish (16) was given to the aluminium surface (17).

18. Necessary apertures in the front panel were punched.

19. Graphics were added to the unit using a silk-printing process.

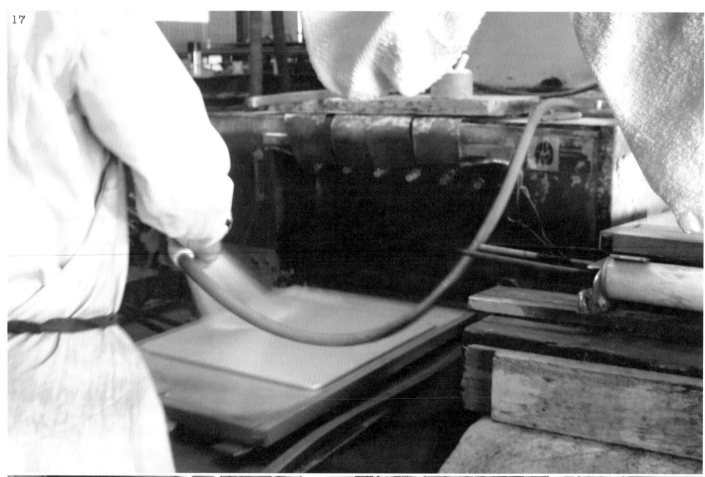

俗
緻密　連続性

20. The inspiration words for the remote control were 'common', 'continuous' and 'precise'.

21–22. Once the design was agreed on, CAD files passed between Sakai and the manufacturer's engineers to refine the details (21) and a prototype was machined in aluminium (22).

23–24. To give the shape and the opening part as clean a finish as possible, the remote was die-cast using eight dies in total.

25–26. The top cover is pressed from an aluminium sheet (25) and finished using a die/anodizing technique. As with the recorders, the process had to be repeated again and again (26).

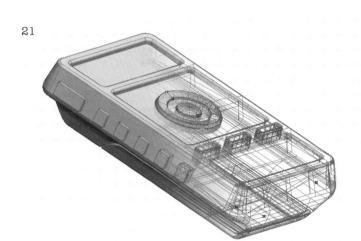

Alyce Santoro is a multi-media sound and visual artist with a scientific background. Her belief system encompasses both the quantifiable and the exact as well as the alternative and ineffable. 'The more I learned, the more I came to value the inexplicable ways of knowing, such as instinct and intuition, and, at the same time, the more I appreciated formulas and theorems designed to describe the invisible. It became clear that my passion was for the in-between.'

After gaining a degree in marine biology, Santoro studied scientific illustration at the Rhode Island School of Design, where she also experimented with printmaking, sculpture and textile design. Her work evolved into installation and performance, and she became progressively more interested in the ancient traditions and rituals of Tibetan Buddhism and Peruvian shamanism. Santoro began to develop the Sonic Fabric with the help of a friend who worked in the textile department of the Rhode Island School. She now lives in the high desert of West Texas, and her work is concerned with social and environmental sustainability.

Sonic is a durable and versatile audible fabric made from 50% recycled polyester and 50% reclaimed audio-cassette tape. The development of the textile started out as a personal project in 2003. Then, in 2007, it was taken up by New York-based manufacturer Designtex, who is producing it in bulk for the contract market. The initial idea was inspired by Tibetan prayer flags and sailboat tell-tails,

an arrow and a small piece of red string. The flags, small squares of printed cotton, have mantras and the symbols of sacred sounds printed on them and are placed in auspicious places to be 'activated' by the wind. Tell-tails are tied to the side-stays or shrouds of boats to indicate wind direction. As a child, Santoro often sailed with her father, who used to tie audio tape instead of string at the apex of his mainsail. She would imagine she could hear music coming from it as it blew in the breeze. Santoro decided she wanted to make a fabric from sound. Collecting tapes of music and words, she started to knit with them but the weave was too loose. She then tried a loom and Sonic Fabric was born.

The first pieces were Santoro's own versions of prayer flags, woven from tapes that were found or donated. Initially she had no idea the textile could be audible. Santoro wanted to create a textile that stored the invisible: memory. She then discovered that by running a tape head over the surface, the fabric could be 'played'. The head picks up four or five strands of tape at once – in other words, 16 or 20 tracks all mixed together. 'The effect sounds like scratching a record backwards,' says Santoro. She started to record her own tapes and made a dress for Jon Fishman, drummer for the band Phish, composed of patches of individual sound. Fishman wore and played it on stage at a concert in Las Vegas in 2004 using specially designed gloves. The sounds were clear, although for them to be audible he had to swipe the head across the

fabric at the speed of the recording. Once the fabric started to be made in greater quantity, Santoro sourced a family-run textile mill in New England to weave it on a standard dobby loom, using a coloured polyester warp and the audio-cassette weft. Individual tapes could no longer be used, as each (30-minute, 60-minute and 90-minute) was a different thickness and length, meaning the loom needed constant readjustment. Instead, 'pancakes' or large spools were employed. These are surplus stock and purchased from a supplier but are blank and have to be prerecorded before they are woven.

Designtex is now distributing Sonic but the method of production stays exactly the same: Santoro even insisted that the handover contract should stipulate that the New England mill be used for all further yardage of the fabric. Designtex had wanted to manufacture a special reader, but once again Santoro insisted that her instructions to create a hand-made device from an ordinary Walkman be followed.

SONIC FABRIC
ALYCE SANTORO

Manufacturer: Designtex
Polyester, cassette tape
Dimensions: W: 132cm (52in)
Design to manufacture: 60 months
Mass-manufactured
www.alycesantoro.com/www.sonicfabric.com/
www.dtex.com

Sonic Fabric is made from
50% recycled polyester
and 50% reclaimed tape. It
is extremely durable, but
remarkably soft, with a
sparkly sheen. The strands of
tape form a collage of sounds
that Santoro recorded on a
tour of New York.

1–4. The inspiration for Sonic Fabric came from two sources: Tibetan prayer flags (1–2) and sailboat tell-tails (4). Santoro was also influenced by her childhood; she would often sail with her father (3) who would tie audio tape to the side-stays of his boat to indicate the wind direction. She imagined she could hear sounds as the tape blew in the breeze.

5. The early fabric was made into Santoro's own versions of prayer flags with screen-printed patterns emulating the symbols on Tibetan flags. They are prerecorded with sounds collected in the Peruvian rainforest, dialogue by Jack Kerouac, Santoro's high-school punk band, the Beatles and of Beethoven.

6. Another early project involved costumes inspired by shamans or superheroes' robes.

7. A custom-made sonic dress for Phish percussionist Jon Fishman was worn and 'played' live on stage during a concert in Las Vegas in 2004.

8. A limited amount of material is being hand-loomed and sewn into handbags at a craft cooperative for Tibetan women refugees in Nepal, in an initiative to support the culture that inspired Sonic.

9–11. Sonic Fabric was woven on a standard dobby loom in a family-run mill in New England, using a coloured polyester warp and audio-cassette weft. Large spools of surplus-stock blank tape were recorded and woven.

12. Santoro is now working on Sonic Fabric sails. Early prototype.

13. Sonic Fabric is available in five colours formed by the hues of the polyester warp combined with the cassette-tape weft.

14. A reader can be created from an old Walkman. Unscrew the head and remount it on the outside of the plastic housing using silicone glue. Plug in the headphones, turn the volume up and press play. The best effect is achieved by running the head in the direction of the tape. Moving it at different speeds creates different noises.

Richard Sapper's career spans four decades and more than 200 products from ocean liners to household products. There are few, if any, designers whose output is so heterogeneous. He is probably best known for the computers he designed for IBM, the iconic singing kettle for Alessi and, most famously, Tizio, the first ever halogen task light. Sapper's work embodies an extraordinary talent for transforming creative research and engineering into functional elegant products, and his polymath experience has resulted in his ability to draw on solutions from a wide range of disciplines and typologies.

Nowhere is this more evident than in the Halley light. In 2003, Sapper was approached by a former IBM colleague, David Gresham, now the Vice-President of Lucesco, a newly formed Silicon Valley-based LED lighting company, who was looking for a start-up product. The revolutionary Tizio desk light was designed 30 years ago, and Sapper, who had not designed a task light since, was interested in the challenge of once again using a new technology in the creation of a ground-breaking product. The Tizio had been developed as a response to a personal need: a light source that could be moved as easily as possible, an unobtrusive head, and long arms that meant that the base could be placed as far away as possible on Sapper's crowded desk. The same criteria were used for the Halley light.

Sapper initially had some doubts about using high-powered LEDs, as he was sceptical about the cold light they cast. He wanted to create the light of the sun on a cloudy day, or in a painter's studio facing north, when colours are at their most true, and it was only when Lucesco sourced LEDs that generated exactly that quality of light that Sapper was convinced to undertake the project.

The first major technical problem was the need to cool the LEDs. Sapper could not use a normal radiator as the large surface area would result in a cumbersome head. Also, as he wanted at least six degrees of freedom in the jointed arms of the light, a complicated counterbalancing system meant that the head had to remain as light as possible. To achieve the necessary miniaturization of components, Sapper drew on his knowledge of laptops. Laptops produce approximately the same amount of heat as the number of LEDs needed for the Halley but have to remain light and portable. They are cooled by a heat pipe, a technology Sapper adapted for the Halley. The LEDs are mounted on a printed circuit board that is fixed to an aluminium plate that absorbs heat. This is attached to a copper tube containing a liquid that carries the heat to a miniature radiator. The liquid circulates through the same pipe without mixing, going along the periphery and returning through the middle. The radiator is made of a series of delicate aluminium fins that absorb the heat and cool the system down with the aid of a fan located at the rear end of Halley's head.

The weight of the head was of paramount importance for the whole idea of creating a light consisting of three consecutive arms, each balanced by a counterweight that provided a light source with six degrees of freedom in its movement without compensating springs and only a minimum amount of friction. As the arms and their counterweights constitute a cascade of elements where each weight must balance all preceding parts, each gram added to the head results in a multiple increase for the lowest part.

The appeal of the light is derived from its movement, which is based on a series of tiny joints housing the electrical connections (there are no wires in these intersections) and supporting the friction system that controls the light's agility. The current travels through six of these to get from the base containing the generator and computer to the head. Once again, Sapper used laptop technology, reworking the hinges that fit the computer's flat profile while supporting the friction that prevents the cover from slipping down and transmitting the current to light up the display. The manufacture of the light is straightforward and not photographed. The joints and head of Halley are aluminium die-cast, the radiator formed in sheet metal and the fan injection-moulded.

HALLEY LIGHT
RICHARD SAPPER

Manufacturer: Lucesco Lighting
Die-cast aluminium, formed sheet-metal radiator, injection-moulded plastic fan
Light source: 16 x high-power LEDs
H: 101cm (40in) x L: 89cm (35in)
Design to manufacture: 12 months
Mass-manufactured
sapper@us.ibm.com/www.lucesco.com

The Halley light has
arms articulated in three
sections. In order to achieve
perfect balance, a lateral
counterweight is needed to
balance the weight of the
arms. This is provided by a
chrome sphere.

1. 'The lamp to me resembles a comet with its luminous head and tail,' says Sapper. 'I named it Halley in honour of the astronomer who discovered the comet that bears his name.' The chrome ball made Sapper think of the comet orbiting the earth.

2. A system to cool the powerful LEDs was borrowed from laptop technology: the lights are mounted on a printed circuit board attached to a heat-absorbing aluminium plate. A copper tube containing a conducting liquid carries the heat to a miniature radiator, which is cooled by a fan. The fan is kept visible, becoming part of the light's aesthetics.

3–4. Sapper's first model, defining the articulated arm of Halley and the head with the 'tail' containing the concept for a cooling element (3) was sent to Lucesco along with a brass model of the base (4). The base was conceived to allow papers to slip on to its gently curving profile to save desk space.

5. Lucesco produced their own model to check they agreed with Sapper's basic concept. The design was developed in an ongoing collaboration between Sapper and Lucesco's engineers in the form of sketches, models, emails and technical drawings.

6–8. First model of the head and fan made by Sapper in foam and paper showing the initial form of the cooling air intake (6–7). Lucesco examined the model and returned a technical drawing, which Sapper amended in pencil (8, amendment centre right) to improve the formal overlap of head and tail.

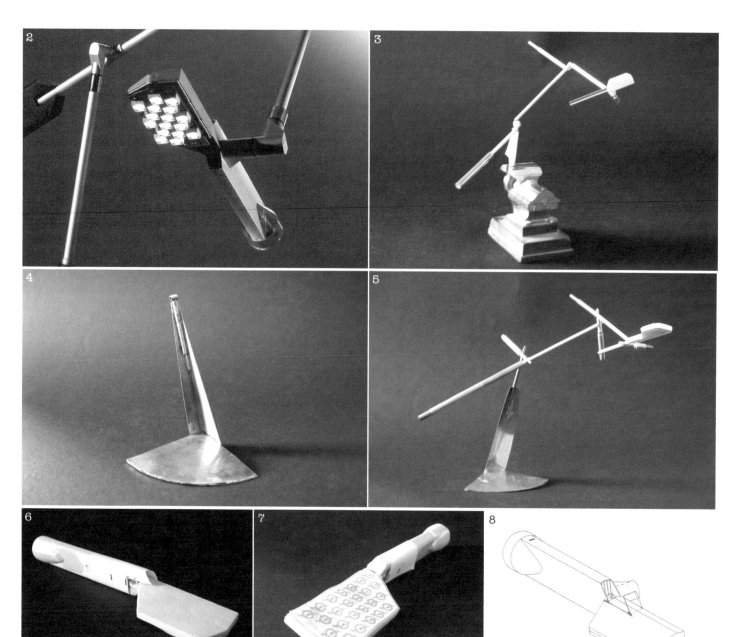

9–13. Models and drawings
showing experiments for the
cooling fins.

14. The cooling fins were
designed to be contained in
the radiator housing. The heat
pipe can be clearly seen in the
centre of the model.

15–17. Various LED
configurations were discussed
between Lucesco and Sapper,
and sketches, models and
technical drawings produced.

18. Alternative light sources.
Two different kinds of LEDs
(left and right) and halogen
(centre) were also examined.

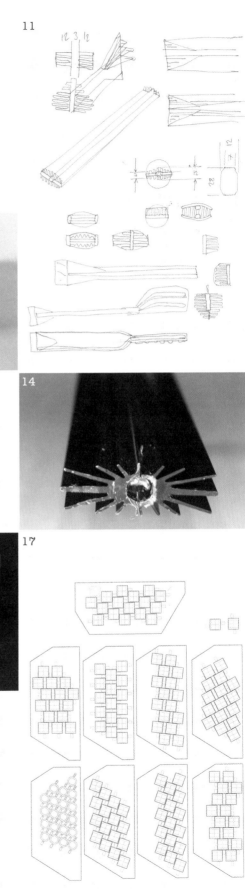

11

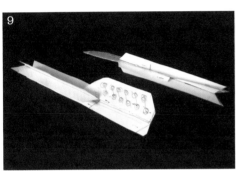

9

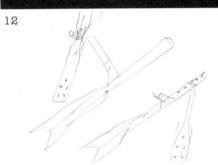

12

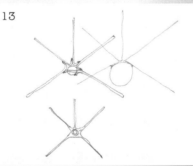

13

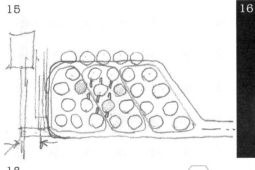

15

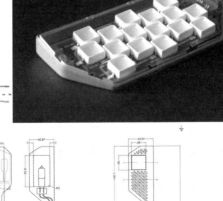

16

14

17

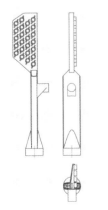

18

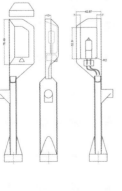

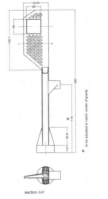

section AA'

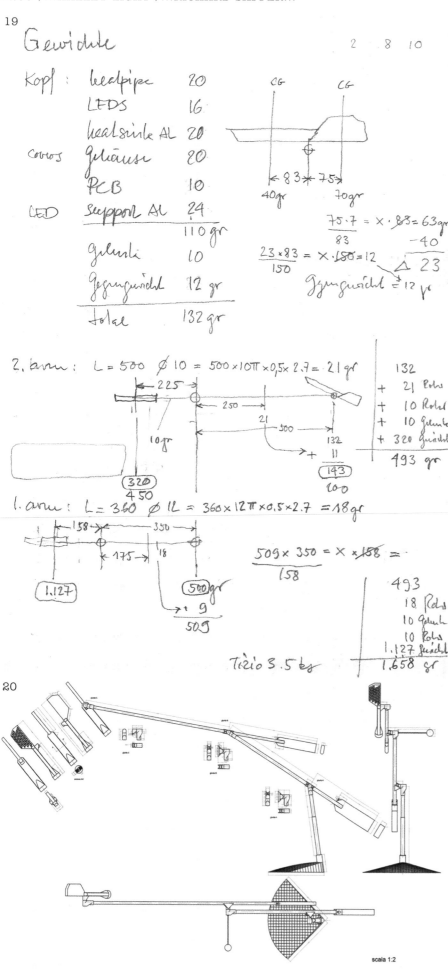

19

20

19–20. Sapper worked out the intricate calibration of the light's movement. His early pencilled calculations (19) were very close to the weights and dimensions of the finished object. Annotated technical drawing (20).

21–22. Sketches (21) and technical drawings (22) define the delicate jointing of the arm. In order to maintain a 360-degree articulation, no wires were used in the joints. As well as containing the electrical connections, the joints support the friction system that controls the light's agile movement.

23. Adaptation of Lucesco's technical drawing of the electrical connection by Sapper. The note reads 'Could we modify the dividing line like this (for aesthetical reasons)? Or is there a danger for short circuits?'

24–25. Remnants of the final full-scale model created by Sapper.

26. Final model of the base made by rapid prototyping.

21

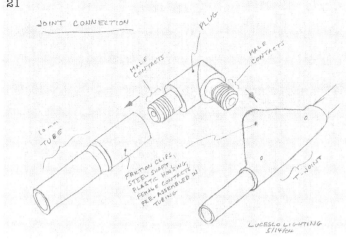

JOINT CONNECTION

PLUG

MALE CONTACTS

MALE CONTACTS

10mm TUBE

FRICTION CLIPS,
STEEL SHAFT,
PLASTIC HOUSING,
FEMALE CONTACTS
PRE-ASSEMBLED IN
TUBING

T-JOINT

LUCESCO LIGHTING
5/14/04

22

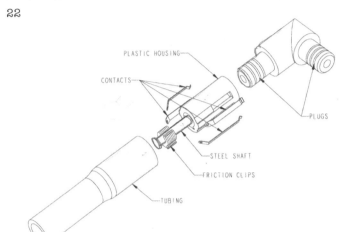

PLASTIC HOUSING

CONTACTS

PLUGS

STEEL SHAFT

FRICTION CLIPS

TUBING

23

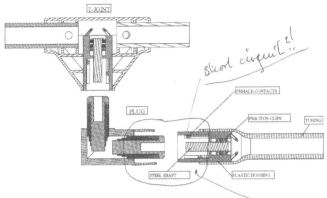

T-JOINT

short circuit?!

FEMALE CONTACTS

FRICTION CLIPS

TUBING

PLUG

STEEL SHAFT

PLASTIC HOUSING

Question No 2:
Could we modify the dividing line
like this (for esthetical reasons)?
Or is there a danger for short circuits?

Regards

Richard.

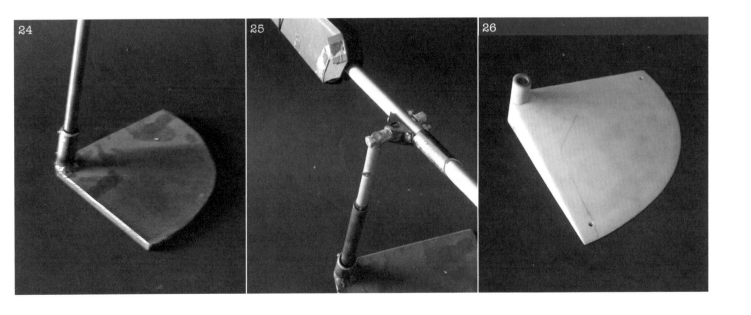

24 25 26

Wieki Somers was trained at the Design Academy Eindhoven and, in common with most of that school's alumni, her work is strongly conceptual. Best known for Bathboat, a bathtub shaped as an inverted rowing boat, and High Tea Pot, a water-rat-fur-covered porcelain skull, the pieces she designs engage the user's imagination. They are playful, eclectic, unorthodox and demonstrate an original use of materials. 'There is in all my products an interaction between function, content and my passion for materials,' she says.

Bellflower was developed for the Dry Tech 3 collection presented in collaboration with Droog Design and the Structures and Material Laboratory in the Faculty of Aerospace Engineering at the Technical University of Delft. It was unveiled off site during the Milan Furniture Fair of 2007. The concept of Dry Tech was developed during the mid-1990s; it put the knowledge and advanced material resources of the laboratory at the disposal of designers who were instructed to 'weave' products with a high-tech lightness and strength from new fibre-based materials. The results, which combined traditional methods with cutting-edge material science, were various and most famously produced the now iconic Knotted Chair by Marcel Wanders.

The same use of material, shape and process was the motivating idea behind the products on show at Dry Tech 3. The brief was unchanged from the 1990s; to design objects that are light and made from advanced materials, or traditional materials used innovatively. In preparation for the commission, Somers visited Eurocarbon, a producer of tubular and flat braids, woven tapes and fabric and was introduced to their overbraiding machine. The carrier, consisting of 144 computer-controlled spools, weaves composite 'sleeves' from carbon, polyester and glass fibres around a mould. The complex shapes are impregnated by epoxy resin and, after removing the mould, are used to cover car and aeroplane parts. Somers recognized the exciting free-form possibilities of adapting this machine to produce a strong, lightweight woven textile that could be shaped at will. Taking as her inspiration the bellflower, which goes to sleep at the end of the day (the time to read a book), she decided to design a lamp. By incorporating electrical cables and LEDs with the high-tech materials, she aimed to weave it out of one piece; the shade, base, connecting arch and light source coming together in one production line. The advantages of overbraiding are that the 'sleeve' can be shaped into many different forms before it is impregnated by resin and, in one material and one technique, all the elements of the lamp are achieved. The epoxy allows the rock-hard shell to maintain a soft textile appearance and, by connecting the 20 LEDs directly to the electrical cables in the fabric of the shade, a star-lit aesthetic is produced.

Starting with hand-drawn sketches, Somers quickly translated the rough concepts into 3D renderings to try out various measurements and shapes. Once a form had been defined, a series of prototypes was constructed, in collaboration with Eurocarbon, to address issues that could not be assessed on the computer. The sleeve was braided over a temporary polyurethane foam mould to form the shade. Once the weaving was complete the mould was removed and the textile bell impregnated with resin. The stem was then bent to create Bellflower's standing curve, using a second mould in plywood. This, too, was impregnated with the resin. The lamp was allowed to dry for 24 hours before the LEDs were connected. Problems were resolved, such as the textile pleating irregularly in the acute curves, and a final prototype made.

Bellflower is still a work in progress, and Somers is in the process of resolving certain issues. She intends to make the shade more transparent and use smaller LEDs. Her latest prototype replaces the coloured polyester with coloured fibreglass, while carbonfibre is used to conduct the electricity, thereby removing the need for electrical cables.

BELLFLOWER LAMP

WIEKI SOMERS

Production: Wieki Somers
Carbon, coloured fibreglass, carbonfibre, epoxy
Light source: 20 x LEDs
H: 18.5cm (7¼in) x W: 13.5cm (5¼in) x D: 50cm (19¾in)
Design to production: work in progress
Prototype
www.wiekisomers.com

1

(Previous page). The Bellflower lamp is a combination of high-tech and braiding technique. The LED lighting gives a true galaxy feel.

1. The shape of the lamp was inspired by the bellflower, or Campanula.

2. From early hand drawn sketches, computer renderings were constructed to work out the final form.

3. One of the advantages of overbraiding is that complex shapes can be formed around cheap moulds; here made from polyurethane foam.

4–5. The mould is put into the 144-spool overbraider designed by Eurocarbon and the sleeve starts to be woven.

6. The original textile was formed from carbon, coloured polyester, glass fibre and electrical cable. The latest prototype replaces the polyester with conductive carbonfibre replacing the need for electrical cables.

7. The textile sleeve is complete and the mould can be removed. The bell is impregnated with resin.

8. The textile is placed over a second mould made from

plywood, bent to create the curved form of the lamp and the stem, and is then also impregnated with resin.

2

Patricia Urquiola trained as an architect in Madrid before moving to Milan where she met Achille Castiglioni, undoubtedly one of the most important designers of the 20th century; it was an event that proved seminal in her career. He became her mentor, persuading her to follow in his footsteps and replace architecture with design, and instilling in her the belief that inspiration can be found in everyday things and ordinary materials. Urquiola's work is at once contemporaneous but not fashionable, and commercially sound while displaying tiny details that have an emotional kick.

Writing in the introduction to The International Design Yearbook, 2007, Patricia Urquiola talks about her current fascination with 'skin'. She says: 'After years of putting function first, it seems that design is becoming more subjective, and adaptive to our needs, desires and pleasures...I am excited by the potentiality of mixing art and craft techniques with modern technologies to achieve a blending of the new and advanced with tradition to generate an emotional response that is connected to something we know and recognize but that has been adapted in an innovative way.'

Urquiola's collaboration with Italian lighting manufacturer Flos dates from the years she worked in the studio of Piero Lissoni, the Italian architect and designer, but Chasen is the first product for the renowned manufacturer created under her own name. Her desire to design for Piero Gandini, the

President of Flos, stems from the close relationship he enjoyed with Castiglioni, which resulted in iconic pieces such as the Taccia, Arco and Brera lamps. In Chasen, Urquiola believed she had the perfect concept for the company. The delicately beautiful light (which, thanks to a mechanism controlling vertical regulation, expands and contracts according to the user's wishes) originated in Urquiola's observation of everyday objects – which, in this case, led to the challenge of transforming the purity and lightness of the traditional bamboo whisk used in the Japanese tea ceremony into something completely different in function by the utilization of modern technologies and materials.

Urquiola sketched freehand, on print-outs and renderings, and even on prototypes, during the creative stages of development, to fix ideas in her own mind as well as to communicate with her staff and Flos' technicians. Due to a short timeframe, it was imperative to maintain close contact with the client at all times. Models are important to Urquiola, as they allow an immediate and interactive reaction. Many were produced in 1:1 scale, the first in paper and cardboard, then polystyrene and foam and finally in metal. Urquiola believes in using readily disposable and inexpensive materials that give her the freedom to make as many changes as she wants. Technical drawings were produced in Rhinoceros® and AutoCad, and renderings were created to give a better comprehension of the project and to avoid misunderstanding.

In total a dozen prototypes were developed by Urquiola, and the same number by Flos, to define as many elements as possible and make the industrialization of the lamp run smoothly; this process extended into the manufacturing.

The selection of material was fundamental to Chasen. The centre of the project (a light that transforms its shape through cuts) is metal, and a compromise was sought between elasticity, resistance and endurance. Extensive research was undertaken to find the right type of steel, the quantity and dimensions of the cuts, and the components necessary to achieve a harmonious movement. Originally laser-cutting was considered but was rejected due to cost, production time and quality of the detailing: the cuts were too sharp. During analysis of the form and function of the light, chemical milling – the erosion of steel using an electro-chemical process – was selected. This transforms sheet metal (traditionally used as a static component) into a kinetic material.

Urquiola has a reputation for finding existing technologies and working with them in pioneering ways, or even, on occasion, inventing industrial processes of her own. For her, the electro-erosion treatment was symbolic of the art and craft involved in the Japanese tea ceremony.

CHASEN LAMP
PATRICIA URQUIOLA

Manufacturer: Flos SpA
Steel, borosilicate glass, heat-resistant double insulation cable
Light source: 150W halogen
H: 64–74cm (25–29in) x Dia: 26–50cm (10¼–19½in)
Design to manufacture: 8 months
Mass-manufactured
www.patriciaurquiola.com/www.flos.com

Lamps are often static.
Chasen transforms its shape
due to an infinity screw that
permits vertical regulation
to expand its structure. It
is available in large (shown
above) and small.

1. The inspiration for the lamp was the chasen, a bamboo whisk used in the Japanese tea ceremony.

2–4. Urquiola's sketches, showing her interpretation of the inspiration (2), the possible movement (3), and the way the different elements might fit together (4).

5. Technical drawings were developed to define details and to communicate with Flos' technicians. Initial drawing showing the solution to achieving the best angle of curvature, and deliberation on the thickness of the 'cuts' to the chemically milled sheet (left), and an early proposal for the inner tube that houses the control of the vertical movement and the container for the double-insulated cable (right).

6. Presentation renderings were used as a working tool to transmit the soul of the concept.

7. Technical rendering working out how to place the various components.

8. Prototypes of the components.

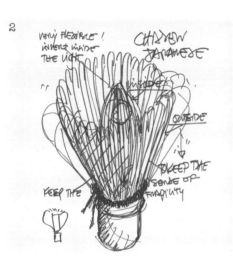

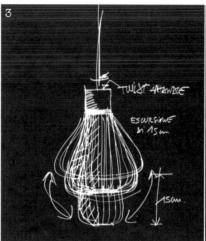

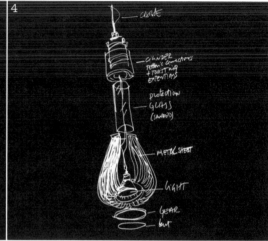

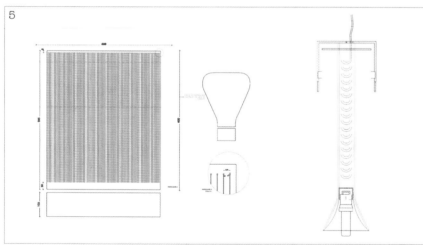

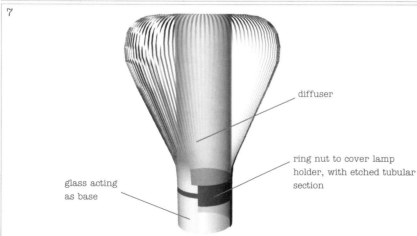

diffuser

ring nut to cover lamp holder, with etched tubular section

glass acting as base

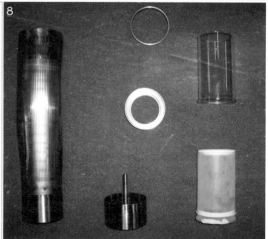

9–11. Computer drawings produced early in the development showed a study of the stabilizers controlling horizontal movement (9), and a cross-section of the light illustrating the detailing of the internal parts including the movement mechanism (10). Detail of the base (11).

12–13. Chemical milling is an electro-erosion technique used to create cuts on thin, flat metal sheets using corrosive elements. It involves a resist – in this case a film similar to photofilm – being printed on the surface of the metal to protect against the caustic action of the acids. Unprotected parts are eaten away. The patterning is plotted on a computer.

14. Prototype of the diffuser. It is made from borosilicate, also known as the brand name Pyrex®. The durable glass was selected for its heat-resistance.

15. A liquid type of varnish with pigment saturation control was applied to make the exterior transparent and the interior opaque.

16–17. The steel base was turned on a lathe (16) and the etched sheet was welded to the entire diameter (17).

18. Early prototype. Different kinds of sheet were cut in various thicknesses to gauge possible movement.

19–20. A later prototype demonstrates different curves and the reaction possible in the materials.

21–22. Different lighting effects were also examined from halogen (21) to spot (22).

Eugène van Veldhoven's fascination with the tactile and optical effects of the surface of materials has resulted in his trademark combination of traditional and high-tech methods. He considers himself an industrial designer. He supplies detailed information on his designs to his clients, from how the pattern is made to the techniques used, and then considers his role at an end. He has little interest in being in the limelight. Van Veldhoven creates patterns from a thorough knowledge of what is possible with the material he is using and the methods he has chosen, whether they be machine embroidery, silicon coating, ultrasonic embossing or, as in the case of Orchid 5, pleating and laser-cutting: he scorns the notion of decoration for decoration's sake.

For a designer who has declared his preference for working behind the scenes, his decision to accept the New York Museum of Arts and Design's (MAD) invitation to participate in the exhibition 'Radical Lace and Subversive Knitting' (January to June 2007) may seem hypocritical. However, for van Veldhoven it was a chance to present a coherent collection, bringing together all that he has learnt to date.

Orchid 5 forms part of the work van Veldhoven undertook for MAD, but also coincided with the Dutch Textilemuseum commissioning him to design and manufacture a series of three 4m-long (13ft) fabrics using its new laser-cutting and engraving machine. Although MAD's exhibition's theme dealt with constructing with yarn rather than the cutting away of material, the end result, an open textile, is the same, and van Veldhoven decided he would create lace effects with the laser.

One of the greatest influences on van Veldhoven's work was a masterclass given by the Japanese textile designer Junichi Arai, who is known for the pleats he made for Issey Miyake. As a result, inspired by hand-folded paper chains, van Veldhoven had experimented on laser-cutting pleated fabrics. He revisited this concept in Orchid 5.

Taking a flower motif from a previous design, van Veldhoven worked with the Textilemuseum's Graphixscan laser-cutter. Abstracting the pattern on Illustrator he produced 20 variations (ten to the scale) before taking the best two to the technicians. They selected the one they considered would work best in combination with the laser (too many lines close together or too small a motif build up heat and cause melting of the fabric).

Van Veldhoven's work is normally very geometric, so he chose to work with irregular pleats to obtain a balance between the organized and the accidental. Choosing the fabric was difficult, as synthetic is best for ease of pleating and laser-cutting without fraying, but burns easily. The obvious choice would have been a lightweight synthetic and natural blend whose layers would not fuse when heated and that would easily reopen on the pleats after cutting. To make his life more difficult, however, van Veldhoven was introduced to an unpredictable heavy 100% polyamide satin and was immediately seduced by its sheen and supple body.

The material was hand-fed into a Klieverik calendar, where two cylinders heated to 180°C (356°F) exerted pressure, reducing the 300cm-wide (118in) fabric to 80cm (31½in), creating a thick fabric with pleats occasionally overlapping. The Textilemuseum's laser-cutter was only capable of carrying out tests on the material as it is operated by means of a small mirror that steers the laser beam in different angles. As such it could not cut through the pleats without burning the adjoining fabric, which consisted of one layer only. To produce the full-size hanging with repeated motifs, the operation was moved to ID-laser, a company with industrial laser-cutters. Here the beam is moved by an X-Y-bar and at a fixed angle, making it possible to blow a neutral gas over the point of cutting, preventing the fabric becoming scorched or worse.

Once the fabric was cut, the suspended 4m (13ft) hangings were allowed to drop, their own weight pulling open the horizontal cuts to create the lacy effect. Van Veldhoven is now working on a more affordable variation on the original piece, to be produced commercially.

ORCHID 5 FABRIC

EUGÈNE VAN VELDHOVEN

Production: Eugène van Veldhoven
100% polyamide satin
4m (13ft) drop
Design to production: 7 months
One-off
www.dutchtextiledesign.com

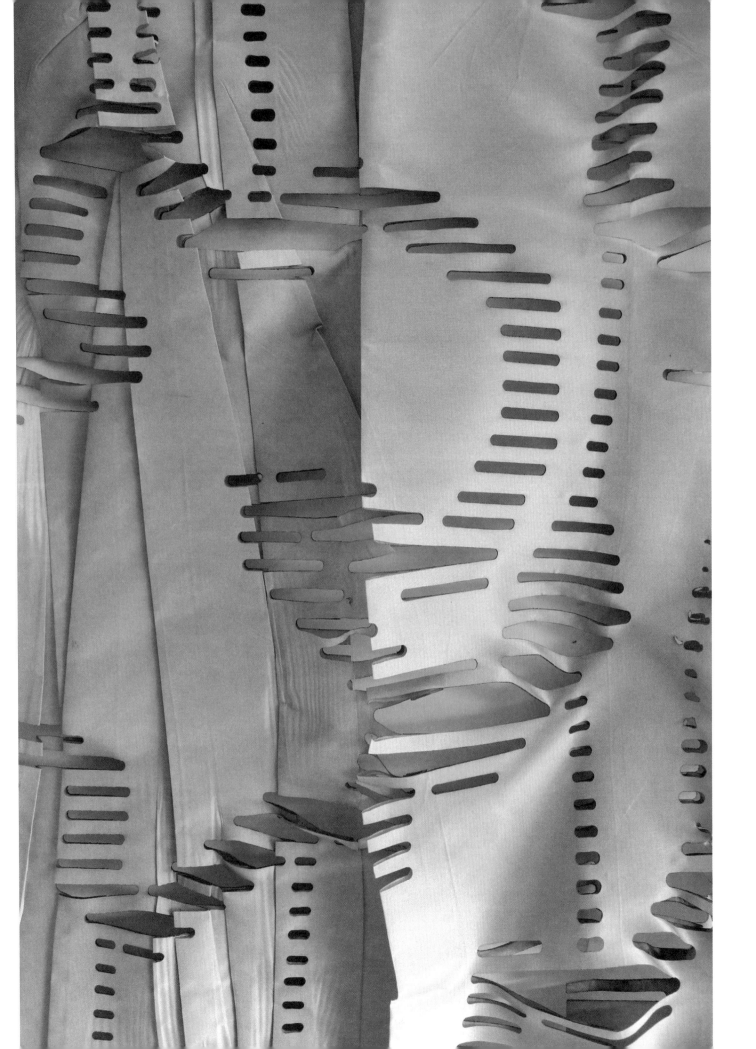

(Previous page). Orchid 5 is created by laser-cutting pleated fabric.

1. Van Veldhoven's open fabric was inspired by the idea of hand-folded and cut paper chains or garlands.

2. Van Veldhoven was greatly influenced by the Japanese textile designer, Junichi Arai, who is famous for the pleated fabrics he created for Issey Miyake. As early as 1998, van Veldhoven was experimenting with pleating and laser-cutting fabric.

3–4. Taking a flower motif from an earlier design (3), van Veldhoven created an abstracted version in Illustrator (4). Many proofs were worked on, but only the best one or two were delivered to the technicians.

5. A test was carried out on a polyester voile, as the designer liked the idea of working on a transparent fabric, which he considered would best show all the different layers. However, it proved too sensitive to heat.

6. In the end, a supple and shiny polyamide satin was selected. Tests were again carried out to experiment with different speeds and intensities of the laser. The labels record the various results.

1

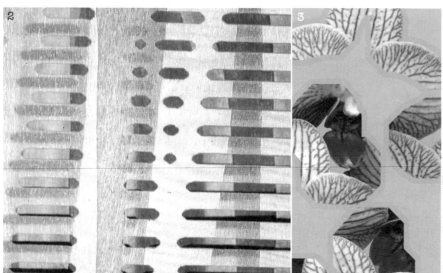

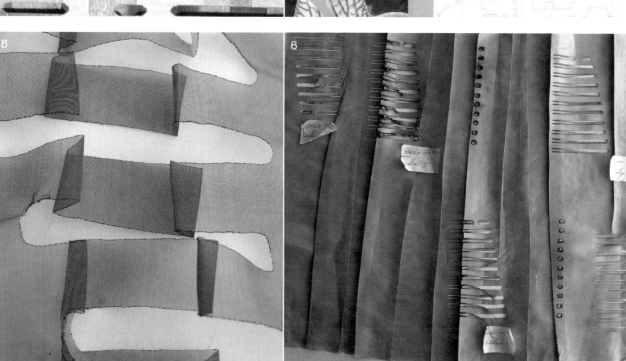

7–8. Information was fed into the Textilemuseum's Graphixscan computer (7) to control the laser-cutting of the fabric (8). Because of its size and the way it is operated, this laser-cutter was only capable of carrying out the tests; it could not cut through the pleats without burning the adjoining fabric.

9. A Klieverik calender heats and presses the fabric, reducing its width from 300cm (118in) to 80cm (31½in) and creating occasionally overlapping pleats.

10. To produce the full-size hanging with repeated motifs, the operation was moved to an industrial laser-cutting facility. Here a neutral gas was blown over the point of cutting to prevent burning.

11. The freshly cut textile was allowed to hang out under its own weight, which opened up the cuts on the pleats and creating the 'lacy' aesthetic (see opener).

12. Van Veldhoven in front of the Orchid 5 wall hanging at the 'Radical Lace and Subversive Knitting' exhibition held at the Museum of Arts and Design, New York, in 2007.

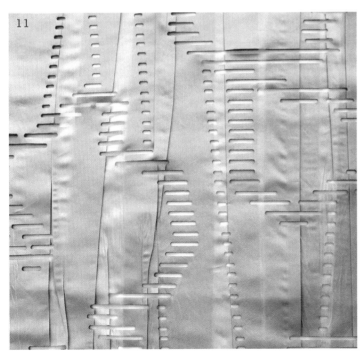

Glass-plating often refers to the technique of creating stained glass, but it's also the term given to the forming of molten glass in any way other than blowing. It has been used by the craftsmen of Murano for centuries in the production of their more traditional pieces and here refers to the stretching of semi-molten glass over a mould. Kundalini commissioned leading figures in the contemporary design world to create objects that would take this classical process and bring it into the 21st century. This was the concept behind both Mandala and Pirouette.

Melted glass is spooned out of the furnace at 1300°C (2372°F) and poured on to an even bronze surface. This is covered with minute glass spheres to help the glass move easily out towards the frame, the 'trappola' that contains the glass within a predicted area. At a later stage in the process these partially embedded micrograins of glass are sand-blasted away to obtain a smooth finish. The cooling glass forms a circular extension (referred to as the 'pizza') with the consistency of treacle, on to which a tool, the 'fracco', is impressed to create the pattern. The glass is then transferred to the mould. As the temperature decreases, the glass slumps and is pulled over the mould to give the piece its definitive shape. The object is then removed and placed on a platform in the furnace to temper, thereby reducing the stresses that could cause the glass to shatter.

The final part of the process is the hand decoration. Kundalini developed a technique of applying paint to the back of the crystal glass, following the patterns impressed by the fracco. The colours project through the transparent glass and give the effect of translucent coloured glass.

Mandala is a work in progress. The idea was for designers of different generations to produce contemporary wall lights based on the oriental tradition of contemplative and curative imagery. Mandala means 'circle' or 'wheel' in Sanskrit and the symbol has been used by various cultures as an aid to meditation. So far, Alessandro Mendini and Karim Rashid have been invited to develop their interpretations, and Ettore Sottsass and Ora Ito will follow.

Once Mendini's drawings had been received and worked up using CAD drawings and 1:1 cardboard models, the information was translated into the physical objects, using the method outlined above, in a collaboration between Gregorio Spini, the Managing Director of Kundalini, and the family-run Murano furnace with whom he has worked for many years.

Guido Venturini's inspiration for Pirouette was the traditional lampshade translated into an exaggerated Flintstone cartoon aesthetic. Originally he had wanted to glass-blow the basic shape and then cut the 'frilled' edge using a 3D water-jet. After discussions with Spini the concept was diverted to glass-plating. To create the dimension of the shade's surface, the hottest possible pizza was needed and the fracco stage was omitted. A solid mould would cool the glass too quickly, so the foundry developed a skeleton of the final form over which the glass was stretched. The invention was fundamental to the design, as the air between the struts kept the glass at a temperature where it could flow and be eased over the mould, to create the largest glass volume ever achieved with this technique. The diffuser was tempered and then decorated. A partially mirrored metal finish was applied, which gives a satin translucency to the shade when the light is on.

Although glass-plating is ancient and simple, translating it into a contemporary idiom was more difficult, especially in the collaboration with artisans whose idea of beauty was diametrically opposed to that of Spini. All the concepts of contemporary design had to be explained to the craftsmen, who are trained for generations in classical aesthetics. Nothing could be taken for granted and Spini remained involved throughout the process, to develop mutual understandings through which solutions could be reached and decisions made.

MANDALA LIGHT
ALESSANDRO MENDINI

PIROUETTE LAMP
GUIDO VENTURINI

Manufacturer: Kundalini srl
Crystal glass
Light source: 2 x R7s 118mm
D: 10–15cm (4–6in) x Dia: 40–60cm (15¾–23½in)
Design to manufacture: 9 months
Mass-manufactured

Manufacturer: Kundalini srl
Crystal glass
Light source: 1 x R7s 78mm
H: 30–43cm (12–17in) x Dia: 23–49cm (9in–19¼in)
Design to manufacture: 9 months
Mass-manufactured, www.kundalini.it

Mandala (right) is a range of
wall and ceiling lights with a
curved plated glass diffuser
pressed with the fracco and
hand-decorated. The Pirouette
crystal lampshade (below) is
available acid-etched and sand-
blasted or mirror-plated.

1. Mandala is inspired by the Sanskrit for 'circle' or 'wheel'. The patterns are ancient; they symbolize our connection to the infinite and are used as an aid to meditation.

2. Mendini prepared a series of drawings exploring his personal interpretation of the mandala.

3. Karim Rashid was another designer invited to design his interpretation of the mandala.

4–5. Glass is heated to 1300°C (2372°F) and spooned out of the furnace on to a smooth bronze surface (4) and spread into the trappola, a frame that confines the flow of the glass, to form a molten disc of glass called a 'pizza' (5).

6. The fracco is impressed on to the surface of the glass and the pattern created.

7–9. The fracco is removed as is the trappola (7) and the pizza is transferred to the mould (8–9).

10. The glass flows and is pulled over the mould to produce the definitive form of the fixture.

11. The light fixture is then hand-decorated. A technique was developed to paint the back of the crystal glass following the lines impressed by the fracco. The impression is of glossy translucent coloured glass.

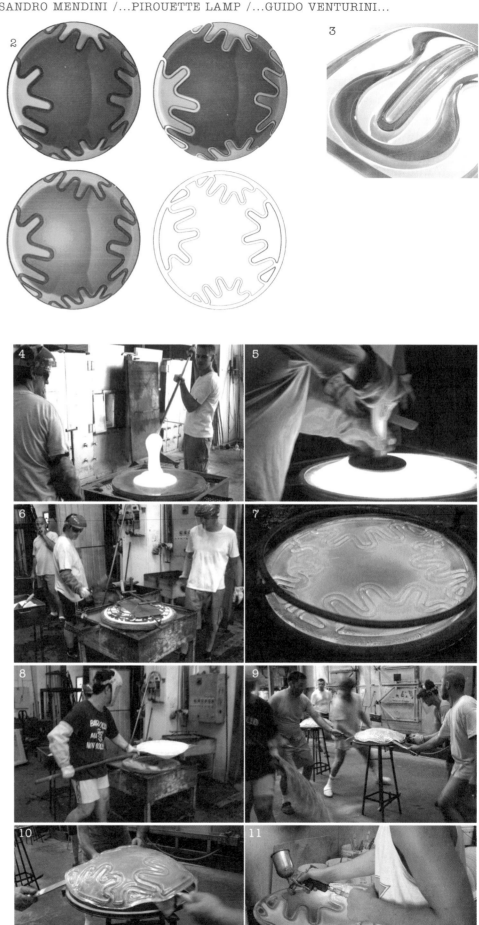

12. Paper models of Pirouette were produced from drawings and used as the basic information to make the mould.

13. Because the glass pizza used in Pirouette needed to be kept fluid for as long as possible, a skeletal steel mould was developed. The air between the struts ensures that the glass does not cool too quickly.

14. To keep the pizza hot, the intermediary stage of imprinting a pattern by using the fracco was left out. The pizza was placed directly on the steel frame.

15–17. The glass was pulled down over the mould as it cooled, retaining the lines of the frame.

18. The latest product in the glass-plating series is Filo by Paola Navone. A furnace has been constructed that is suspended above the heads of the artisans. A 10mm (½in) hole allows a continuous thread of molten glass to cascade down, which is formed into a woven plate. The process is still partially secret and could not be photographed.

19–20. The plate was pulled over a mould similar to that created for Pirouette (19), allowed to harden and then removed (20).

21. The artisans have a very traditional understanding of aesthetics and Gregorio Spini wanted to bring the age-old technique of glass-plating into the 21st century. A crystal version had very beautiful reflections but was too classical. Spini had the idea of painting it black to make it look as if it had been created by rapid prototyping, to the bemusement of the decorator.

Kevin Walz works as architect, designer, curator and artist and is well known for his research into structures and materials. In 1996 he received international recognition for a collection of furniture in compressed cork for KorQinc, which was followed by pigmented cork flooring and tableware.

When Walz was approached by Ralph Pucci, international manufacturer of custom-made artistic furniture and mannequins, to design a collection comprising a wooden chair, table and side-table, he started to ponder exactly what that meant in this day and age. Most manufactured wooden furniture today is not wood at all but veneered plywood or, worse still, veneered composite board. Plywood has been one of the most ubiquitous building products for decades, but over the last 50 years nothing new has been attempted. For Walz the material was looking dated: heavy, bulky and, with the current preoccupation with green design, more than a little environmentally unfriendly. Walz set out to invent a modern-day equivalent. 'I wanted to make a timber-based material that harnessed wood's structural properties and allowed its characteristics to be seen, but which was lighter and more malleable than plywood', he says.

His inspiration came from a canoe that had been given to him by his brother Barry, boat designer and craftsman. Here was a lightweight product, made from solid layers of wood sandwiched between layers of a technical fibre that was strong and even waterproof. Together they thought of using the technology of canoe manufacture to develop a new material that could be used in the Pucci furniture collection.

The creation of the furniture and the three versions of the laminates produced are co-dependent. An idea of what the design of the pieces would involve was needed to judge how the material should be made to behave, yet without realizing the exciting new properties of the laminates the evolved profile of the objects could not have been imagined. The laminates – walnut mixed with different thicknesses of carbonfibre – allowed Kevin and Barry Walz to design as if they were working in metal. Combining technology with natural materials, the five layers of wood and fibre flex in a gentle way but can be cut very specifically with none of the shrinking found in natural woods. Undulating forms were possible with planes meeting in precise points with no fear of shifting.

The three variations were devised to suit the different functions required of the furniture series: vertical, horizontal and formed, but produced in essentially the same way. The vertical laminate is 8mm ($^5/_{16}$in) thick and designed to hold weight. By adjusting the proportions of the layers of wood and fibre, a balance was found between a rigid strength and appropriate thinness. The horizontal version was conceived for tabletop surfaces. It is composed of fine layers of solid wood, a light core and a solid wood frame to create the thinnest possible top that would remain taut and not warp even in long measurements. Both vertical and horizontal laminates are laid up as flat planes. Starting with wood, the layers are placed on a level surface, the carbon sheets are soaked in resin and the next wood layer is placed on top until all five layers are together. They are then set in a vacuum press and allowed to dry. The skin laminate is just 3mm ($^1/_8$in) thick. It was used to form the two complicated curves of the seat and the sinuous, flexible profile of the chair's backrest. In this case the five layers are sandwiched between male and female moulds, vacuum-pressed and left to dry. In all cases, the laminates are produced individually and cut precisely to avoid waste, and then joined together with epoxy in accordance with the furniture designs. Walnut was chosen as it has a linear strength but is flexible. It also has a wide pigment range, making each piece of furniture distinctive.

The furniture was designed to emphasize the lightness and flexibility of the material. The chair weighs only 0.68kg (1½lb). The wood layers are left unstained and the grains carefully balanced, to reinforce their natural beauty and to contrast with the technologically assisted performance of the now patented laminate.

PATENTED FLEXIBLE WOOD LAMINATE

KEVIN & BARRY WALZ

Production: Kevin and Barry Walz
Walnut and carbonfibre, cut to measure
Design to manufacture: 9 months
Small-scale production
www.walzworkinc.com

The development of the
laminate was in response
to a commission received to
design a plywood furniture
collection. The patented
alternative produced is
lighter and more malleable.

1. The inspiration for the flexible walnut and carbonfibre laminate came from examining a canoe. The construction of the canoe, with thin panels supported by wood ribs, was instrumental in the variations of laminates produced: vertical for strength and skin for shape.

2. Close-up of the laminate. The base material is walnut, which is layered with resin-soaked carbonfibre. The five-layered sandwich is vacuum-pressed and allowed to dry.

3–5. Kevin and Barry Walz were involved in the creation of the patented laminate and the prototypes of the furniture series commissioned and manufactured by Ralph Pucci. The collection has now gone into mass production and is fabricated by East Coast Interiors, a high-tech aeronautical manufacturer.

6. Barry Walz preparing the vertical laminate, which is laid up as a flat plane. Starting with wood, the layers are placed on a flat surface, the carbon sheets are soaked in resin and the next wood layer is placed on top until all five layers are together. They are then set in a vacuum press and allowed to dry.

7. Walnut layers and carbonfibre roll. To the rear can be seen the skin laminate of the mould-formed seat.

8. The laminates are laid up as needed. They are not produced in a fixed sheet size but are slightly over the size required for the furniture, to avoid wastage.

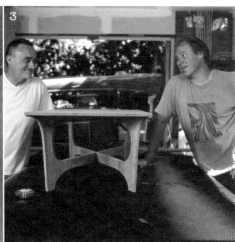

9. The chair design was worked up via a series of sketches and 20 cardboard models.

10. Image of the model presented to Ralph Pucci.

11. Information was fed into the computer and CAD drawings produced. Walz's studio use AutoCad 2007, Rhinoceros® and Cinema 4D.

12–14. A foam model of the seat was made, and the data fed into the computer from which a tool was created and the skin laminate formed between the male and female parts. Male and female mould of the chair seat (12). Female mould of the chair seat (13). Male and female mould of the chair back (14).

15. Three prototypes assess and address structural issues. It was found the laminate was being asked to bend too much in two directions. The solution was to make the front edge of the seat curve up in the centre to remove some of the stretch. The relationship between the seat and the crossed leg planes was also examined. The positioning of the meeting of the 'x' under the seat impacts on the size of backrest needed and the centre of gravity of the chair.

16–17. A full-scale model was made using the formed laminate seat to correct the 'x' so that the backrest could be rethought.

At the age of 40, Tokujin Yoshioka is one of Japan's leading designers and one of the few to have made an impression on the European market. He is known for products that mix poetry with innovative technical processes, creating pieces that have a strong artistic appeal but sell commercially. He works in materials that are not necessarily new but in a way that liberates their full potential in innovative ways. Tokujin's constant experimentations ensure that his products transcend banality. His first designed chair, Honey-pop, presented in 2002 during the Milan Furniture Fair, is already iconic. Tokujin comments: 'My concept has always been to create something new, something no-one has done before.'

Pane chair is certainly, as Tokujin says, 'a chair that no-one has ever dreamed of creating'. 'Pane' is the Italian for bread and this unique piece is literally baked in an oven; its form created by the cooking process. Tokujin frequently uses catering analogies: 'My design philosophy might have some similar principles to the spirit of Japanese cuisine. When you look at the finished dishes, you can't discern how much time and preparation have gone into their presentation. Simple food does not mean simple cooking: that is the way of Japanese cuisine, and that is the way I want to design.'

Three years in the making, Pane's uncomplicated form belies the research and experimentation that has gone into the end result. The concept for the chair sprang from an article that Tokujin read in National Geographic magazine. The feature examined fibres from the natural to the advanced and scientific. Tokujin was struck by the fibrous structures, which, despite their softness, demonstrate their strength in their capacity to absorb forces. If numerous cells come together to form an intense group, they gain strength by spreading the stress. His idea was to create a new type of seating in which the fibres themselves form the structural body but, because they are soft, the effect of sitting on the chair would be like sitting on air.

Tokujin's normal working method is to develop a concept in his head; he rarely uses sketches. He then conducts tests to give a tangible form to his ideas, producing computer graphics in order to communicate the notion to other people. For Pane chair, Tokujin experimented with various fibrous materials, finally settling on a translucent and spongy polyester elastomer normally used in medical and agricultural applications. From an early sketch he developed the form and typology of the chair by way of CAD drawiings. To test the physical and tactile qualities of the chair he then produced a model in sponge. Ten prototypes refined the process of 'baking' the chair.

The process begins when a semi-cylindrical block of fibres is rolled and shaped by hand, then fixed with a plastic ring. The block is wrapped in a cloth, which, when twisted and secured, creates the eventual armrests. The block is inserted into a tube made from the kind of paper normally used to pour concrete on construction sites. The tube is baked in a kiln at 104°C (219°F) for 30 minutes; the fibres memorizing the shape of the chair as they are heated.

The Pane chair is the first of its kind. The factory that helped with the production of the chair had never witnessed its like before. By systematically organizing small, light fibres, great strength can be achieved that eliminates the need for hard materials, creating what Tokujin refers to as 'structures for the future'. The result of the process is a chair with an 'uncertain finish' (no two pieces are alike) that is autonomous, accidental and organic.

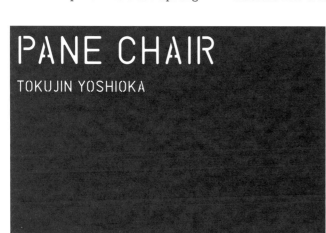

PANE CHAIR
TOKUJIN YOSHIOKA

Production: Tokujin Yoshioka
Polyester fibre
H: 80cm (31½in) x W: 90cm (35½in) x D: 90cm (35½in)
Design to production: 36 months
Limited batch of 39
www.tokujin.com

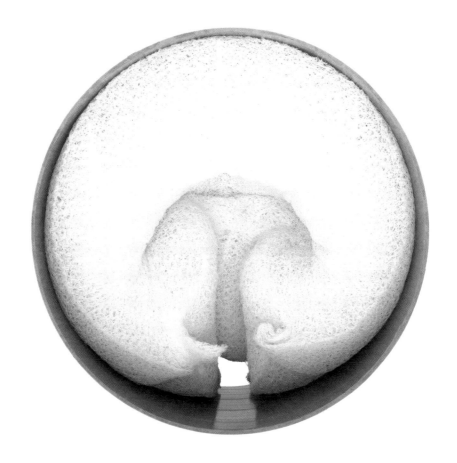

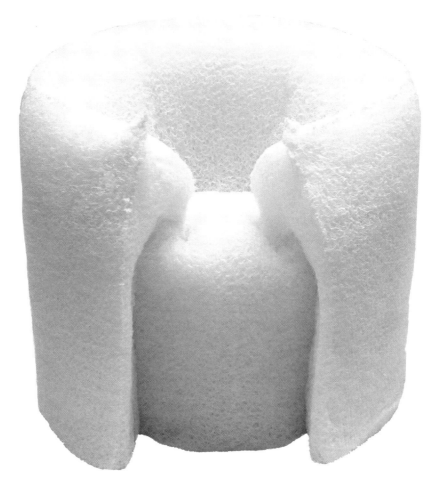

The 'baked' Pane chair, viewed in its cooking tube (above) and without (below).

1

1. The Pane chair is named after the Italian word for a food that everybody in the world is familiar with: bread. Developing this innovative seating, which contains no internal structure, is like baking a loaf in the oven.

2. Freehand sketches are unusual for Tokujin. Normally he produces them retrospectively for magazines. For Pane, he did a series of freehand drawings that gave an idea of the fibrous and simple form of the end-product.

3. After numerous experiments with different fibres, a translucent polyester elastomer normally used in medical and agricultural applications was selected.

4–10. A semi-cylindrical block of fibres is rolled by hand and shaped into a tube (4–5). The block is secured with a plastic ring and wrapped in a cloth, which is then twisted and secured (6–7). The block is then placed in a paper tube and baked in a custom-made oven (8–9). When cooked, the fibres memorize the shape of the chair (10).

2 .

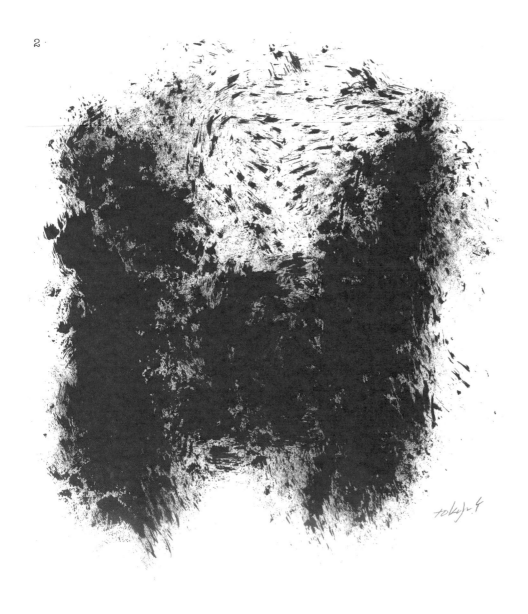

4

5

6

7

8

9

10

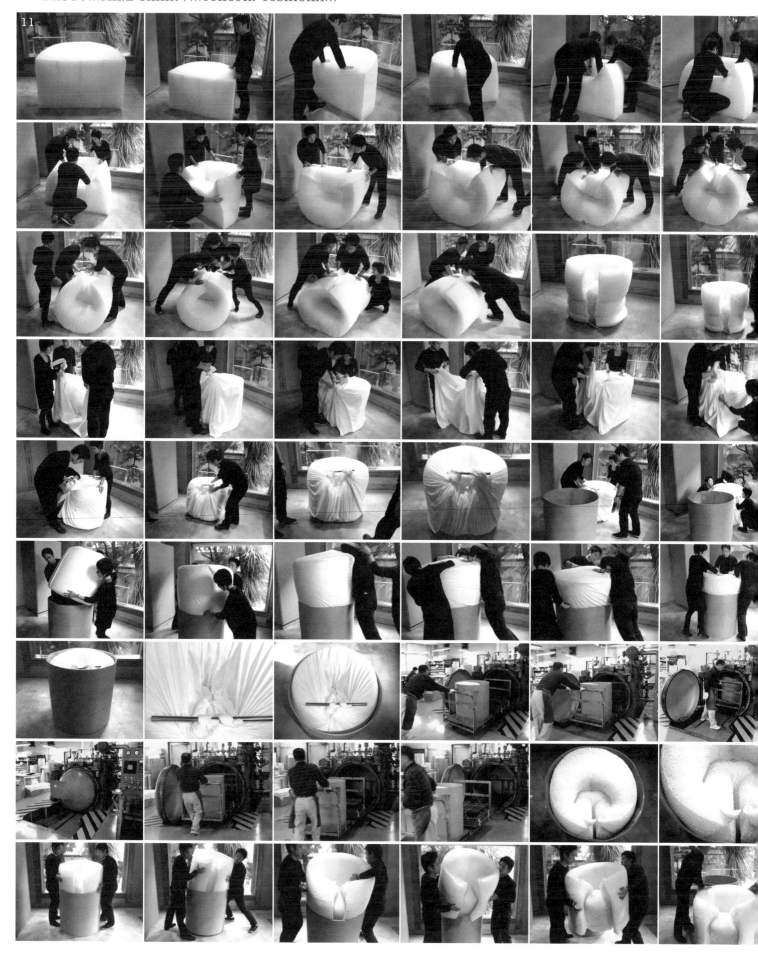

11. Tokujin Yoshioka and colleagues develop one example of the chair in their studio, showing in detail the complete development process. For the designer, whose other work includes interactive exhibitions and displays, the theatre of the object's manufacture is as beautiful as the final piece itself. From initial fibre block, to rolling, wrapping, and then placing in the cooking tube and in the oven, each finished chair has the additional feature of always being completely unique.

12. 'I believe that a "deliciously" comfortable chair, with an original feel, has been baked by the innovative process of a new idea, material and structure,' says Tokujin.

GLOSSARY

abrasive Typically a very hard, brittle, heat-resistant substance that is used to grind or smooth the rough edges and surfaces of an object.

ABS (Acrylonitrile Butadiene Styrene) A common thermoplastic polymer used to make light, rigid moulded parts.

algorithm A logical sequence of instructions that explains how to accomplish a task going from one phase to the next with a finite number of steps.

anodizing An electrolytic process used to increase the thickness and density of the natural oxide layer on the surface of metal materials.

artist's proof An almost, but not quite, identical impression of a finished work. Often used to check the quality of reproduction or to make small refinements.

axis An element of the Cartesian coordinate system where points in 2D space can be specified by a coordinate in the x and y axes. Points in 3D space have coordinates in X, Y and Z. Translations and rotations can be defined by these axes.

azote Nitrogen (N) with the atomic number 7. A common non-metallic element, azote is a colourless, odourless, tasteless inert gas used in a range of manufacturing processes, notably gas injection moulding.

Bakelite The first plastic produced from synthetic components, used for its heat-resistant and electrically non-conductive properties.

Baydur® A rigid, microcellular engineering RIM (reaction injection moulding) polyurethane material, suitable for the production of large mouldings.

bead The raw material for injection moulding is usually in pellet or granule form and is melted by heat and shearing forces before being injected into a mould or within the mould itself.

bell metal A hard alloy used for making bells. It is a form of bronze (usually 3:1 ratio of copper and tin). In some parts of India it is used for the manufacture of utensils.

bi-injection moulding A process whereby two different polymer melts are simultaneously injected at different locations in the same mould.

biomechanics The research and analysis of the mechanics of living organisms or the application and derivation of engineering principles to and from biological systems.

blow moulding The process of forming hollow objects or parts by expanding a piece of hot plastic, glass or aluminium against the internal surfaces of a heated mould using compressed air.

blowpipe In glass-blowing, an iron or steel pipe through which air is blown to inflate the gob of glass at its end.

borosilicate A particular type of glass, better known under brand names such as Pyrex®. It is economical to produce and, because of its superior durability and chemical- and heat-resistance, is used in laboratory equipment, cookware and lighting.

brake bending The creation of sharply angular linear bends in sheet metal using a press brake that forces the metal over a die.

breadboard A reusable solderless device used to build a prototype of an electronic circuit to experiment with circuit designs.

CAD (Computer-Aided Design) The use of a wide range of computer-based tools that assist designers, engineers and architects in their work, involving various software programs ranging from 2D vector-based drafting systems to 3D solid and surface modellers.

CAE (Computer-Aided Engineering) The use of information technology to support engineers in tasks such as analysis, simulations, design, manufacture, planning and repair.

CAID (Computer-Aided Industrial Design) A subset of CAD that includes software that directly helps in product development. Typically involves free-form drawing and modelling tools.

calender A finishing process in textile and paper design and production. Synthetic fabric is run through a series of steel rollers and heat and pressure are applied to stabilize it. Calendering is also used, for instance, to laminate two layers of fabric with an adhesive in between, to heat set pleats and to create a shiny surface. Industrially, it can be used to form high volumes of PVC sheet at a fast rate.

CAM (Computer-Aided Manufacturing) The use of computer-based software tools to assist manufacturers in producing components through the use of numerically controlled machine tools (CNC). Often referred to together with CAD as CAD/CAM.

casting Manufacturing method in which a molten material is injected or poured into a mould to form an object of the desired shape. It is used to make parts of complex shape that would be difficult or uneconomical to make by other methods.

cathode An electrode through which positive electric current from a polarized electric device is emitted out of a polarized electrical device.

cavity In mould design, the space inside a mould into which material is injected or poured to create the desired shape.

chemical milling Sometimes referred to as electro-chemical milling and involves the exact removal of material from thin metal sheets. A resist is printed on to the surface of the metal to protect against the corrosive chemicals used. The sheet is then exposed to acid and the uncovered parts are eaten away.

chill zones Channels located within the body of a mould through which a cooling medium is circulated to control the mould surface temperature and ensure that the melt cools and hardens evenly, avoiding deformation.

clamp In injection moulding, the part of an injection-moulding machine that incorporates the platens that provide the force necessary to hold the mould closed during injection of the melt, and that open the mould to eject the part.

clamping line The edge of the mould tool that clamps/grips the material to be formed.

clamping plate A plate fitted to a mould and used to fasten the mould to the platen.

CNC (Computer Numerical Control) A computer controller that drives a machine tool. The process of operating this from CAD is known as CAM.

CNC-bending The application of CNC to fold flat metal sheets into three-dimensional forms.

CNC-cutting The application of CNC to cutting various materials into largely 2D shapes.

coefficient of thermal expansion Solids typically expand in response to heating and contract on cooling; this response to temperature change is expressed as a material's coefficient of thermal expansion.

co-injection moulding A process that employs the sequential injection of polymer melts into the same mould with one material as the core and one as the skin.

cold work A term for an operation performed on glass when it has already formed and cooled, such as cutting, acid-etching or engraving.

composite Material formed from two or more substances. Usually describes materials with advanced properties made from the combination of a matrix material and a fibre or powder reinforcement.

Desmopan™ A thermoplastic polyurethane elastomer, which combines the characteristics of rubber with the strength of polyurethane.

diamond saw Powder metal and diamond crystals are combined, then heated and pressed into a moulding to form a cutting surface for various types of saw.

die Tool used to cut, shape and form a wide variety of components. The words 'die' and 'mould' are virtually interchangeable. They are forms, usually made from metal, into which a melt is forced and from which it is ejected when hardened, retaining the shape of the form.

die-casting Metal-forming process in which molten metal is forced into a cavity or mould under pressure.

die-cutting Process involving a sharp edge cutting a predetermined form in a thin material. The die-cutting tool both incises shapes and creates creases to permit the bending of the material into 3D shapes.

dobby loom A type of loom that increases the number of cloth designs available to the weaver and allows longer sequences in a cloth pattern.

double-shot moulding A moulding process for making two-colour or two-component thermoplastic objects. Typically, it consists of injection-moulding the first part and inserting it into a second mould in which the second part is moulded on to the first.

draft The degree of taper of a mould-cavity side wall, or the angle of clearance designed to facilitate removal of parts from a mould.

draw The direction in which the core and cavity separate from each other.

Durometer Indicates the hardness of a material, defined as the material's resistance to permanent indentation. Typically used for polymers and elastomers/rubbers.

EBM (Electron Beam Machining) A process used to cut or drill components. It involves a concentrated stream of electrons being focused on to the surface of the work causing the material to heat up, melt and vaporize. The process is performed in a vacuum chamber to stop air molecules causing the electrons to veer off course.

EBM (Electron Beam Melting) A rapid-prototyping process that uses a beam of electrons to melt small particles of metal powder into a 3D form. The electron beam scans cross-sections generated from a 3D CAD file on to the surface of the powder bed. After each scan the bed is lowered by one layer of thickness, more powder is added and the process is repeated until the part is complete. The process is similar to SLS (Selective Laser Sintering).

EDM (Electrical Discharge Machining) A machining technique used for hard materials that would be impossible to machine using traditional techniques. Sparks from an electrode are used to erode the material along a computer-controlled (CNC) path.

ejector pins Pins that are pushed into a mould cavity from the rear as the mould opens, to force the finished part out of the mould. Also called knockout pins.

ejector rod A bar that actuates the ejector assembly when a mould opens.

Ekotek A bi-component resin containing a charge of ore (aluminium tri-hydrate). It is similar to Corian® in both texture and appearance but unlike Corian® it is a cost-effective product which is totally recyclable and is based on mould manufacture.

elastomer Often used interchangeably with rubber. The word comes from 'elastic' (describing the ability of a material to return to its original shape when a load is removed) and 'mer' (from polymer, in which 'poly' means many and 'mer' means parts).

electro-forming A highly specialized process of metal-part fabrication using electro-deposition in a bath of electrolyte solution over a base form, which is subsequently removed. A metal skin is built up on any surface that has been rendered electro-conductive. Essentially, a metal part is fabricated from the plating itself.

electronic ballast A device to limit the amount of current flowing in an electric circuit. It is often used in fluorescent lighting to eliminate flicker and reduce energy consumption.

EPS In this book EPS refers to expanded polystyrene and should not to be confused with the common file format used by graphic designers.

ergonomics The application of scientific information concerning humans to the design of objects, systems and environments for human use.

extrusion A manufacturing process used to create long objects of a fixed cross-sectional profile. A material is pushed and/or drawn through a die of the desired profile shape. Hollow sections are extruded by placing a pin or piercing mandrel inside the die.

failure analysis The process of collecting and analysing data to determine the cause of a failure and how to prevent it recurring.

FDM (Fused Deposition Modelling) A rapid-prototyping process that extrudes a molten polymer or metal to create cross-sectional layers of material generated from a 3D CAD file. The layers are then built up one at a time until the part is complete.

FEA (Finite Element Analysis) A computer simulation technique used in engineering analysis. It allows the determination of effects such as deformations and stresses that are caused by applied structural loads such as pressure and gravity. Can also be applied to thermal, electro-magnetic and fluid analyses.

felting A process used in textile design to change the face of a woollen fabric. Various methods are used to agitate the surface fibres causing them to mat together: washing in hot soapy water, chemical treatment or the use of special felting needles.

flange An internal or external rib or rim (lip) on a component, normally used for strengthening it or for attaching it to another object.

flash Any excess material that is formed with, and attached to, the component along a seam or mould parting line. It is generally unwanted and removed.

flock technique The process of depositing millions of individual fibre particles on a surface coated with a layer of adhesive, using mechanical and/or electrostatic force. It is used for creating tactile, aesthetically pleasing and also anti-slip surfaces.

foam moulding A thermoplastic injection-moulding technique that introduces gas into the melt, creating a foam core to the moulded part.

form-cutting Cutting a shape in a flat surface of a material using a tool of a particular form. An example is the cutting of gear wheels, in which the cutting tool has the same form as the space between two teeth. The form-cutting in the EPS chair (see page 74) was done by hand using hot wires and templates.

fracco A tool used to impress a pattern on semi-molten glass.

free needle sewing machine Lacks the conventional feed plate that normally keeps the fabric in a fixed position so that it can only move backwards and forwards. A free needle allows the fabric to move in any direction.

galvanization Refers to any of several electro-mechanical processes. Typically relates to a metallurgic process that is used to coat steel or iron with zinc to prevent corrosion.

gas-assisted injection moulding The injection of an inert gas into the centre of the flow of plastic. The process can be used to overcome problems with shrinkage, and to make parts that combine thick and thin walls, or hollow sections and elongated shapes. It allows for more complex forms than are possible in multi-part assembly.

gate In injection moulding, an orifice through which the melt enters the mould cavity.

glass A hard, transparent substance made by melting a mixture of sand and other materials such as soda and lime at a high temperature and allowing it to cool. Short glass (hard) A potash-lime glass with a high silica content, used for making brilliant glassware. Also known as Bohemian glass. Long glass (soft) Usually of soda-lime composition. Its low softening point and high coefficient of thermal expansion make it suitable for blowing and forming. Float glass An extremely flat and smooth glass used for windows (among other things), produced by floating molten glass on molten tin until it has cooled sufficiently to be removed to cool independently.

glass-plating A traditional and ancient technique of glass crafting. Relates to the forming of molten glass in many ways except blowing, and is commonly used in relation to stained glass.

glass-slumping Occurs when glass is heated sufficiently to soften enough to slump into or over a mould.

gob In glass-blowing, the ball of molten glass attached to a blowpipe to be hand-blown or moulded.

green sand A slightly moist mixture of sand and clay, and other possible binding additives, used to produce moulds for sand-casting.

hairline finish A brush finish with a continuous grain that runs the length of the metal sheet to be treated. Due to the grain, repairs can be made to minor scratches.

halogen A series of non-metallic elements. Halogen lamp An incandescent lamp in which a tungsten filament is sealed into a small transparent envelope filled with a halogen gas.

heat-sink An environment or object that absorbs and dissipates heat from another object using thermal contact. Used in the cooling of refrigerators, heat engines, electronic devices, lights, etc.

high-density polyurethane Polyurethane foam that has expanded within a mould. The confinement of the foam creates the higher density.

HiREK™ A multi-layered techno-polymer composite made from polyolefine and polyester. Feels like Corian® but performs like plywood.

infinity screw A screw with infinite thread, the action of which is determined solely by the dimensions of the object in which it is contained.

injection moulding A shape-forming process in which a polymer melt is injected into a mould to form parts with a broad range of sizes and shapes. See **RIM (Reaction Injection Moulding)**.

injection pressure In injection moulding the pressure required to push molten polymer into the mould, usually expressed in psi.

insert moulding (over moulding) A moulding process in which an insert is incorporated into the component during the moulding processes. The insert is used to provide additional strength, or different characteristics or functionality to the part in a specific location.

investment-casting Also known as lost wax casting. The process involves coating an expendable wax pattern in a ceramic to form a mould. The wax is then removed by heat to leave the completed mould into which the molten metal is poured. When cool, the ceramic mould is broken away. The process is capable of producing high-quality parts with complex shapes.

iteration (computing) The repetition of a process within a computer program.

jig A tool for holding parts of a component or material, or the guiding tools during the manufacturing process.

Kelvin A unit of temperature (K) where absolute zero (the lowest possible temperature) is 0 K or –273.15°C on the Celsius scale.

laser (Light Amplification by Stimulated Emission Radiation) An electronic-optical device that emits a highly focused beam of light.

laser-cutting An industrial process that uses a laser to cut or decorate material. The laser melts, burns or vaporizes away the material leaving an edge with a high quality of surface finish.

laser-machining A machine tool that uses laser-cutting to generate 3D objects.

laser-sintering A high-powered laser beam is used to heat a particulate material to just below its melting point until the particles fuse together. See **SLS (Selective Laser Sintering)**.

LED (Light Emitting Diode) Electronic device that emits light when electric current flows through it. LEDs are available in a range of shapes, sizes and colours and are extremely long-lasting. In addition, they are very efficient which makes them suitable for low-power and battery-operated applications.

LOM™ (Laminated Object Manufacture) A rapid-prototyping process that involves building up 3D forms by the layering of laser-cut paper. Each layer is cut and then bonded to the next using adhesive and a heated roller. Variants that use plastic and metal layers are starting to become available.

lost wax casting See **investment-casting**.

machining Turning, shaping, drilling, boring or otherwise finishing by machinery. All these processes involve cutting in one way or another and are referred to as chip forming (the production of chips of material as a result of the cut) or material removal processes.

marver A tool used in glass-blowing. It generally consists of a polished steel or bronze surface attached to a metal or wooden table. The warm glass is rolled on it to control the temperature of the glass and adjust its shape.

matrix The material to which reinforcing materials (fibres, powders, etc.) are added in the creation of a composite. The matrix can be any binding material but is typically a polymer or metal.

melt In injection moulding, is the liquefied polymer injected into a mould.

metal stamping A process employed in manufacturing metal parts with a specific design. A metal alloy sheet that is malleable and able to flow easily is stamped on a press using dies (female component) and punches (male component). Progressive stamping A metalworking method that encompasses punching, coining, bending and several other ways of modifying sheet metal into complex profiles. A feeding system pushes the sheet metal through a series of different sized die and punch combinations.

Micarta A composite material created in 1910 as a by-product of the development of Bakelite. It has an organic substrate of silk, linen, or cotton or paper held together by a resin matrix.

Microscribe™ G2 A mechanical arm used to trace over the surface of an object to digitize the surface and create a 3D model in a CAD system.

milling The cutting and shaping of metal or other solid materials into products or parts using a milling machine. Milling machine A machine tool for the complex shaping of solid materials. The range of motion of the rotating cutter and the platform to which the material to be cut is fixed define the complexity of the form that can be milled. This form-creating complexity is often related to the number of axes of the milling machine. Milling machines can be manually operated or numerically controlled (CNC).

mirror polishing The highly reflective finish produced by polishing with successively finer abrasives, and buffing (polishing with a soft material) until the surface is free of marks.

mould (or mold) A series of machined steel plates containing cavities into which melt is injected to form a part. Positive mould (male) Presses the liquefied material into the negative mould. Negative mould (female) Mirror image of the object.

multi-cavity mould A mould which has two or more cavities for forming multiple finished items per each machine cycle.

multi-material injection moulding The use of injection moulding to mould different types of materials together. The process can be divided into three primary types: multi-component which includes co-injection moulding and bi-injection moulding; insert moulding; and multi-shot injection moulding.

multiplex board A multi-layered wood-veneer board ideally suited for furniture manufacture because of its appealing appearance and hard-wearing properties.

multi-shot injection moulding A process where several distinct injections of material (shots) are applied to produce the final component.

Neoprene The DuPont Performance Elastomers trade name for a family of synthetic rubbers. Used in a wide variety of environments, such as wetsuits, laptop sleeves, electrical insulation and car fan-belts.

nozzle In injection moulding, allows transfer of the melt from the plasticator to the mould.

overbraiding A composite material production technique that braids resin-impregnated fibres over a former (mandrel) and is then cured.

parametric computer model A numeric and visual representation of a process or object that can be manipulated by changing individual parameters in real time. Often associated with CAD, it allows changes to the model to be made easily and in a controlled manner.

parting line On a finished moulded part, shows where the two mould halves met when they were closed. It is typically located by the tool designer with input from the design engineer and there is always a trade-off between aesthetics, design considerations and the ease of moulding. It is also known as a witness line.

PCB (Printed Circuit Board) Used to support and electrically connect electronic components using conductive pathways integrated into the board.

photosensitive materials Materials which, when exposed to light, chemically change their properties.

plasticator The complete melting and injection unit on an injection-moulding machine. Takes polymer granules and other additives and creates the melt through the application of heat and shearing forces from the rotation of a long screw inside a cylindrical barrel. Injection is achieved by pushing the whole screw along the barrel, forcing the melt out of the nozzle.

platens In manufacturing, the mounting plates of a press on which the mould halves are attached.

Polariscope Instrument for examining the properties of polarized light or the interactions of polarized light with transparent materials. Can be used to examine the stresses in glass.

powder-coating A type of dry coating that is applied as a free-flowing, dry powder. It is added electrostatically and then cured under heat to allow it to flow and form a 'skin'. The powder may be a thermoplastic or a thermoset polymer, and the finish is tougher than that of conventional paint.

press Another name for an injection-moulding machine. It comes from the clamping unit that applies force to the mould to keep the halves from separating. The other part of the injection-moulding machine is the injector unit or plasticator.

pressing laminate A process that presses resin-treated laminates together to form a board.

product testing Testing the performance characteristics of a product or product part. Loads or forces are applied to the product to determine the circumstances under which it might fail. The process includes static load testing (the magnitude of the force is steadily increased) and dynamic load testing (the product is subjected to cyclic forces to determine the effects of fatigue).

psi (pounds per square inch) A unit of pressure.

PUR (polyurethane or PU) A polymer with a broad range of forms and uses.

rasp Woodworkers' rough file used for shaping wood.

RE (Reverse Engineering) The process of discovering the technological principles of a device or object through analysis of its structure, function and operation in order to duplicate or enhance it. As CAD has become more popular, RE has become a viable method to create a 3D virtual model of an object for use in 3D CAD, CAM, CAE and other software. The process involves measuring an object using laser scanners, structured light digitizers or computed tomography, and then reconstructing it as a 3D model.

refractory mould A mould made from a material that is strong at high temperatures, and has low thermal conductivity and low coefficient of expansion.

restricted gate A very small orifice between the runner and the cavity in an injection mould.

RIM (Reaction Injection Moulding) This is similar to injection moulding except that a reaction occurs within the mould. The process uses thermoset polymers (commonly polyurethane) instead of thermoplastic polymers used in standard injection moulding. Before the injection of the polymer takes place, two components are mixed that react in the mould to form a solid thermoset polymer. The bi-component fluid is of much lower viscosity than molten thermoplastic polymer, which enables the economical production of large parts with complex geometry.

riser Used in metal casting as a reservoir from which molten metal can be drawn to offset shrinkage.

rotational moulding (roto moulding) A process used to produce hollow products by building up liquid material on the internal cavity of a mould. As the mould rotates the liquid solidifies on the outer surface of the cavity leaving a void in the centre. Heat and rotation are the only methods employed, which eliminates the possibility of making complex shapes or angles.

RP (Rapid Prototyping) Takes virtual designs from CAD software and transforms them into thin, virtual, horizontal cross-sections that are then created in physical space, layer by layer, using liquid, powder or sheet material. The cross-sections are fused together until the part is complete. Prototyping technologies include SLS (selective laser sintering), FDM (fused deposition modelling), LOM™ (laminated object manufacturing), SLA (steriolithography), three-dimensional printing and EBM (electron beam melting).

runner When applied to mould design, the channel that connects the sprue with the gate for transferring the molten material to the mould cavities.

sand-blasting Special finishing treatment in which sand is sprayed at high velocities over a surface to smooth, shape or clean it.

sand-casting The production of metal castings using a mould made from sand, formed round a replica of the object to be cast (pattern). A range of sand-casting types exist but they generally fall into two categories: permanent pattern, in which the pattern is removed prior to the metal being poured into the cavity; and expendable pattern in which the pattern is left in the mould and vaporizes when the metal is poured into the cavity. The benefit of leaving the pattern in place is that it damage to the relatively fragile sand mould when the pattern is extracted is avoided. In both cases the mould is destroyed when the finished part is removed, though the sand can often be reused.

satin stitch Also known as damask stitch. A series of flat, closely packed stitches used to completely cover a section of the background fabric.

serif Any of the short lines stemming from, and at an angle to, the upper and lower ends of the strokes of a letter. Typefaces with serifs are serif fonts, those without are sans-serif fonts.

servomotor A type of geared motor that has the benefits of being generally compact, powerful for its size and capable of accurate positional control. It is used for many applications including robotics, industrial automation, CNC machine systems, etc.

ShapeHand™ glove A motion-capture device that translates the motion of a real hand and fingers within the glove to computer data that can be used to provide input to a number of software programs. Predominantly used for animation and special effects, but can also be used as an alternative input for a CAD system. The glove is capable of integration with other motion-capture systems to capture movement from the whole body.

shore A unit of measurement that denotes the hardness of plastics and rubbers in terms of their elasticity. A shore is gauged by using a Durometer to apply a force in a consistent manner, without shock, for a specified time and then measuring the depth of the indentation. The smaller the indentation, the higher the number, and thus the harder the material.

shot In injection moulding, the total amount of melt injected during a moulding cycle, including that which

fills the runner system. The failure to completely fill the mould or cavities of the mould with the melt is referred to as a short shot.

shrinkage The dimensional differences between a moulded part and the actual mould dimensions. Occurs due to the natural tendency for the molten polymer to shrink while cooling, but can be minimized through the design of the mould or the operating parameters of the injection-moulding cycle.

silk (screen) printing A method of printing based on stencilling. Can be used to print on most surfaces, including paper, plastic, fabric and wood. A fine mesh (originally silk) is stretched across a wooden frame to form the screen. An impermeable stencil (paper or other coating) is applied to the screen. The screen is then placed on the surface that will receive the pattern and ink is pressed through it where the stencil has been cut to allow the ink to pass.

single-cavity mould A mould that has one cavity, for forming only one finished item per machine cycle.

sintering (to sinter) Causing powdered materials, including metals and ceramics, to become a coherent mass by heating without melting.

SLA (Stereolithography) A rapid-prototyping process that uses a UV (ultraviolet) laser to cure a photopolymer resin into a 3D form. The laser scans cross-sections generated from a 3D CAD file on to the surface of a vat of liquid resin. After each scan the bed is lowered by one layer of thickness, more resin is added and the process is repeated until the part is complete.

slide In injection moulding, a movable section inside a more complex mould. It is inserted into the mould to form features that cannot be formed using only a core and a cavity.

SLS (Selective Laser Sintering) A rapid-prototyping process that uses a high-power laser to fuse small particles of plastic, metal or ceramic powders into a 3D form. The laser scans cross-sections generated from a 3D CAD file on to the surface of the powder bed, selectively fusing the particles. After each scan the bed is lowered by one layer of thickness, more powder is added and the process is repeated until the part is complete.

soft-touch paint A urethane paint that creates a rich, soft feel on any surface it coats, transforming hard surfaces with its tactile texture.

solenoid valve An electro-mechanical valve for use with liquid or gas, controlled by running or stopping an electrical current through a solenoid (a coil of wire), thus opening or closing the valve.

sprue The passage through which molten material enters the mould.

substrate In materials science, the base material on to which a secondary layer of material is added.

superforming aluminium A process whereby sheet aluminium is heated until it is malleable and is then forced over or into a single surface tool to create complex shapes. There are four main methods: cavity forming (air pressure forces the sheet into the mould); bubble forming (the sheet is blown into a bubble and a mould is pushed up into it; the air pressure is then reversed forcing the aluminium on to the mould); back pressure forming (similar to cavity forming but air pressure is also used in the opposite direction to control the flow of material into the mould); diaphragm forming (the sheet is formed on to a non-super-elastic alloy which then forms both materials over the mould). See **thermoforming** and **vacuum forming**.

tempering (to temper) In metallurgy, the heat treatment of metals, alloys and glass. It involves reheating the material to a sufficiently high temperature without melting it, and then cooling it quickly.

template The design, mould or pattern of an item that serves as a basis or guide for designing or constructing similar items.

theoretical physics Employs mathematical models and abstractions of physics, as opposed to experimental processes, in an attempt to understand nature. The goal is to rationalize, explain and predict physical phenomena.

thermoforming The process of forming a thermoplastic sheet into a 3D shape. The sheet is heated until it is soft and pliable, then stretched over or into a single-sided mould until cooled. See **vacuum forming**.

thermoplastic A polymer that melts or flows when heated. Unlike a thermoset it can be reheated and remoulded.

thermoset (thermosetting plastic) A polymer that is cured through heat, chemical reaction or irradiation to create a stronger form. Thermosets are not usually solid prior to curing, and are designed to be moulded or used as adhesives. Once cured, they cannot be reheated and remoulded like thermoplastics.

three-dimensional printing A rapid-prototyping process that prints cross-sectional layers of material generated from a 3D CAD file. The layers are then built up one at a time until the part is complete. The printing can consist of photopolymers that are cured by ultraviolet light, adhesive to which a powder is bonded, or molten polymer formed directly on to a support structure. Unlike other rapid-prototyping processes, 3D printing is optimized for speed, low cost and ease of use.

TIG (Tungsten Inert Gas) welding An arc-welding process that uses a non-consumable tungsten electrode to produce the weld. The weld is protected by a shielding gas (normally argon) and a filler metal is often used to add filler material to the weld. The technique is used for a variety of metals, is especially suited to thin materials and gives the operator greater control, which results in excellent quality and surface finish.

toggle In injection moulding, a type of clamping mechanism. A toggle is used to close, and exert pressure on, a mould in a press.

tool A piece of equipment that is used to gain some mechanical advantage or provide some ability that is not otherwise available to the user of the tool. The verb form, 'to tool', is the use of a tool for some purpose.

trappola A frame that contains molten glass within a predicted area on the marver.

triangulation A trigonometric operation for finding a position or location by means of bearings (angles from some known datumsuch as the magnetic north) from two fixed points a known distance apart.

tube forming The forming of tubular material (normally metal) after initial production of the tube form. Includes bending and forming the tube into different cross-sectional forms. It can be carried out manually or using a CNC machine.

turning The process used to produce cylindrical components in a lathe. The lathe is a machine tool that rotates the material to be cut, to which a tool is applied to create the cylindrical form. Turning can be carried out manually or with a CNC machine.

ultraviolet (UV) light bonding A process used primarily in glass and plastic bonding. Ultraviolet light is used to rapidly harden and cure a UV-reactive adhesive. The adhesive can be completely transparent so that the join between transparent materials is not visible.

undercut When applied to mould design, a protuberance or indentation that impedes withdrawal of a form from a two-piece rigid mould.

unrolling A computer program facility that translates a three-dimensional shape into a two-dimensional surface.

vacuum forming Consists of a former in the exact shape of the part required and a thermoplastic sheet. The former is lowered into a chamber that is covered by the sheet. The sheet is firmly clamped to a frame creating a sealed environment. The plastic is heated from above until it is flexible and the former is then raised. Air is sucked out of the chamber forcing the plastic over the mould. This method can also be applied to malleable grades of aluminium.

vent When applied to mould design, a shallow channel or opening cut in the cavity to allow air or gases to escape as the molten substance fills the cavity.

vibra finishing A process in which parts to be treated are vibrated in a machine to deburr, descale, clean or otherwise modify their surface finish. The parts are placed in the machine together with some form of granular media that acts like an abrasive on the surface of the part.

voids In cast or moulded parts, cavities that have opened due to shrinkage or the encapsulation of air or other gas during moulding, or that were not filled with material, leaving holes that may well not be visible from the exterior of the part.

Wacom® Pen Tablet (graphics tablet) A computer input device that allows images to be drawn, replicating the use of pencil and paper. It consists of a pen-like stylus and a flat surface called the tablet. Images are drawn directly to the screen and do not appear on the tablet itself. While its main purpose is to supporta natural style of drawing, it also supports more traditional operations that would be performed with a mouse.

warp In weaving, a set of lengthwise yarns through which the weft is woven.

water-jet cutting A cold process in which high pressure (up to 60,000 psi) forces water (optionally mixed with abrasives) through a small orifice (typically 0.1–0.5mm) at speeds up to three times the speed of sound. It produces a working power able to cut any shape of metal, glass or other material. As there is no tool contact there is no edge deformation or heat-affected zone.

weft Sometimes known as the woof. The yarn that is drawn under and over parallel warp yarns to create a fabric.

wireframe model A visual presentation of an object in 3D computer graphics. It is created by specifying the edges where two continuous smooth surfaces meet or by connecting an object's constituent vertices using straight lines and curves. As only edges are drawn, faces or surfaces are shown empty, giving the wireframe appearance. The technique allows the visualization of the underlying design structure of a 3D model.

Zamac An alloy of zinc, aluminium, magnesium and copper. Used for die-casting.

zebra curve A series of curves projected on to a surface in computer graphics. The curves conform to the underlying geometry of the surface on to which they are projected giving a feeling of three-dimensionality to an otherwise flat-looking form. When projected, the shape and arrangement of the curves leads to their zebra-like appearance and allows the transitions to be evaluated.

INDEX